LIBERTY
The Statue and the American Dream

By Leslie Allen

LIBERTY
1886·1986

THE STATUE OF LIBERTY-
ELLIS ISLAND FOUNDATION, INC.

with the cooperation of the National Geographic Society
and a grant from the Kimberly-Clark Corporation

Read	Write	THE COUNTRY OF WHICH THEY ARE CITIZENS	NATIVE COUNTRY	LAST RESIDENCE	STATE CITIZENS OF THE U. S. A.	INTENDED DESTINATION, STATE OR TERRITORY
Yes	"		Hamburg			Rock Isld
"	"	Prussia	Sburg			"
"	"	Austria	Holesova			Herbesville
"	"	"	"			Texas
"	"	Bohemia	Fishtenbach			Buffalo
no		"	"			"
yes	"	Roumania	Piontre			New York
"	"	"	"	"		"
no	"	"	"	"		"
"	"	"	"	"		"
yes	"	Russia	Grodno			New York
"	"	"	"			"
"	"	"	Seeny			"
"	"	Austria	Czorthow			"
"	"	Hungary	Bereez			"
"	"	Austria	Hawtze			New York
"	"	"	"	"		"
"	"	"	"	"		"

Liberty: The Statue and the American Dream By Leslie Allen

Consultant

Dr. Alan M. Kraut, *Professor of History, The American University*

Produced by the National Geographic Society as a public service

Gilbert M. Grosvenor, *President*
Melvin M. Payne, *Chairman of the Board*
Owen R. Anderson, *Executive Vice President*
Robert L. Breeden, *Vice President, Publications and Educational Media*

Prepared by the Special Publications Division

Donald J. Crump, *Editor*
Philip B. Silcott, *Associate Editor*
William L. Allen, *Senior Editor*

Staff for this Book

Mary Ann Harrell, *Managing Editor*
Anne D. Kobor, *Illustrations Editor*
Barbara Grazzini, *Senior Researcher and Assistant to the Editor*
Cinda Rose, *Art Director*
Marianne Koszorus, *Associate Art Director*

Margery G. Dunn, Merrill Windsor, *Contributing Editors*
Elizabeth W. Fisher, Sallie M. Greenwood, Carolinda E. Hill, Bonnie S. Lawrence, Rebecca Lescaze, *Researchers*
Simone A. Andrus, Michael J. Castellon, Daniel J. Hammel, William A. Timmons, *Research Assistants*
Victoria Garrett Connors, Brooke Kane, *Additional Research Assistance*
Thomas B. Allen, Jody Bolt, Seymour L. Fishbein, Patricia F. Frakes, Jane R. McCauley, Tom Melham, H. Robert Morrison, Cynthia R. Ramsay, Pamela Black Townsend, Jennifer C. Urquhart, Suzanne Venino, *Picture Legend and Portfolio Writers*
Elizabeth A. Brazerol, Rosamund Garner, Pamela Black Townsend, *Editorial Assistants*
Carol Rocheleau Curtis, *Illustrations Assistant*
John D. Garst, Jr., Virginia L. Baza, Donald L. Carrick, Gary M. Johnson, Daniel J. Ortiz, *Map and Graph Production*

Marvin J. Fryer, *Copy Preparation*
George Menish, *Decorative Initials*
Dianne T. Craven, Lori E. Davie, Brenda J. Davis, Bernadette L. Grigonis, Virginia W. Hannasch, Nancy J. Harvey, Joan Hurst, Artemis S. Lampathakis, Katherine R. Leitch, Cleo E. Petroff, *Staff Assistants*

Engraving, Printing, and Product Manufacture

Robert W. Messer, *Manager*
George V. White, *Production Manager*
David V. Showers, *Production Project Manager*
Mark R. Dunlevy, Gregory Storer, George J. Zeller, Jr., *Assistant Production Managers*
Mary A. Bennett, Timothy H. Ewing, *Production Assistants*
Kevin P. Heubusch, *Production Staff Assistant*

James Enzinna, *Index*

PRECEDING PAGES: *The statue's torch comes aglow at sunset.* OPPOSITE: *Immigrants crowd the deck of S.S.* Amerika, *arriving in New York in 1905.*
FOLLOWING PAGES: *Towers mark Ellis Island's Main Building; arched windows identify the Registry Room.*
HARDCOVER STAMP: *Drawn from a photograph by Peter B. Kaplan.*

Contents

Foreword

Fourth of July fireworks in holiday splendor frame the year-round glow of the torch of the Statue of Liberty.

he words and pictures in this book tell the story of millions of people who left everything they knew for a chance at something better. Some were drawn to America by ideals such as democracy and liberty, but many were driven by hardship. A few expected streets of gold, but most expected only a shovel and a chance to work. The Statue of Liberty was the first American landmark for the millions of immigrants who landed at Ellis Island between 1892 and 1954, so she became an enduring symbol of hope to them. And to the hundred million of us who are their children and grandchildren, the Lady with the Torch remains a symbol of what those people and this country gave to us.

She reminds us of the courage it took for them to come, and the sacrifices they made once they got here. She also reminds us that their sacrifices paid off because of the opportunities that America gave them.

Theirs was the largest and most successful mass migration in modern history. They found the dignity and security they sought, and in the process they built a country that became the wonder of the world.

But it didn't happen without pain, and sweat, and tears.

It wasn't because the country was rich in natural resources: It was because people dug into the ground and took them out, often under terrible conditions. It wasn't because of miles of open prairies: It was because people broke their backs to till the soil. It wasn't because of a few industrial geniuses: It was because millions of people fired the furnaces and stamped the metal. And it wasn't because of a piece of paper called a Constitution: It was because people fought, and sometimes died, to fulfill its promise of a just and humane society.

The American promise of opportunity would have been barren without the courage and sacrifice and hard work of the people in this book, and of those who came before them.

The pictures are of Germans, and Slavs, and Italians, Irish, Chinese, and others. But the story is about Americans.

And the story isn't over. The Statue of Liberty is being restored not just as a monument to the past, but also as a challenge for the future. She'll stand, stronger and brighter than ever, to remind us of what we've been given, and of what we owe.

The story is being told here through the generous assistance of the National Geographic Society, the Kimberly-Clark Corporation, QuadGraphics Inc., and the National Park Service.

Lee Iacocca

Chairman, The Statue of Liberty-Ellis Island Centennial Commission

Introduction

By ALAN M. KRAUT, *Ph.D.*
Professor of History
The American University

Americans are a people of many pasts. Beginning with the Siberian hunters who crossed the Bering landbridge about 30,000 years ago, America has been populated from around the globe. Whether their relatives arrived on foot thousands of years ago or several months ago on a plane to the Los Angeles airport, Americans all have a past somewhere else. Even the Statue of Liberty, the great lady who reigns in New York's harbor, symbol of American diversity, can claim French ancestry.

Immigration into the United States has been almost continuous since independence, but the nations of origin have changed. Most of the 4.5 million who came between 1841 and 1861 were Irish or German, the balance also coming from northern and western Europe. In the 1880s southern and eastern Europe became significant—Italy, Greece, the Russian and the Austrian Empires. Thousands from China and Japan, as well, joined this second great wave. Meanwhile, hundreds of thousands of French Canadians and Mexicans crossed America's borders, often without being counted or questioned. From 1880 through 1920, more than 23.5 million "new immigrants" arrived.

The new "new immigrants" are still arriving, and some historians are talking of a third great wave. Of the twenty countries that have sent the most immigrants to the U.S. since 1965, only five—the United Kingdom, Germany, Italy, Canada, and Mexico—were previously major sources of immigration. Besides the familiar Chinatowns and Little Italies of our cities, there are now a Koreatown in Los Angeles, a Little Havana in Miami, a Little Odessa in Brooklyn, a Little Saigon in Orange County, California, and another in Arlington, Virginia.

No matter how or why they have come, immigrants have changed the United States even as they have been transformed. American government, arts, letters, cuisine, and sports reflect Old World forms recast. "The land flourished because it was fed from so many sources . . . so many cultures and traditions and peoples," President Lyndon B. Johnson reminded us as he signed a 1965 immigration law eliminating the old national-origins quota system. Under the new law, what you can offer is more important than where you are from. And the immigrants have brought a bounteous harvest of talent and labor.

In focusing upon the sheer number of immigrants and the different national groups, historians often lose sight of the individual. Yet, in the end, it was the individual or the family who decided to go or stay. Most people in other parts of the world stayed put. Only a bold minority sought to improve their lives by venturing abroad. And even manacled slaves, forcibly herded aboard ship by others, retained their individuality, passing down from mother to child tales and customs of the African past and the tribal wisdom of their forebears.

Not all who left home chose the United States over Canada, Australia, Brazil, Argentina, and other lands of opportunity. Most who did choose the States knew that success would come only with hard labor. It is perhaps still more the miracle, then, that those who knew the United States was no paradise—that its streets were not paved with gold if paved at all—came anyway.

From the gray-haired grande dame of the Daughters of the American Revolution to the black child at the microfilm reader pursuing his own Kunta Kinte, Americans want to know about the individuals in their own past who left another country and came to this one. In the stories of such individuals—in our own families, then—is the story of America, its past and future.

I saw my paternal great-grandfather, Markus Kraut, for the first time only recently, in a yellowed photograph: a small, bent figure with flowing white beard, wearing the earlocks and *yarmulke* traditional among orthodox Jews. The picture was taken in the 1920s, to be sent from the little village of Moscisker, in Poland, to a son in America.

That son, my grandfather Elchonan, arrived in New York in 1902. Already, in London, he had found a place where Jews could live without fear of mobs. He came to America pursuing good fortune—like many of the 648,742 others tallied by American officials that year. I do not know if Elchonan saw the Statue of Liberty when he arrived, or what he thought of it. But he passed through Ellis Island and established a tailor shop in New York; after two years he could bring his wife and children to join him. In his shop and in the city streets—in the Lower East Side, East Harlem, the Bronx—he met men and women of every race, religion, and nationality. He never ceased to marvel at the richness and diversity of American life.

Such diversity is taken for granted by my four-year-old daughter, Julia Rose. She attends nursery school with children of many races and religions. She has seen a picture of her maternal great-grandmother, Rose Heskes: a young woman with her coworkers in a sweatshop. My daughter does not know what a sweatshop is. She does not spend her Sunday afternoons listening to old men talk of strikes. As the distance grows between the immigrant and the descendants, something of value is lost, though much is gained.

Perhaps what is gained is a feeling of proprietorship. Like many immigrants, a great-granduncle of mine could never quite forget that America was his adopted country. A pants cutter from Prussia, Nathan Schoenbart was a law buff. After his retirement, he would go to the

FOLLOWING PAGES: *Looking down with compassion worthy of a Mother of Exiles, the Statue of Liberty watches the struggles of her immigrants—men, women, and children toiling in New York's sweatshops. Flames in the background evoke a famous tragedy: the Triangle Shirtwaist factory fire of 1911, when young women trapped on the upper floors jumped to a quick death on the pavement below. At center, artist Philip Reisman has placed leaders of a 1909 strike by shirtwaist makers. Samuel Gompers, president of the American Federation of Labor, stands next to teenage Clara Lemlich, who has thrilled a meeting of two thousand by her call for a general strike. The audience roars approval. At the lectern, chairman B. Feigenbaum challenges them to take an oath of loyalty: "Do you mean it in absolute faith?"*

Bronx County Courthouse almost every day. On his way home he would stop at our apartment to regale us with tales of mesmerizing lawyers, quick-witted judges, and unrepentant criminals never punished harshly enough. On one such evening, I was huddled in a corner, hoping for a mention of a gun battle. Nathan noticed me and, smiling, roared, "Ah, there he is, the little American. Come, promise the uncle that some day you will work in the court. If not a lawyer, at least be a court stenographer." It took more than thirty years before I understood that from Nathan Schoenbart's perspective, he would always be a guest here. However much he admired the United States, it could never be his country as it was mine. Decades after he had crossed the Atlantic, an ocean still separated us.

As the experience of America varies from one generation to another, so does the meaning of its symbols. To Julia, both the Statue of Liberty and Ellis Island mean exciting boat rides, "America," and something about Daddy's job. To her immigrant forebears, the Statue surely represented hope for the future. For them Ellis Island seems to have embodied the uncertainties that the United States posed. Besides the dread of being turned away, there was the anxiety of coming to a land where many cherished habits of daily living would be traded away for a chance to become part of American society. There was another fear, too. In America, failure could not be excused by blaming a repressive government. Here you could succeed by your own merit—or be crushed by your own flaws.

Such has been the experience of millions: neither glamorous nor sordid, neither triumph nor failure. The majority succeeded.

In my classroom, I meet those whose ancestors rode the *Mayflower,* those whose forebears came in steerage, those who rode the last helicopters out of Saigon with their parents. I try to integrate the history of those groups with the larger history of the United States, so that many pasts become one. I try to present the unvarnished truth, hoping that my students will reject facile stereotypes and bias.

As a member of the History Committee of the Statue of Liberty-Ellis Island Centennial Commission, I have listened to my colleagues from around the country express the hope that the centennial anniversaries of these monuments would trigger appreciation for their unique history, as well as for the larger history of immigration to the United States, and the marvelous diversity of American life. This book has been crafted with those worthy goals in mind.

Julia Rose Kraut has looked at all the pictures and pronounced many of them "OK," the highest compliment she bestows. I hope that someday she will read it, too—and that its story will remain a compelling one for the children's children of our land.

Liberty: The Story of the Statue

Conceived to celebrate the ties between France and the United States, "Liberty Enlightening the World" proclaims the ideals of democracy as her second century begins.

nveiling ceremonies for the colossal statue of "Liberty Enlightening the World" were under way on Bedloe's Island the afternoon of October 28, 1886. Ignoring a cold, wind-driven drizzle, 2,500 invited guests strained to hear the speakers through a persistent blare of tugboat whistles. Now Senator William M. Evarts of New York was at the podium, presenting the completed shrine to President Grover Cleveland on behalf of the American fund-raising committee and the generous citizens of the land.

"Louder! Louder!" The cries rang out as Evarts delivered his first lines. At last he paused, for emphasis. Someone thought he had ended his speech, and 200 feet above the crowd, in "Liberty's" crown, the sculptor Frédéric-Auguste Bartholdi received a signal to loosen the cord that held a French flag over his statue's 14-foot-long face.

As the Tricolor fell away, a 21-gun salute thundered across New York's harbor. For a deafening quarter-hour, whistles, cannon, fog-horns, bands, and screaming crowds sent up a frenzied cacophony. "A hundred Fourths of July broke loose," as one excited reporter put it. New York was in a mood to celebrate. A million spectators turned out for the festivities; the police had been rounding up pickpockets and con men for days. The "billows of humanity" had splashed "sprays of small boys to every ledge and cornice" along Manhattan's five-mile parade route. Under a blanket of ticker tape, 20,000 marchers had filed along. "It seemed to have rained brass bands . . . windy bands from Boston with vociferous horns; mild bands from Buffalo with a dropsical tuba . . . bands from Washington that could be heard a mile; bands from Philadelphia that couldn't be heard at all. . . ." As soon as the last unit had gone by, the crowds surged down to the Battery to watch a naval parade, largest in the nation's history.

Twenty tugboats led the van, whistles shrieking, with steamers and scows and yachts and dredges behind them. Lesser craft, thronged with merrymakers, jockeyed bow to bow around them and vied for position around Bedloe's Island. They were waiting for the moment when "the brazen voice of steam lifted its utmost clamors . . . bell spoke to bell and cannon to cannon, till all men of the thousands gathered in her honor knew that Liberty had been given and received."

Of course the conclusion of Evarts's speech was not heard at all. Nor were the comments of the European immigrants who crowded the decks of an inbound steamship. Only the *New York Herald* mentioned their presence: "The cannon smoke and the vapor rolled up, and, ringed in a huge, fire-fringed semi-circle, they saw before them the

Images for a new nation: Liberty presents the arts and sciences to blacks to encourage emancipation. Patriotism and Quaker aversion to slavery inspired this painting by Samuel Jennings of Philadelphia, who gave the goddess a contemporary dress of 1792. A French artist of the same period drew America as a conventional "Indian Queen."

For a gold Liberty medal presented to the King of France, Benjamin Franklin chose classical motifs—Minerva, goddess of wisdom, holds the shield of France over the infant Hercules (the United States). Art of that era often showed Britain as a leopard or as a maneless lion.

mighty figure of Liberty. Imagination can hardly conceive what to their tired eyes, weary with the hardships, the hopelessness, and the cruelties of the Old World, this apparition must have conveyed. . . ."

"Liberty's" long career as an American symbol had just begun. Many years would pass before the monument became a supremely eloquent image, identified with the immigrant experience. For the time being, the fact that more than 200 tons of copper and iron had been shipped across the Atlantic and reassembled into New York's highest structure, the world's tallest free-standing statue—the bravado of it all—was source enough of wonderment to the cheering crowds.

Officially, the statue came as a gift from the people of France to the people of the United States. It commemorated, according to a plaque on the pedestal, "the alliance of the two Nations in achieving the Independence of the United States of America" and attested "their abiding friendship." The date of July 4, 1776, inscribed in Roman numerals on the tablet in the statue's left arm, emphasized the theme. In reality, more recent events in the nation of her origin had brought her into being.

The idea for the monument was already twenty years old. In 1865, as the Civil War ended and Americans approached their centennial, Frenchmen chafed under the regime of Napoleon III, who, like his legendary uncle, had appointed himself Emperor of the French. Among the Second Empire's most vocal critics were the "liberals," or "republicans," who revered the American model of government.

Their leader was Edouard René Lefebvre de Laboulaye—jurist, professor of comparative law, and devoted friend of America. He never visited the United States, but he published a three-volume work on its history and a biographical study of Benjamin Franklin. His antislavery tracts, widely read during the Civil War years, put him further at odds with Napoleon, who had favored the Confederacy. Seven decades after the French Revolution, its ideal of *liberté* was a dangerous topic, closely watched by the police and the censors of the press.

Writing about America gave Laboulaye an indirect way of referring to political realities in France. Thus the notion of a sweeping symbolic gesture, to strengthen the liberals' association with America—and to remind the French of liberty—came naturally to him one evening in 1865 at a dinner party at his home near Versailles.

Laboulaye's guests, like himself, were eminent liberals. They had seen in Abraham Lincoln what they admired in the United States, and the assassination of the President had prompted an outpouring of grief in France. Laboulaye may well have thought of the words inscribed on a

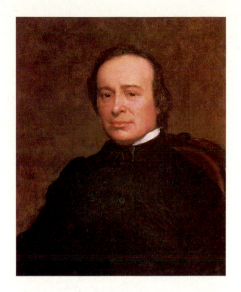

Ideals of a free republic—secure in the United States, but not in France—inspired Edouard René Lefebvre de Laboulaye, jurist and scholar. In 1865, dining with friends, he proposed the monument that became the Statue of Liberty. Not only a gift to America, it would stand for values repressed by the Emperor Napoleon III. Collapse of the Empire in 1870 and founding of the Third Republic gave Laboulaye the chance to develop his plans.

Nobody welcomed the project more than its sculptor, Frédéric-Auguste Bartholdi. In 1869 he had begun sketches for his heroic "Liberty." His first surely dated model (second from left), from 1870, suggests an earlier design (center) for a colossal lighthouse by the Suez Canal. Other models for Suez show him refining his theme. He made the torch the dominant feature, trying it in left hand as well as right. For "Liberty" he straightened the torso, and added the radiant crown.

gold medal sent in the name of the French people to Mrs. Lincoln: "Lincoln, man of honor, abolished slavery, restored the Union, and saved the Republic, without veiling the statue of liberty."

As the guests discussed gratitude among nations, Laboulaye invoked the American Revolution and the Frenchmen who died in its service "for the principles that they hoped to see prevail in France and in the world." He said that if a monument were built in America to honor independence, it ought to be the work of both nations.

This account of the evening was penned years later by Bartholdi, who had been one of the guests. The conversation, he wrote, "interested me so deeply that it remained fixed in my memory"—and not surprisingly. The word "monument" was music to the sculptor's ears, and Bartholdi had the energy to turn ambitious ideas into reality.

Born in 1834 to a prosperous family in the Alsatian town of Colmar, Bartholdi was brought up in Paris by his mother after his father's death in 1836. He studied painting, and then sculpture. As a dashing youth of only 19, he exhibited his "Good Samaritan" group at the 1853 Salon. Three years later, he traveled to Egypt, where the ancient monuments of the Nile Valley fired what would become his trademark passion for the colossal.

Already, French engineers and men of finance were planning a modern project on a grand scale in Egypt—the Suez Canal. It offered Bartholdi a splendid setting for a statue: a towering, torch-bearing female figure to serve as a lighthouse. She would rival the Colossus of Rhodes, one of the seven wonders of the ancient world. She might be called "Egypt Carrying the Light to Asia" or, simply, "Progress." In 1867 and again in 1869, Bartholdi had a chance to woo the ruler of Egypt, Ismail Pasha, with drawings. But he never got this commission.

Later in his career, he insisted that this project had no connection at all with "Liberty." Yet the sketches and models for the two projects show considerable similarity. Moreover, as the art historian Marvin Trachtenberg has pointed out, both great statues were planned for "key points astride major waterways of the world, symbolizing twin deities in the nineteenth-century pantheon—Liberty and Progress—in both cases actively passing their message from one continent to another."

However touchy about the uniqueness of "Liberty," Bartholdi was an idealist by nature and a republican by conviction. The theme of liberty took on deeper meaning for him after the Franco-Prussian War of 1870-71, in which he served as an officer. A debacle for France, the war brought the end of Napoleon's rule, violent social unrest, and the loss of Alsace to Germany. The United States had given tacit support to

One of many commissions, a "Liberty" model stands to the side as Bartholdi poses in his Paris studio. His concern for his colossal "American" led to a promotional visit to the U.S. in 1871, which encouraged the formation of the French-American Union in 1874 to raise funds. Bartholdi's strong emotional attachment to his mother inspired the use of her stern face as a model for that of "Liberty."

Prussia; one and a half million German-born immigrants had been a potential bloc of support for the fatherland, while Napoleon III had angered the leaders of the Lincoln Administration. For Laboulaye, all this made the idea of an American monument more timely than ever. The statue would help to reestablish the old alliance.

"Go to see that country," Laboulaye reportedly advised Bartholdi in the spring of 1871. "You will study it, you will bring back to us your impressions. Propose to our friends over there to make with us a monument, a common work, in remembrance of the ancient friendship of France and the United States. We will take up a subscription in France." A month later Bartholdi was on his way, armed with letters of introduction from Laboulaye to his friends.

Traveling tirelessly, Bartholdi spent three and a half months ranging the country. Its foreignness constantly amazed him. Facetiously, he characterized the nation as "an adorable woman chewing tobacco." His letters to his mother overflowed with detail. New York, his port of entry, was a confusion of "hurrying crowds, neglected cobbled streets, the pavement scarred with railroad tracks, roadways out of repair, telegraph poles on each side of the street, lampposts not uniform, signs, wires, halliards of flags hanging across the streets, open fronts of stores such as one sees at a fair. . . ." Washington's stately avenues, by contrast, reminded him of Versailles. Boston of a Sunday was so quiet that "one might imagine himself in Pompeii," while Chicago, throbbing with motion, seemed to Bartholdi "the most American of all cities." Everywhere, hotels were "immense bazaars" where everything was big—"even the *petits pois.*"

In the grandeur of the landscape, he found scale appropriate to his project. He had found his site as soon as he sailed into New York's harbor. Bedloe's Island was occupied by the massive old Fort Wood, but that seemed less of a difficulty than finding "a few people who have a little enthusiasm for something other than themselves and the Almighty Dollar."

Hundreds of potential supporters listened, with varying degrees of interest, as he described his statue again and again. He gained access to notables of the day—the abolitionist Senator Charles Sumner, the editor Charles Dana, the millionaire Cyrus Field, the writer and landscape architect Frederick Law Olmsted. Near Boston, he smoked cigars and watched the sunset with white-bearded Henry Wadsworth Longfellow. In Salt Lake City he met Brigham Young, "very intelligent" and also "very shrewd." President Ulysses S. Grant displayed "an affability that is reserved and simple." At Grant's summer home in Long Branch, New

"Liberty's" torch on display at the 1876 Centennial Exhibition in Philadelphia reminds visitors of France's gift and America's part in the project. Bartholdi attended in a French delegation, enlisting support, as always. Even the modest fee charged to go up in the 32-foot structure went to the statue fund. Sheet music (opposite) for a Centennial march, adorned with the new emblem, manifests its growing popularity as a symbol.

Jersey, "one is received as by the simplest bourgeois. I met his children, and his gouty father-in-law seated by a spittoon."

Bartholdi returned to France with an enthusiastic report, but Laboulaye and his allies had no time to spare from their struggle to win support for a republican government. The sculptor occupied himself with a variety of projects, focused on French heroism in the late war and the historical amity with the United States. He created the bronze "Lafayette Arriving in America" which now stands in Union Square, a gift from France to the city of New York. He produced models and drawings for "Liberty," and waited for the project's official start.

He was far from the only sculptor with a constant flow of commissions, for it was the heyday of the public monument in the Western world. The Industrial Revolution had bred not only the wealth but also the advances in technology to support ever grander endeavors. It was an age of urban growth, and newfound civic pride.

French sculptors devoted themselves to timely ideals: images of *la Nation, la France, la Révolution, la République, la Liberté*. And because public subscriptions were becoming a common way of paying for new monuments, the French took in their stride what might have seemed an outrageous proposition: a call for hundreds of thousands of francs to build a monument for another country.

The fund-raising drive opened with fanfare in 1875. "Let us each bring his mite," exhorted the sponsoring French-American Union in a nationwide newspaper appeal. Its signers included descendants of Lafayette, Rochambeau, and Tocqueville. The union's manifesto announced that the statue would honor the American Centennial the following year, and that the American people would give the pedestal for the shrine.

Glittering events on "Liberty's" behalf studded the social calendars of Paris. At a banquet in the ornate Hôtel du Louvre, 200 guests enjoyed a 14-course meal—including *filet de boeuf Lafayette* and *croustades à la Washington*—and, at 11 p.m., a 45-minute address by Laboulaye. At the Opéra, artists performed Gounod's cantata to "Liberty." Money flowed in—primarily from wealthy liberals and larger cities, but also from small municipalities and anonymous individuals.

The American press began to take note. In New York, one paper thought Lafayette a more fitting subject than liberty. Another called Bedloe's Island a poor site "because the thousands of persons who would be anxious to write their names in pencil on its legs would dislike the trouble of being compelled to hire a small boat in order to reach it."

Few commentators discussed the question of imagery. What, went the unasked question, should "Liberty" look like? For the sculptor, the partial answer was simple and personal. The statue's countenance reflects that of Mme Bartholdi, a formidable woman who dominated her son throughout her life and who—ironically—saw her Alsatian homeland denied its own liberty under German rule.

Considering appropriate attributes, Bartholdi could draw upon the European art of two thousand years, starting with the personified *Libertas* of ancient Rome. His statue's upstretched, torch-flaunting arm, the tablet, the radiant crown, the broken shackles—all were ancient symbols. Probably the best-known modern *(Continued on page 30)*

Hand in the making dwarfs workmen, a top-hatted visitor and its creator (lower center) in the Paris workshop of Gaget, Gauthier et Cie. A full-scale plaster sleeve encases the wooden skeleton. For the separate sections, carpenters constructed massive wooden duplicates of the plaster shapes to act as molds for the copper "skin." Artisans hammered the copper into these molds to perfect details. This hammering by hand—a process called repoussé—*added resilience, strengthening the metal. Three hundred sheets of copper, each less in thickness than two pennies, comprise the visible image. "Liberty" reached her final size—151 feet, 1 inch from base to torch-tip—through a series of models, about 4, 9, and 37 feet in height.*

Waiting for her ship to come in, the scaffolding-clad "Liberty" looms above Paris streets in an 1884 painting. After contributions from 181 towns and 100,000 subscribers, a French lottery assured her completion. The work in progress attracted some 300,000 visitors. Although Congress in 1877 authorized acceptance of the statue and a site for it in New York Harbor, it voted funds for its maintenance only. In America, contributions for the pedestal lagged despite numerous appeals to the wealthy. Hoping to spur these efforts, Bartholdi presented the monument to the American Minister to Paris on July 4, 1884. Though the sum in hand barely covered the costs of the foundation, the American committee went ahead with the ceremony of laying the cornerstone on August 5, 1884 (below). Exasperated by the delays during the following months, Bartholdi decided to dismantle the statue and send "Liberty" to her American home. On May 21, 1885, the French naval vessel Isère sailed with two hundred-odd crates containing the copper skin and iron skeleton of a monument still unsure of a base. A contemporary cartoon (left), mocking the delays, shows a dejected goddess "one thousand years later" still awaiting her pedestal.

Liberty: A Shrine Assured

The pedestal fund found a champion in Joseph Pulitzer, immigrant from Hungary, veteran of the Civil War, and now owner of the New York *World*. Seeing an opportunity to serve the public interest—and attract new readers—Pulitzer launched a campaign to raise the final $100,000. He challenged the citizens of New York and the nation to provide the pedestal denied by the rich. He promised to welcome any amount and to publish the name of every donor, "no matter how small the sum given."

Each day inspirational editorials and stories of fund-raising activities filled the newspaper. Published letters accompanying the donations encouraged others to give: "why cannot a healthy rivalry of $1 subscriptions be made between 'the butchers, the bakers, and the candlestick-makers'? all for the good cause." "I am a little girl only six years old and have 25 cents in my savings bank, which I send to help build the Pedestal."

On August 11, 1885, a *World* headline proudly announced complete success—in just five months. (When Pulitzer put up a new office building in 1890, a stained-glass window echoed a revision of his paper's logotype, with "Liberty" triumphant.)

Completing the pedestal took a full eight months. Designed by Richard M. Hunt, Paris-trained and the acknowledged dean of American architects, it rose 89 feet above its base in the foundations of the star-shaped old Fort Wood. It combined motifs from several periods

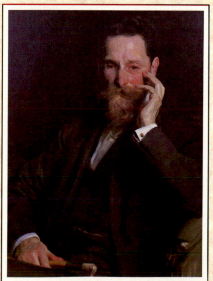

Pulitzer in 1905, by John Singer Sargent

of architecture. A great hollow concrete trunk, faced with granite, anchored in rock, it was said to be so strong that to overturn the statue one would have to upturn the island.

Gen. Charles P. Stone, chief engineer of the project, set the last block in the pedestal on April 22, 1886, as workmen sprinkled coins into the mortar—a reminder of more than 120,000 gifts, most of them less than a dollar, that made it possible.

work was Eugène Delacroix's painting "Liberty Guiding the People to the Barricades." This depicts a muscular woman, her breasts bare, with a musket in her left hand and the Tricolor in her right, striding forward among the fallen of the 1830 revolt in Paris. Napoleon III thought this painting subversive, and had it kept from public display. Bartholdi needed a balanced pose; moreover, he needed a treatment appropriate for the United States.

Americans themselves had already acquired a tradition of national images, some homegrown, others transplanted from Europe. The oldest New World symbol was the Indian Queen, popular since the 16th century. As a young princess, she had represented Britain's North American colonies—and then the new young nation. Given a classical reworking, she donned the drapery of a goddess and discarded her plumes. As American Liberty, the goddess appeared on coins with 13 stars in her hair, or wore the peaked cap that identified the freed slave in ancient Rome. As Columbia—a stately rival to Britannia—she carried the Stars and Stripes, or an American eagle. Cartoonists favored Uncle Sam or Brother Jonathan in political scenes, but chose either white-robed goddess to personify the idealized nation. In the later 19th century, Uncle Sam survived; but Bartholdi's distinctive figure became the reigning symbol of ideals and aspiration.

Symbols of two nations convey the genius of one man: Gustave Eiffel, a world-famous master of wrought-iron construction and the mathematics of stress. Bartholdi asked him in 1879 to find a way of supporting "Liberty" in her 88 tons of thin copper. Eiffel designed a core pylon of four iron columns linked for maximum strength at minimum weight (diagram, opposite). Later he designed his 1,000-foot tower for the Paris Exposition of 1889—the same year that a 36-foot bronze "Liberty" based on a Bartholdi model was installed on the Île des Cygnes, an islet in the Seine.

His "Liberty"—"my dear daughter"—fitted neatly into the American iconographic family. But persuading the American public to adopt her was a task for the future. The project lagged behind the original hopes for completion by 1876. To salvage the situation, Bartholdi concentrated on the arm and torch, enlarging them to full size for display at the Centennial Exhibition in Philadelphia. He arrived in May, with a French delegation; 21 crates' worth of arm and torch followed in a sweltering August.

Though highly publicized, the statue was subject to ridicule, and misinformation abounded. The *Cincinnati Commercial*'s Paris correspondent wrote that he had "visited the studio of the Italian Bartolomi." Almost every newspaper reported that the statue would be cast in bronze. And why bring just the arm? The *New York Times* ventured a risqué comment: If the sculptor honestly intended to complete the work, "he would have begun it at its foundation, modeling first the boot, then the stocking, then the full leg in the stocking." New York, it suggested, should ignore the project.

Chaos finally yielded to a kind of order early in 1877, when an American committee on the Statue of Liberty was formed in New York. It secured a joint resolution of Congress accepting the statue and

designating either Bedloe's or Governor's Island as its site. (Gen. William T. Sherman, chosen to decide the location, obliged the sculptor with Bedloe's.) Bartholdi in the meantime had sailed for France with his new bride. He had married the doe-eyed Jeanne-Emilie Baheux de Puysieux, who may have been his mistress, and a model for "Liberty."

In Paris, Bartholdi had technical questions to resolve as the project proceeded in the shops of Gaget, Gauthier et Cie. He used progressively larger models—1.25 meters high, then 2.85 meters. A model 11.4 meters (about 37 feet) tall gave him his last chance to see the statue whole. It was divided into sections, each to be enlarged four times according to standard procedures for huge sculpture. Using plumb lines, workmen took careful measurements from selected points and multiplied each by four. On the basis of these calculations, full-scale sections were executed in plaster. Then carpenters built wooden forms that duplicated the plaster shapes. The thin copper sheets for the statue's "skin" were placed on these forms and hammered into shape by the firm's skilled metalsmiths. Sometimes thin, highly malleable sheets of lead were pressed into shape over the plaster, and the copper sheets were checked against the leaden ones. For simple sections such as smooth drapery, the workman might have hammered out the copper on an anvil, working "by eye." The sheet could be checked against the measurements and reworked as necessary until it was accurate.

Fanciful in detail, this early view reveals an interior spiral stairway and a ladder to the torch. It omits or distorts structural elements: the pylon, and eight levels of horizontal struts extending outward, with diagonal bracing. The three uppermost levels anchor a 60-foot support for the upraised arm. Today specialists think workmen adjusted the position of this arm when they assembled it in Paris in 1883—they made an 18-inch change in the support, bringing the arm and head closer together.

Bartholdi's own account of the project never mentions this alteration, possibly done for technical reasons. Subtleties of his design required corresponding variations in the flat bars that link the central framing to the skin. Eiffel allowed for this in calculating the overall stability of the statue, the play of stress in its frame, the strength of iron, the effect of wind. "Liberty" has stood serenely in gusts as strong as 90 miles per hour.

Techniques of hammered—or *repoussé*—metal were known in classical antiquity. Metal-casting had almost made them obsolete, except for projects like this. Metal can be hammered thinner than it can be cast, and the difference of weight is all-important for immense works. Since less metal is needed, money can be saved. Moreover, the repoussé technique produces sections easily packed for shipment—a significant factor in this project.

For "Liberty," the skin was only 2½ millimeters, or 3/32 of an inch, in thickness. It needed extensive support from inside. But what? Here the past gave Bartholdi little help. The best precedent, a copper colossus in Italy, rested its 76 feet 9 inches of metal on a ponderous core of masonry. Bartholdi, with a figure measuring 151 feet 1 inch of copper from base to tip of the torch, needed a different framework.

Eugène Emmanuel Viollet-le-Duc, the famous architect, art historian, and restorer of medieval buildings, was consulted. He suggested internal compartments filled with sand; any one of these could be emptied for repairs if necessary. He died in 1879, leaving his plan unfinished, and the problem was referred to a man who solved it brilliantly.

At age 47 and the peak of his career, Gustave Eiffel had become famous building iron bridges for the burgeoning railroad network in France. He had ventured into other huge projects before turning his attention to the statue and to his final masterpiece, the 300-meter (almost 1,000-foot) tower that bears his name. Like the other major figures associated with "Liberty," he was a man of his times: confident, energetic, daring, entrepreneurial, and an ardent believer in technology.

Eiffel's vision allowed no distinction between form and function. Scorning embellishment for its own sake, he would mutter "stupid as an architect" when he saw a design lacking in purity. As he pared his own designs down to their functional essence, he achieved in his enormous works a spindly, almost gossamer elegance.

Eiffel was Bartholdi's complementary opposite. While the sculptor labored over a traditional, even sentimental image, the engineer applied his talents to a framework revolutionary in the realm of art. He began with an Eiffel trademark: a pylon of four wrought-iron columns, 96 feet 11 inches high, similar to the soaring piers that held his bridges over deep valleys. For the torch and arm, an awkward feature to support, dense cross-bracing and reinforced platework—a box truss, in technical terms—provided stability.

Eiffel's design solved the unprecedented problem of connecting the pylon to the irregular contours of the copper skin. Projecting from the pylon were eight levels of L-shaped iron bars, horizontal struts with diagonal bracing between them—the secondary supports. The struts would be bolted to flat bars—the tertiary supports. These, connected in turn to iron strapwork on the skin, would function like springs. Thus the statue would literally float on its framework, in a brilliant demonstration of the resiliency of wrought iron. With iron placed against copper, harmful chemical changes could be expected, so a protective layer of asbestos was set between them.

Even before the pylon rose over neighboring rooftops, Gaget and Gauthier's workyards had become a tourist attraction. Some 300,000 visitors paid to watch the work. Celebrities came too—among them, former President Grant. The site, it is said, turned into a public forum for impromptu speeches about *liberté, egalité, fraternité.*

In France, at least, Bartholdi's financial worries had come to an end, thanks to ingenious fund-raising ploys; but publicity stunts continued. On one occasion, 20 reporters and their hosts were fed lunch on a platform inside the statue's right leg.

On the Fourth of July in 1884, the American Minister to France, Levi Morton, formally accepted the statue on behalf of the American people. Ferdinand de Lesseps, builder of the Suez Canal, made the presentation—he had become chairman of the French committee after Laboulaye's death in 1883. When the ceremonies were over, the proud

Eerie closeups of the uncrated face suggest the artist's vision and the engineer's insight. The view from inside the face (opposite) shows the wrought-iron strapwork that reinforces the copper skin throughout the structure. Copper strips or "saddles" hold this iron armature to the skin. Flat iron bars linked to the pylon by angle bars provide resiliency and transfer the load to the main columns. Thus no part of the skin must support the weight of any other. All of these components had to wait on Bedloe's Island more than a year before the final assembling could begin. That took more than three months.

sculptor led a trail of dignitaries up a helical staircase to the statue's crown, "with nothing to guide our steps," wrote Morton, "but the thousand and one little eyelets of sunlight that came through the rivet holes." An American eyewitness called this "perhaps the most notable celebration of the day that has ever been held in the Old World."

Embarrassment might have been the most appropriate sentiment for Americans. The statue was, so to speak, all dressed up with no place to go. In New York, work on the pedestal hadn't even begun.

Since the American committee was formed in 1877, every fund-raising effort had fallen short. In the aftermath of the Civil War, the rush of westward expansion and rapid industrialization, the turmoil of a boom-and-bust economy, this project had little resonance. If Americans considered the statue at all, it stirred misgivings. If this really was a gift, why pay ransom in the price of a pedestal? Average citizens seemed willing to leave the cost to millionaires, and the rich of the Gilded Age found other uses for their money.

Moreover, newspapers often referred to the statue as "New York's lighthouse," and suggested that New Yorkers foot the bill. Other cities—San Francisco, Boston, and Chicago among them—offered to take the statue and pay for her footstool. When Baltimore made a bid, the *New York Times* gibed that it came too late: "Painted Post, N.Y., and Glover, Vt., applied . . . more than two years ago." Meanwhile, the *Providence Journal* reported that a plan was afoot to erect the Statue of Liberty atop the half-finished Washington Monument.

Still, the committee had more than $100,000 in hand when work began on Bedloe's Island in 1883, supervised by the Civil War general Charles P. Stone. He had to dig through old Fort Wood, a coast-defense work dating from the early 1800s. Its bomb-proof masonry doubled the projected cost. After excavating 20 feet to schist and granite, Stone produced an engineering feat of his own—23,500 tons of foundation, the largest single mass of concrete anywhere at the time.

If Stone was the man for his task, which took a year, the designer of the pedestal came equally prepared for his. This was Richard Morris Hunt, the most fashionable American architect of his day. After many revisions, he worked out an 89-foot structure of concrete faced with granite. It combined mass with detail to link the star-shaped fortress below, elegantly but unobtrusively, to the statue above.

On August 5, 1884, the cornerstone—a six-ton block of granite quarried on Leete's Island, Connecticut—was hoisted into place, to be dedicated with elaborate formalities and full Masonic ritual. The event garnered much-needed publicity; but four months later, with only 15 feet of pedestal in place, work stopped for lack of funds.

By early 1885 the situation was desperate. In Paris, Bartholdi was dismantling his statue to ship it to New York. In Washington, a Congressional bill appropriating $100,000 for the pedestal died in committee. In Albany, the state legislature had already approved a $50,000 expenditure for the project, only to see it vetoed by Governor Grover Cleveland on constitutional grounds. As the statue was a gift to the nation, he explained, local authorities could not assume its cost. By a pleasant irony, Cleveland as President would witness its unveiling.

By a further irony, a man who had championed Cleveland's presidential campaign also rescued "Liberty." Hungarian-born Joseph Pulitzer, a man of great ambition and boundless energy, had arrived in 1864 in time to serve in the Union's ranks. His meteoric rise in publishing began in St. Louis, where by 1873 he controlled the German-language *Westliche Post* and by 1880 he owned the *Post-Dispatch*. In May 1883 he bought the faltering New York *World* from its robber-baron owner, Jay Gould. Within two years he had increased its circulation from about 15,000 to more than 100,000, given its support to Cleveland and the Democratic Party, and opened a campaign for "Liberty" as an ideal cause for working-class readers. An earlier effort had fizzled; this would be different.

In a spirited editorial, Pulitzer pointed out that the statue had been paid for "by the masses of the French people"—workingmen and artisans, tradesmen and shop girls: "by all." It was a gift from people to people, not from French millionaires to American ones. Every reader should give something, "however little," and every single donor would be named in print.

Now the *World* offered prizes to the biggest contributors; it encouraged such special events as a Bartholdi Day at the Brighton Beach race track, and these raised thousands of dollars. Day after day, Pulitzer's editorials hammered away at "croakers and laggards" and, especially, at the rich. He announced that William Vanderbilt and Jay Gould together had contributed one $500 Confederate note—"so that we may no longer be called the 'closefisted millionaires.'"

Especially compelling were the thousands of letters printed as the money started flowing in. They came from adults: "I am a young man of foreign birth and have seen enough of monarchical governments to appreciate the blessings of this Republic." Or "Since leaving off smoking cigarettes I have gained twenty-five pounds, so I cheerfully inclose a penny for each pound." They came on behalf of infants: "Although I cannot creep, I can shout for the cause of Liberty when my papa and mama want to sleep. Enclosed please find one dollar from a little boy eight months old." "Inclosed find 50 cents, collected at a birthday

"A hundred Fourths of July" rolled into "a delirious and glorious one"—so a newspaper summed up the jubilation at the statue's unveiling on October 28, 1886. Fog and drizzle, with smoke from saluting cannon and countless boats, obscured her from admiring thousands afloat and on shore. But President Grover Cleveland, undaunted, vowed on behalf of the nation that "a stream of light shall pierce the darkness of ignorance and men's oppression until liberty shall enlighten the world."

party." Or from gamblers: "inclosed please find $10, the contribution of a poker party to the Bartholdi Fund." A few, perhaps, came from staff ghost writers. One declared: "I am a little girl nine years old . . . and I will send you a pair of my pet game bantams, if you will sell them and give the money to the Statue." The *World* preferred to keep them and report on their well-being until new owners were found.

"ONE HUNDRED THOUSAND DOLLARS!" A headline shouted the news on August 11, 1885—the goal had been reached. It had taken 120,000 contributors from around the country a mere five months to accomplish what nine years of genteel haggling could not. And not a moment too soon. The statue had already arrived in more than 200 cases aboard a French naval transport. Off Sandy Hook, in midnight darkness, a pilotboat had hailed an odd-looking, bark-rigged white vessel: "What ship?" A voice with a strong accent answered: "*Isère*, from Rouen." "It's all right," said the pilot, getting ready to board her and to take her into harbor; "she's got that big Liberty aboard." Small boys in Manhattan yelled a welcome—"Three cheers for the Eye-sore!" "Hurrah for the Iseree!" And all the travail faded into dimming memory while the last preparations went forward.

On the great day of unveiling, President Cleveland called Bartholdi "the greatest man in America today," and the long-suffering sculptor became the toast of society. One of the occasion's few discordant notes came from a boatload of suffragettes who, in the maritime traffic jam near Bedloe's Island, tried to point up the significance of "Liberty's" embodiment as a woman.

According to the *New York Herald,* no tickets to the ceremony were issued to ladies. Its reporter warned "the fair sex" that accommodations would be limited; and in fact few ladies braved the nasty weather. Among those not included was the poet Emma Lazarus.

In 1883 she had composed a sonnet, "The New Colossus," for an exhibition to raise funds for the pedestal. A member of a prominent New York Jewish family, she was inspired by her horror at the anti-Semitic riots in Russia and the sight of the refugees who fled them—"men of brilliant talents and accomplishments," she said, reduced to "menial drudgery." No mere token of Franco-American ties, Lazarus's statue was the "Mother of Exiles" who silently welcomed the world's "huddled masses yearning to breathe free," its "wretched refuse," and its "homeless, tempest-tost" to the "golden door" of America. A great new wave of immigration was rising, and was already highly controversial; neither Lazarus nor her poem was mentioned at the unveiling.

Only in 1903—and then, only through the efforts of an admiring philanthropist—was a plaque bearing the poem affixed to a wall inside the pedestal. Only in the late 1930s did the poem begin to win recognition as an American classic.

It was the immigrants of the late 19th century and early 20th—most of whom entered the United States through New York's harbor—who gave the statue the identity defined by Lazarus. Not all of them were waiting eagerly to see her; some were below decks struggling with luggage as their ship passed by; but their experience of their new homeland began where she stood. She became a symbol of welcome, and of America itself.

In time, that symbolism was adopted by the entire nation; and today, the Statue of Liberty remains the most poignant image of America—to friend or foe—throughout the world. Her French parentage now all but forgotten, it is appropriate that "Liberty's" new symbolic meaning came to life through those who themselves sought new life in the United States of America.

The Wanderer finds Liberty in America

Americans eagerly adapt the image. Mae West poses in 1934 to publicize the movie Belle of the Nineties. Goldie Mabovitz Meyerson—later famous as Golda Meir, prime minister of Israel—plays "Liberty" in a 1919 pageant in Milwaukee. An Anglo-American ball in London in June 1914, attended by 4,000, features Mrs. John Astor in a midnight tableau as Columbia with attributes of Bartholdi's goddess—tablet, torch, and crown.

Shackles of oppression and alien rule lie broken at the feet of "Liberty."

She has stood for a hundred years as a symbol of a new world and a new life to the millions who come to America seeking opportunity.

Old Lands, New Nation

A son of Erin assesses the cost of escape from Dublin around 1855. A heritage of anti-Catholic laws, poverty, and starvation drove more than 4.5 million Irish to America between 1820 and 1920.

"**W**e are not a nation, so much as a world. . . ." Thus Herman Melville, writing at the 19th century's midpoint, defined an America given form and essence by the varied people who arrived on its shores to make a new life. They were borne, in Melville's day, on the first flood tide from western Europe: the famine-stricken Irish whom the novelist saw languishing on Liverpool's quays and the German peasants whose brave hymns rose amid the howl of ocean storms. They were the English artisans, Scandinavian farmers, and all the others who in ragged armadas set sail with their hopes and belongings. In the decade before the Civil War, two and a half million new immigrants joined America's twenty-three million inhabitants.

There had been nothing to compare with it in diversity, avowed a newspaper, "since the encampments of the Roman Empire."

Human migrations began, unrecorded, long before the rise of Rome. Yet in the entire history of human mobility, the epic of American immigration stands out in scope and speed and magnitude. To speak of an America without immigrants is to imagine a blank, unpeopled wilderness. The ancestors of today's "Native Americans" were themselves immigrants of a sort when they began spreading into North America from Siberia some 300 centuries ago. By the time white explorers appeared, the Indians of the Americas had developed a striking cultural and linguistic diversity, comparable to that of Europe.

In their turn, the colonial settlers were, at first, immigrants as well. They laid the cultural groundwork—English and otherwise—for the western Europeans who followed them, mostly from the same countries, in the 19th century. They fixed a pattern that endured for those who began to arrive later from different lands and continents.

Even in the context of the colonial era, a Frenchman-turned-American could ask, "What then is the American, this new man?" He gave a lengthy, but incomplete answer: "a mixture of English, Scotch, Irish, French, Dutch, Germans, and Swedes. From this promiscuous breed, that race now called Americans have arisen." He might have added the Swiss, or the Sephardic Jews, expelled from Spain in 1492 but still speaking a medieval Spanish. He might have included the three-quarters of a million Africans, mostly in bondage, who were the colonies' largest non-English group, or the dwindling Native American population. And to the west and south, beyond the British colonies, were strong tribes of Indians, as well as Spaniards and Frenchmen, in regions that would later become part of the young nation.

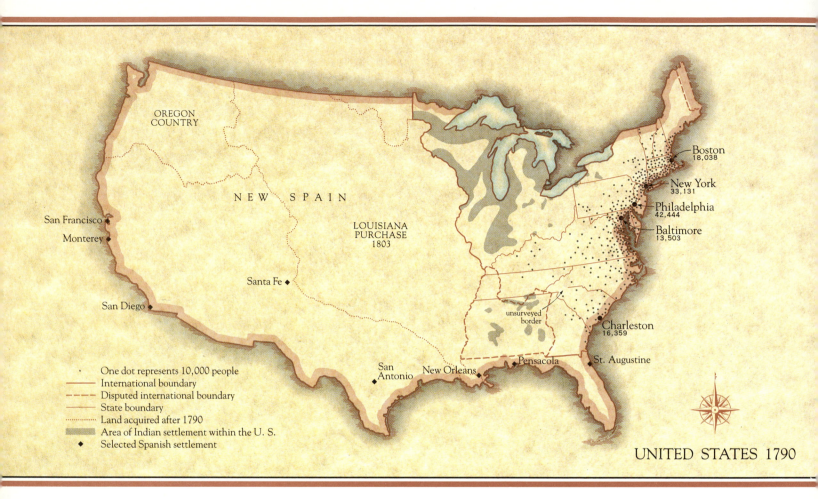

OREGON
COUNTRY

NEW SPAIN

LOUISIANA
PURCHASE
1803

San Francisco ◆

Monterey ◆

Santa Fe ◆

San Diego ◆

unsurveyed
border

San
Antonio ◆   New Orleans ◆   Pensacola ◆   St. Augustine ◆

Boston
18,038

New York
33,131

Philadelphia
42,444

Baltimore
13,503

Charleston
16,359

- · One dot represents 10,000 people
- —— International boundary
- – – Disputed international boundary
- —— State boundary
- ····· Land acquired after 1790
- ▒ Area of Indian settlement within the U. S.
- ◆ Selected Spanish settlement

UNITED STATES 1790

Land of hope: The first United States census, taken in 1790, numbers its people at 3,929,214. Most Americans live along the coast; the center of population lies 23 miles east of Baltimore, Maryland. Five harbor towns—Boston, New York, Philadelphia, Baltimore, and Charleston—have grown to cities of more than 10,000. Land remains available farther west, although settlers have already pushed Indian tribes into the Appalachian Mountains and beyond. In the Northwest Territories west of Pennsylvania the Chippewa and other tribes live on ancestral woodlands somewhat diminished by diffused pioneer settlements. In far-off New Spain, a handful of soldiers hold scattered outposts; mission priests live among Native American converts. Too few to control the area, they provide a basis for Spanish claims to East and West Florida and the largely unexplored lands west of the Mississippi River. (France will take Louisiana from Spain in 1800, then sell it to the U.S.) Within the 13 states, the English supply about half the settlers, leavened by measures of Scotch-Irish, Scots, and Germans, with sprinklings of Dutch, French, Swedes, Welsh, Finns, Swiss, and others. Blacks number roughly 750,000—a fifth of the total—and southern planters import more slaves. Although the free population increases rapidly, the economy, based on agriculture, has work for the willing. In return for their passage, many of Europe's poor bind themselves into servitude for some years—four, on average. Newspapers regularly carry advertisements like those opposite. Historians estimate that more than half the white immigrants to the English colonies south of New England arrived in the New World as indentured servants.

The non-Indian inhabitants of the English colonies had come for a variety of reasons. Most were of humble origin; nearly half came as indentured servants, bound to an employer in return for the cost of their passage. Some came voluntarily, others involuntarily—a few on the *Mayflower* but thousands more in the infernal holds of slave ships. Among other things, the colonists were refugees, convicts, and adventurers, representatives of all occupations and most creeds.

"Europe, and not England, is the parent country of America," as Thomas Paine pointed out. At first the offspring sought in their new homeland the comfort of familiar traditions. Each ethnic group added its distinctive features to the dominant English culture. Skillful German farmers raised livestock, flax, grain, and vegetables in Pennsylvania as they had in Europe. The Scotch-Irish took their sturdy independence to the frontier, in rugged conditions reminiscent of Ulster or of their earlier country, Scotland. Finns introduced their log cabins, the Dutch their windmills, the Scots their looms and whisky.

A nd while some groups quickly became assimilated, others clung fiercely to their own customs and tongues. In 1753 Benjamin Franklin crustily complained of the difficulties of communicating with Pennsylvania's German population, since "few of the English understand the German language, and so cannot address them either from the press or pulpit. . . ." A Marylander who visited New York in 1744 declared in exasperation: "I never was so destitute of conversation in my life as in this voyage. I heard nothing but Dutch spoke all the way." In old age the black evangelist Sojourner Truth remembered her girlhood in Ulster County, New York: Born a slave about 1800 among Dutch-speaking Protestants, she didn't know a word of English at the age of ten.

Isolation, literal and cultural, made it possible for such differences to survive. Most of the population lived in rural areas; and for even the most prosperous, existence had its risks. For many, it lacked comfort. In 1733, one of the largest plantations on Virginia's frontier struck the wealthy William Byrd as "a poor dirty hovel, with hardly anything in it but children that wallowed about like so many pigs." Other families lived in caves and lean-tos until they could put up a house. The frontier's threats to life and limb included unfriendly Indians, white outlaws, wild animals, accidents, and disease.

Frontier dwellers became, of necessity, self-reliant, independent, and resourceful—more so, in all probability, than their European contemporaries. The ease of acquiring land worked to bring down the barriers of class. So did the prospect of success based on individual pluck, for

Sounding horn signals the departure of the mail coach carrying emigrants from a village in County Kerry, Ireland, in 1866. By the early 1800s, fast-growing populations in many countries were causing a division of farmland into plots too small to support a family. Disaster struck Ireland after blight hit the potato crop in 1845 and other crops failed across the continent. Immigration became the great hope for millions of Europeans—the only hope for some. Opposite, Ireland pleads on behalf of her starving people in an American cartoon of the mid-1800s. Desperate folk looted potato storehouses in Galway during the famine.

which Benjamin Franklin, once a poor printer, served as the era's most cherished example.

But it was in the crucible of the Revolution that this new man, the American, confirmed his public character. People of English background differed on the issues. At least 80,000 colonists chose to leave the rebellious states rather than disavow the Crown, and other Loyalists, however reluctantly, remained. Patriots of diverse ethnic backgrounds struggled together to cast off England's yoke. Those who made common cause were linked together in a new and profound sense, and staked their claim, whatever their origins, to full and equal standing in the new nation.

While the Declaration of Independence defined the grievances of the people by the rights of Englishmen, it asserted the dignity of the people by a grander norm: ". . . that all men are created equal . . . endowed by their Creator with certain unalienable Rights. . . ." Thus it emphasized the idea of America as a haven for those of all backgrounds—as an "asylum," Thomas Paine said, "for the persecuted lovers of civil and religious liberty from every part of Europe."

Few immigrants arrived in the United States during its first half century. War on both sides of the Atlantic disrupted travel. Europe's rulers imposed restrictions to keep their military manpower and skilled labor at their command. With few newcomers to join them, America's ethnic communities dwindled, while their languages were passing out of use. A common tongue was a proof of unity: As DeWitt Clinton wrote in 1814, "the triumph and adoption of the English language have been the principal means of melting us down into one people." In fact it was a vigorous, homegrown hybrid speech that flourished, as Noah Webster's book of American spelling proved in 1783.

Thus Americans were indeed a homogeneous people at the dawn of the 19th century, when the first flowering of nationhood coincided with a lull in immigration. In Europe, meanwhile, changes were taking place that would give the United States more than four million newcomers between 1840 and 1860—an influx roughly equal to the number of residents in 1790.

For the great migrations of the 19th century to begin, the pull of America had to be galvanized by factors tending to push Europeans out of their homelands. Those factors influenced northern and western Europe first, southern and eastern Europe later.

By far the most important of them was an enormous increase in the European population after 1750: from 140 to 250 million people within a century. Mortality rates declined sharply, for a number of reasons. Medical knowledge grew and sanitation improved; killer pandemics of plague and smallpox disappeared. New farming techniques, such as crop rotation and the introduction of chemical fertilizers, increased the food supply. So, significantly, did the widespread cultivation of the potato, a South American contribution to the Old World. Potatoes fed more people per acre than did grain, and soon became a staple.

In human terms the "expansion" of population usually meant just the opposite: the constriction of peasant families into ever-smaller plots of land. Law or ancient custom required, in some areas, that all sons or all children inherit equally. Since more children were surviving into adulthood, their portions would inevitably be smaller. In such regions, the holdings often became too small to support new families. Plots of less than an acre were the norm in some villages along the Rhine. Even worse was the situation in Ireland. "Every patch produces a new family," wrote one observer in 1822, "every member of a family, a new patch. . . . Hence a country covered with beggars . . . a complete pauper warren."

Although Scandinavian farmers usually bequeathed their land to the eldest son, leaving the others to find a different livelihood, they also could foresee trouble. The population was growing; agricultural land was not. In Norway, one future immigrant commented with sad irony that his countrymen, who had obeyed the Biblical command to "multiply and replenish the earth," would be forced to seek a new Canaan.

Other changes conspired to uproot peasants from the soil. Growing cities created new markets for foodstuffs. The larger the farm, the greater the profit to its owner. Powerful landlords enclosed common lands that independent farmers and tenants alike had relied on for firewood and pasturage. Or the landlords simply consolidated their estates and evicted their unhappy tenants.

In Ireland, where industry was almost nonexistent, the plight of the evicted became especially wretched. "For God's sake give us work," scores of villagers begged a traveling surveyor. Another traveler saw barefoot girls who had walked for miles to a town market in hopes of selling a few eggs or an apronful of raw wool.

Elsewhere smallholders fared better than tenants, but few could compete with the richer landowners and many went bankrupt buying equipment or fields for the effort.

The entire economic system was in upheaval. Beginning in the mid-1700s in England and spreading to the continent, the Industrial Revolution was mechanizing the production of all kinds of goods.

Rallying to the standard, Berliners throw up a street barricade during the uprising of 1848, one of many in western Europe at mid-century. The ideals of the French Revolution and the defeat of Napoleon Bonaparte fostered among many Europeans expectations of greater freedom and economic security—hopes dashed by the refusal of their rulers to institute reforms. Although only a few thousand individuals immigrated as a direct result of these revolts—or their failures—their decisions reflect the social unrest that prompted millions of others to leave their homelands for America.

Formerly, individual artisans had fashioned by hand life's necessary craftwork. Their finely honed skills, passed from father to son and mother to daughter for generations, inspired pride in the makers themselves and respect in society at large. Now factory machines and unskilled labor produced such items in quantity at a fraction of the old cost. Thousands of artisans were thrown out of work.

Some moved to factory towns and found jobs. The change usually meant low wages, drudgery, loss of status, loss of independence. Others tried to halt the march of industry by attacking the machines that were replacing them. In Germany, wagoners tore up railway tracks and boatmen fired shots at the sleek new steamers on the Rhine.

Farmers were affected too as industry placed new demands on land. Rolling emerald farmscapes in Wales and England, yielding to needs for coal and iron, gave way to the gray dross of new mines. Legions of displaced farmers and craftsmen longed to return to the familiar security of life in the countryside.

Against a background of sweeping change, the idea of emigration was at first most appealing to those who still had hopes and resources but feared a future of want and desperation. Often enough, local events or conditions—such as a single killing frost in a vineyard—gave an immediate reason to leave. Emigration was spurred by bitter winters and high food prices in the 1820s, by crop failures on the continent in the 1840s, by unemployment in England late in the same decade.

None of those events compared with the Irish famine which started in 1845. Ireland had become so dependent on the potato that a third of its people ate almost nothing else. The plant was subject to various diseases, and a new peril appeared in the 1840s, a blight not understood for years and not successfully dealt with until 1885. Its cause is a fungus that flourishes under moist, calm, warm conditions: *Phytophthora infestans* can kill the infected plant quickly, or lurk in the stored tuber. Slightly diseased potatoes, if used for planting, can yield a doomed crop. If stored where they get damp, they rot into a reeking mess.

Blight struck scattered areas in 1845; and when it struck again in 1846, the devastation was as sudden as it was total. Father Mathew, a priest on his way from Cork to Dublin that summer, took heart upon seeing the plants in bloom. Returning just a week later, he saw only "one wide waste of putrefying vegetation. . . . The wretched people were seated on the fences of their decaying gardens, wringing their hands and wailing bitterly the destruction that had left them foodless."

Private relief efforts could not feed a population of more than eight million. Invaluable but inadequate gifts came from the United States, including $170 sent by Choctaw Indians and hundreds of thousands sent by Irish-Americans. The English government's attempts at aid were, at best, ill-informed and ineffective. It bought hard "Indian corn" from America for mills incapable of grinding it, sent flour to women who didn't know how to make bread and lacked the ovens to try. The death toll rose in the ferocious winter of 1846-47.

A million people starved or froze or died of relapsing fever and typhus during the famine, which lasted till the 1849 harvest. By 1860 another million and a half had managed to reach the United States.

Though nowhere as desperate as the famine, or as pervasive as economic change, religious discontent inspired thousands of Europeans to seek a new homeland. The first Norwegians to emigrate to America were Quakers at odds with the official state church, which was Lutheran. Jews from many German states felt the spur of hostile policies. Ulster Presbyterians as well as Irish Catholics had chafed under the Penal Laws of English rule, which had forced them to pay taxes that supported the Anglican "church of Ireland."

Decades of war and political upheaval also fostered emigration. The French Revolution had spread radical new notions of liberty and equality, which prompted revolutionary movements in various countries during the 19th century. Unsuccessful uprisings produced successive groups of exiles, and focused political thought on the distant young republic where democracy reigned.

Becoming an American citizen was easy. The alien would report his arrival at a court of record; its clerk would give him a dated certificate. After five proven years of residence, after renouncing his old allegiance and avowing the new, he could receive his certificate of naturalization. Now he could vote, even run for office.

By the 1830s, America was on its way to becoming the cherished goal it has remained ever since. Its obvious lure was economic. Good land had become even more abundant after the Louisiana Purchase of 1803. Jobs were ever more plentiful. Ships were ready to take passengers across the Atlantic.

Awareness of these conditions was spreading in countries where education was improving. True, old legends and vague ideas survived— of a wilderness cursed with earthquakes, or an Eden blessed with Noble Savages. As late as 1827 a major German newspaper put reports from Virginia, Texas, and Mexico under the heading "South America." But as more accurate accounts came on the market, they fanned interest in the United States into the rage known as "America fever." Cheap newspapers and journals sprang up in Britain and Germany solely to inform and advise would-be emigrants, and were passed from hand to

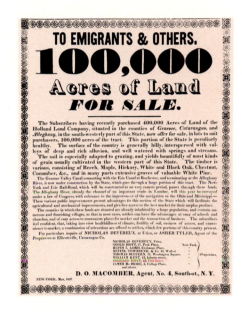

Promise of land, more than any other inducement, attracted 19th-century immigrants to America. Broadsides like this 1837 example from New York promised rich valleys watered with streams and springs, soil especially suited to grazing, and good timber. Opposite, the frontispiece of an 1869 guide for immigrants, one of thousands distributed in Europe, appeals to their hopes. At the top, pioneers camp at a wilderness homestead; below, the same scene, transformed by their labor, has developed into a prosperous community.

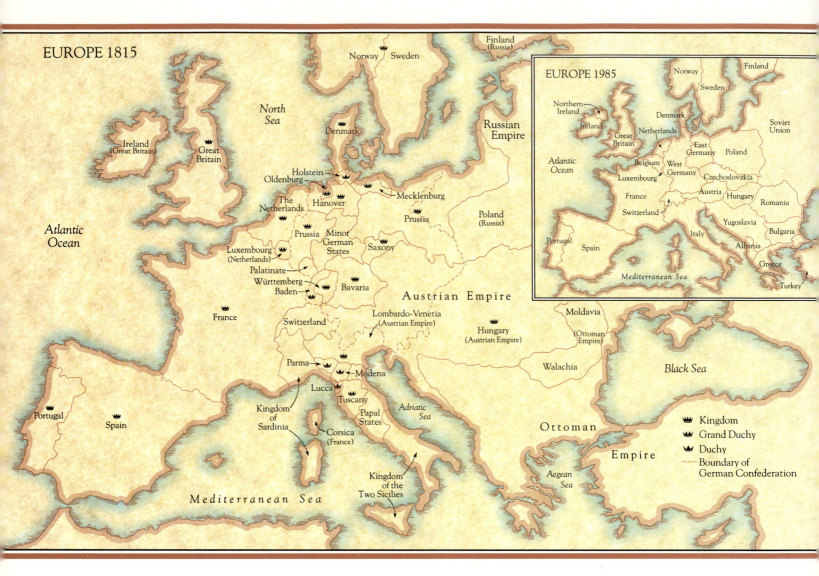

EUROPE 1815

Norway · Sweden

Finland (Russia)

North Sea

Denmark

Russian Empire

Ireland (Great Britain)

Great Britain

Atlantic Ocean

Holstein
Oldenburg
The Netherlands
Hanover
Mecklenburg
Prussia

Prussia
Minot German States
Saxony

Poland (Russia)

Luxembourg (Netherlands)
Palatinate
Württemberg
Baden
Bavaria

France

Austrian Empire

Switzerland

Lombardo-Venetia (Austrian Empire)

Hungary (Austrian Empire)

Moldavia

(Ottoman Empire)

Walachia

Black Sea

Parma
Modena
Lucca
Tuscany
Papal States
Kingdom of Sardinia
Corsica (France)

Adriatic Sea

Portugal

Spain

Kingdom of the Two Sicilies

Ottoman

Empire

Aegean Sea

Mediterranean Sea

♛ Kingdom
♛ Grand Duchy
♛ Duchy
— Boundary of German Confederation

EUROPE 1985

Norway
Sweden
Finland

Northern Ireland
Ireland
Great Britain

Denmark
Netherlands
East Germany
West Germany
Belgium
Luxembourg

Soviet Union

Poland

Atlantic Ocean

France
Switzerland

Austria
Czechoslovakia
Hungary
Romania

Portugal
Spain

Italy

Yugoslavia
Bulgaria
Albania
Greece

Turkey

Mediterranean Sea

hand "as long as the texture of the paper holds together." Several publications ran a question-and-answer column, encouraging readers to go or to stay according to their circumstances. A correspondent with experience as a teacher, sailor, farmer, and railway construction supervisor was "just the man to go and prosper." A narrow specialty was another matter: "On a bell-hanger's prospects we cannot speak."

In general, it was agreed that life in America was best suited to folk of the humbler classes, good at manual labor. Even they, however, were warned away from the western frontier: "It will be as well to let the Americans take the rough edge off the country."

Pamphlets and guidebooks for prospective emigrants were sold in hundreds of thousands. Typical of such works was the *Emigrant's Guide to the United States of America,* published in London in 1818. It began with notes on Canada, which was drawing "considerable numbers" of British settlers, but concentrated on her southern neighbor, which was attracting "the great stream of emigration." It sketched the basics of geography and reviewed each state and territory in fair detail, because emigrants should carefully choose their destination before setting out.

Climate was always noted—Massachusetts: "salubrious and healthy." Maine: "spring, hardly any." District of Columbia: "summer pretty warm." There was advice on how to survive hot, humid weather: "The labourer or mechanic should put off his ordinary clothes, and wear next his skin a loose flannel shirt. . . ." Soil received equal attention—Ohio: "Generally excellent." Kentucky: "Every kind, from the best to the worst." Louisiana and Indiana: "Generally rich and fertile."

No less than 150 million acres lay in the public domain east of the Mississippi River, surveyed and ready for development. (To the west of the Mississippi, far more would soon be available.) The federal government was offering this for sale in quarter-section parcels: 160 acres at $2 an acre on a four-year installment plan, or $1.64 an acre cash. An industrious farmer who could make the $80 down payment could "easily" earn enough to cover the rest. His *"equal share"* of taxes would be "but a trifle," without excise or rent. "Such is the system!"

Farmers were warned that they "must learn a number of things not connected with agriculture in some other countries"—how to wield an ax with dexterity to cut down trees, to recognize different species of trees and useful wood. A year as a farmhand would turn the immigrant into an expert, earning $12 to $15 a month plus room and board.

Artisans and laborers were given wage rates for various places. Carpenters and masons in Geneva, New York, could expect $1.50 a day;

Crazy quilt of states covers the land the immigrants left. It resulted from the Congress of Vienna, where European rulers met in 1814 and 1815, following the defeat of Napoleon Bonaparte, to carve up a continent. They created buffer states on France's borders to preserve the balance of power, and parceled out territory to allies in the fight against imperial France. Prussia and Austria each annexed portions of Poland, leaving a shrunken and nominal kingdom ruled by Tsar Alexander I of Russia. In their negotiations, the rulers paid scant attention to the surging ideas of nationhood that would eventually lead to the far more unified Europe of today (inset map). Prince Metternich of Austria emerged as the strongest figure of the Congress, and probably of mainland Europe. His unflinching support of the old dynasties drove his crusade to stamp out what he knew as "liberalism"— the increasing demands of European commoners for a measure of constitutional protection and a degree of representation in their governments.

A cartoon (lower) published in 1849 depicts Austrian emperor Francis Joseph I (at right) putting down rebellious subjects in Hungary. Frederick William IV of Prussia sweeps intellectuals and liberals toward France, where Louis Napoleon waits to hurry them onto ships sailing for America.

mechanics in Cincinnati, $2; common laborers in rural Ohio, about 75 cents. A cobbler in Pittsburgh would get $2.50 for making a pair of boots, 94 cents for shoes. Expenses were stated, for comparison. The mechanic in Geneva would pay $2 a week for board. The best hotel in Cincinnati charged $5 a week. Markets in western Ohio sold beef and mutton "3 to 4 cents per lb," fowls $6\frac{1}{4}$ cents apiece, peach brandy 40 cents a gallon. In Pittsburgh, cabbages cost 5 cents each. Prices in Richmond, Virginia, ran much higher, for provisions "of bad quality."

Perhaps less objective than the *Guide* and its later counterparts was the flood of material circulated by American commercial interests after mid-century—shipowners and railroads, especially. Not far behind in time and zeal were the new states beyond the Appalachians, in search of men to break sod, clear forests, drain marshes, and to bring the skills of business and professions. States appointed immigration commissions and competed fiercely for newcomers. Kansas portrayed Minnesota as a land "where, if the poor emigrant did not soon starve to death, he would surely perish with cold." Minnesota boasted a lower death rate than Wisconsin's, and a tract for the latter state devoted chapters to dispelling "Untrue Rumors." Such materials were commonly printed in German, Dutch, Welsh, French, Norwegian, and Swedish as well as English, and distributed accordingly.

But the most effective advocates of America were those who had already succumbed to its lure. Their letters, as all still at home well knew, contained better evidence than the propaganda of American companies or states. With plain-spoken eloquence, many correspondents described America's fruitfulness. "Norway," wrote one, "cannot be compared to America any more than a desert can be compared to a garden in full bloom." A Welshman reported simply, "We can eat our beefsteaks or ham every morning with our breakfast." As proof of their prosperity, many enclosed large remittances or even prepaid fares with their "America letters." Others dwelt on American social equality: "Here, it is not asked, what or who was your father, but the question is, what are you."

Often the prospect of reunion with loved ones would be decisive. A tone of pleading underlies homely detail in a letter penned on Sunday, March 20, 1796, by a man in Monmouth County, New Jersey: "Dear Mother I want you to come here very much and live with Me and you can live better than in Best Mans house in Ireland. . . . Dear Brother Come here without fail as you Can work at your trade. . . . you can get a shilling a yard for weaving anything. . . . Bring your loom. . . . Dear Brother if you have any spare money bring me a good riding saddle as they are dear here. . . . likewise Coper tea kettles is very Dear here. Buy two or three and use them once and you wont Pay any Duty for them. . . ."

Not all correspondents wrote glowingly of life in the United States. Some found much more to object to than the price of copper kettles. But any letter could be expected to draw a gathering at which the local clergyman or schoolmaster might read the contents to a rapt audience. Even more exciting was the reappearance of the emigrant himself—an event that grew more likely as passenger service improved. Sporting a new gold watch, perhaps, or a dapper serge suit, the former peasant might amuse as much as dazzle his countrymen. He might brag

Capturing the attention of a Danish carpenter and his family, a Mormon agent describes a new Zion (now Salt Lake City, Utah). Beginning in 1850, the Church of Jesus Christ of Latter-day Saints sent missionaries to Denmark and other countries on the continent. By the end of the century, 12,000 Mormons had emigrated from Denmark alone— and nearly 180,000 other Danes as well. Many of them came not from the poorer regions but from the most fertile agricultural areas, where farmland had become so expensive that young couples setting up housekeeping could not afford to buy their own farms.

Dream of self-satisfied prosperity
contrasts with the grim reality of flybitten
penury in caricatures published in Prussi
in 1838. Concerned about loss of

Danish children's view of America: Lollipop trees flourish in a fabulous land where it rains lemonade, where chocolate bars substitute for bread, where grown-up delights like wine and cigars abound, and where school hardly exists. This fantasy illustrated a Danish poem of 1830 that gained and held widespread popularity. By its definition of liberty, "you spit on the floors when you feel like that / and play with cigars and fire."

Opposite, giant eggs and a monstrous potato overshadow the even greater wonder of owning a horseless carriage— a comic postcard of the early 1900s. Published in Kansas, it sold widely in the United States and Canada. Such humor merely exaggerated the glowing reports successful immigrants sent home.
In 1863, a family in San Francisco wrote to relatives still in Wales: "Potatoes grow here to an immense size; it is very common to see them weighing a pound, three pounds, and also seven pounds, and I saw a report that some grow here that will weigh twenty pounds. . . . Carrots and parsnips grow very big here; I have seen plenty here that would measure as long as my arm, and some even longer than that."

until they compared him, in the phrase used of one Irishman, not to "a blow but a constant blast." But in general he was taken most seriously. One Norwegian expatriate remarked that "the rumor of my homecoming passed like a flame through the country. . . . Many traveled 20 Norwegian miles [equal to more than 130 American miles] in order to talk with me about my trip." In the light of such conversations, some would begin to plan trips of their own.

Fewer than 150,000 Europeans reached the United States during the 1820s; during the 1880s, more than five million came. Between 1820 and 1890, the British Isles sent the largest contingent, followed closely by the German-speaking states, with the Scandinavian countries and the other lands of northwestern Europe far behind. Gradually, southern and eastern Europe were being drawn in too. By 1890 nearly 300,000 Chinese and more than a million Canadians had arrived.

In some instances, the immigrants did not pay the full cost of their journey. German officials sometimes reckoned a one-way ticket to America cheaper than long-term relief. In the deepening shadows of the potato famine, some Irish landlords paid the fares of evicted tenants. Yet most of the individuals who left for America relied completely on their own resources, unassisted and uncontrolled by either public or private agencies, and many set out entirely alone.

The Perils of the Journey

Sober faces of a couple leaving England in 1855 bespeak the mingled emotions of departure: bitterness over hopes frustrated in the homeland; grief; resolution; apprehension. Inevitably, they faced a risky voyage, an uncertain future.

I f any one trait distinguished the America-bound migrant, it was probably the sheer courage to leave behind all that was familiar and strike out for a world of unknowns. Guidebooks or letters might reassure literate travelers, but uncertainties always remained. Even when emigrants knew that some security—in the form of familiar faces or jobs or both—awaited them across the Atlantic, the voyage itself remained a daunting prospect. Many of the early emigrants had never even seen a ship; many had, however, heard tales of a harrowing ocean passage, and much human knavery along the way.

"They go aboard; the old man stands motionless on the shore gazing at the ship, like Mother Norway herself lamenting the going of her children." So runs a poetic description of one incident among many. For those who stayed behind and those who left, the emigrant's departure from the local harbor or the native village was a wrenching moment; all knew they were not likely to see one another again. In the early 19th century, emigrants often faced a complicated, trying journey simply to get to a major seaport—Liverpool, Bremen, Hamburg, Le Havre, Antwerp, and a few others—from which ships bound for America would sail.

In 1820, for instance, a German from Bavaria or Baden or Württemberg would meet infuriating delays trying to go down the Rhine, making his way by foot or cart until he could get passage on a barge or other boat. At state borders the vessel would stop to pay tolls or deal with cargo; he might wait for days until the next departure. From Mainz to Cologne, he might travel on a grain boat, camping out on deck. Disembarking, he could make his way to Utrecht and from there to Amsterdam—slowly—by horse-drawn canal boat.

In later years, more prosperous Europeans enjoyed a much quicker journey by railroad and river steamer. Emigrants from Ireland sometimes sailed direct to America from ports like Dublin or Cork, but more often took a small steamer across the Irish Sea to Liverpool. There transatlantic service was more regular, and competition among shipping lines brought the fares down. The Irish Sea boats were so crowded that passengers often had to stand during the entire crossing, which might take 36 hours. These vessels had little shelter; women and children could use it if cattle and pigs, the valuable cargo, didn't need it.

Once in Liverpool or another major port, emigrants fell prey to an astounding variety of swindlers, despite the efforts of benevolent societies and local officials. The first parasites the travelers encountered were known in English as "runners." Let the bewildered strangers appear, wrote one observer, and immediately "there come as many runners,

who snatch up their luggage as quickly as possible, and carry it away; they are like so many pirates." A gang in Liverpool, nicknamed the Forty Thieves, was notorious for the sums its members extracted from emigrants before releasing their belongings.

Runners led unsuspecting travelers into the clutches of the shady boardinghouse keepers, provisioners, agents, and brokers with whom they were in league. Such "hosts" overcharged their lodgers or tried to delay their departure. In overcrowded Amsterdam, emigrants seeking shelter might wind up in brothels, whose permanent inhabitants would cheerfully call, "Come in, farmer!"

Provisioners swindled emigrants by selling them bad food and drink—a trick that could lead to extreme hardship. Before the 1850s, when regulations outlawed self-provisioning, only cabin class passengers received provisions from the crew. Long afterward, however, steerage food was often barely "sufficient to stave off starvation." Careful planners took precautions. Norwegian housewives began, months before setting out, to salt meat, bake bread, prepare cheese, and pack butter in watertight kegs. Jews traveling in any class could never count on finding kosher facilities, and many left home carrying hundreds of flour-and-sugar wafers; "they were to be our only nourishment for the entire journey." In 1834 a British handbook of "Practical Advice" suggested appropriate quantities for a family of five, including 300 pounds of oatmeal or flour, 56 pounds of ship's biscuit, a gallon of molasses and one of spirits, a 20-pound keg of butter and a 50-pound keg of herring. "A few pounds of tea or coffee, and 28 lbs. of sugar, will be an additional comfort to the females," noted the writer, and luxuries might include "a few oranges (if sound)." But the herring might rot, the butter spoil, or the flour grow moldy—in which case, a captain's compassion was the only hope, and an undependable one.

Dishonest provisioners could tally up additional profits by convincing emigrants that they needed items like bowie knives and telescopes. These ruses would seem plausible because reliable guides suggested bringing "light articles in general, of constant usefulness," such as gunlocks. Not to be outdone by other specialists in fraud, currency dealers often tormented the confused traveler, as a Norwegian blacksmith reported, with wheedling—"I am making you so good an offer . . . at this moment that I cannot promise to stand by it another time"—or insults like "You fool . . . you have lost a lot of money; why did you not come to me?"

In this welter of fraud, sharp practices pervaded the ticket-selling business during the years of sail. Fares fluctuated with demand; ticket

Finding ways across the miles between their inland villages and seacoast cities posed one of the first obstacles for many America-bound emigrants. As in an 1805 woodcut (opposite, lower), boats conveyed those leaving Basel, Switzerland, on the Rhine to the North Sea port of Rotterdam. Subject to fickle weather, and numerous delays for tolls at customhouses, such craft took as long as six weeks to reach saltwater ports. For other travelers, however, treks on foot or in wagons proved even longer and costlier. Legal formalities at the borders of Europe's various statelets delayed them even more, especially if they lacked passports, proof of military service, or birth certificates. But by the 1860s, a new era in transportation had dawned, revolutionizing travel by land and sea.

Frail vessels gave way to sturdier and more comfortable ones (opposite, upper) on the Rhine, still a principal artery to the busy harbors along the North Sea.

In the 1850s mail coaches accepted riders, conveying them to coastal cities with rest stops in way stations like this pleasant one in Prussia. Colorful travel posters—one appears here—announced specific sailing dates. With tedious and costly delays at seaside reduced at last by predictable departures, the number leaving home swiftly burgeoned. Cities and shipowners competed for their patronage. American captains unloaded cargoes of timber, cotton, or tobacco, then recruited passengers for the trip home.

A free city-state until 1871, Bremen managed to capture the north German trade with its new port Bremerhaven, the first regulations to ensure passengers' safety in 1832, ample accommodations reserved at dockside, and special agents to advise travelers. While Le Havre, Hamburg, and Liverpool rivaled Bremen with their steady flow of traffic, they offered few such amenities for some years.

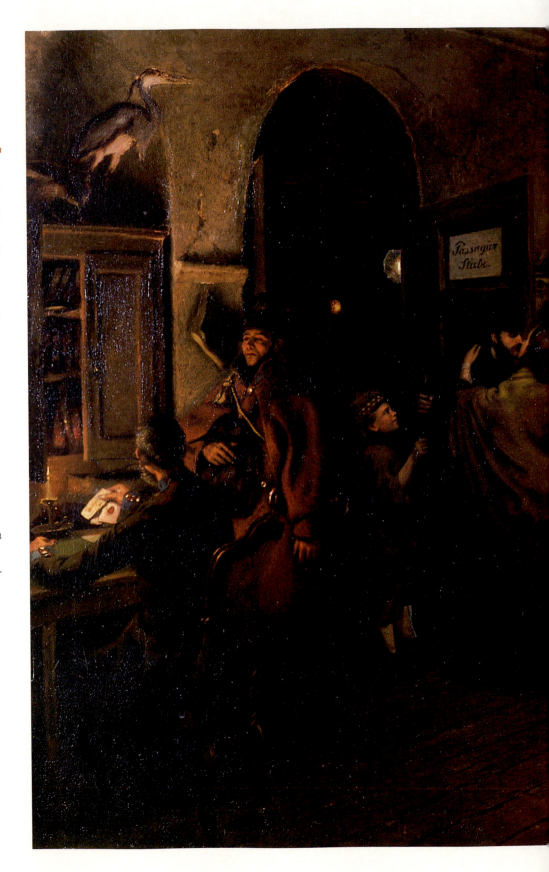

Pioneering as a steam packet for travelers on the Atlantic, the Washington *chugs into Bremerhaven on June 19, 1847. Sweeping changes accompanied the supplanting of sail by steam between the 1840s and 1870s. No longer at the mercy of whimsical breezes, ships adhered to schedules for the first time; several weeks at sea decreased to three, or two; in turn, the risks of death from contagious diseases or starvation also diminished. Increasingly competitive carriers and more stringent laws eventually assured better living conditions on board, but not until late in the century.*

A poster (opposite) from the early 1870s puts a price of $32 on tickets in steerage—the poorest quarters—from Liverpool and Queenstown to New York. Earning a sum equal to about $7 a week by this time, a semiskilled British laborer could set aside enough for his family's fares.

agents took advantage of this to renege on agreed-upon terms and raise fares, alleging that the rates had risen between sailings. Sometimes they sold passages that shipowners refused altogether to honor. But they invariably advertised "the most favourable terms" and "the lowest possible rates." Filthy cargo ships were touted as "floating palaces." A few of the early packet steamers *were* luxury liners, single-class ships fitted with "rosewood, mahogany and bird's eye maple, polished and varnished, and gilded." It was said that "the finest lady in the land has no such boudoir." Many more passenger ships, steam and sail, were second-class vessels, defined by Lloyd's of London as "unfit for carrying dry cargoes, but perfectly fit for the conveyance, *on any voyage*, of cargoes not in their nature subject to sea damage." Ships below this minimal standard undertook the voyage in years of peak demand. Emigrant guides urged travelers to evaluate a ship's seaworthiness, comfort, and crew before booking passage.

An intelligent choice of a ship—sometimes a matter of life or death—was completely beyond the ken of most travelers. Some of them, wrote Herman Melville, were "the most simple people I had ever seen. They seemed to have no adequate idea of distances; and to them, America must have seemed as a place just over a river. " But even the more sophisticated—"an honest family of the green-grocer kind," for instance—would find such decisions bewildering. They received little honest advice during the 19th century's early decades.

For much of that time, official interest, when it existed, focused on other human movements. The Napoleonic wars had broadened the horizons of countless young soldiers, and the Industrial Revolution had forged new trade and transport links. Europeans were leaving home—from the countryside to the city, at first, or from one country to another. About 250,000 German farmers and artisans moved into Russian-controlled areas of Poland between 1818 and 1828; in those years, fewer than 10,000 Germans left for the United States. Or officials might concern themselves with subsidized migrations to overseas possessions. Canada received more British subjects than did the United States in the early 19th century.

Then, officials cared little about the American traffic. They tended to view it as the concern of shippers, who were bridging the Atlantic with cargoes of cotton, tobacco, grain, and timber—and seeking additional profits from emigrant fares on the return.

But as "America fever" began gaining a momentum all its own, the emigration business—honest or otherwise—grew to such proportions that in some ports, whole city blocks contained nothing but establish-

ments devoted to it. Governments started to intervene. Bremen, then an independent city-state, took the lead in 1832. Its ordinances required shipowners to post schedules, draw up passenger lists, keep provisions for passengers, and provide proof of their vessels' seaworthiness. Merchants built a model lodging house for travelers. Official information booths gave honest advice to the bewildered. All this was designed to bring more business to the city, which, for most emigrants, was not as conveniently placed as Rotterdam, Antwerp, and Le Havre. The plan succeeded, and Bremen's rivals began to follow her example.

Sometimes nature itself conspired to deplete the emigrants' funds by prolonging their stay in European ports. Even after steamships made their debut in the passenger trade in the 1840s, many emigrants still traveled on sailing ships, and adverse winds might delay departures. In 1854, for instance, a Dutch farmer named Johannes Remeeus arrived with his family in Antwerp, where he found "2,700 emigrants, mostly Germans, waiting for ships to take them to America. For four weeks the winds had been blowing out of the wrong quarter; hence no ships had entered the harbors of Holland, Belgium, or Germany."

Such delays must have been a special torment for a farmer hoarding as much money as possible for his tract of America's fine soil. Urging thrift upon the traveler, an earlier writer had noted: "Two dollars, saved in Pennsylvania, will purchase (Continued on page 75)

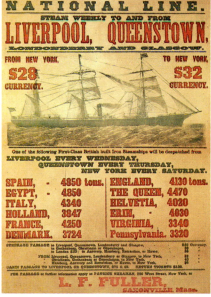

Confronting a surly cook, late risers besiege the galley on the packet Acasta. On sailing ships, a stove or open fire on deck served the whole steerage—unless weather made it unusable. After weeks at sea, spoiled food and tainted water weakened travelers already wearied by overcrowding and seasickness.

Violent storms would pour water into the hold, where terrified people could do little more than pray or hang on for dear life. In such conditions, contagion added its toll to hazards like childbirth. In the somber scene at right, a devout passenger brings dignity to a routine burial at sea, praying for a stricken companion. Aboard the

Leibnitz on a winter crossing from Hamburg in 1867-68, cholera claimed 108 of 544 passengers.

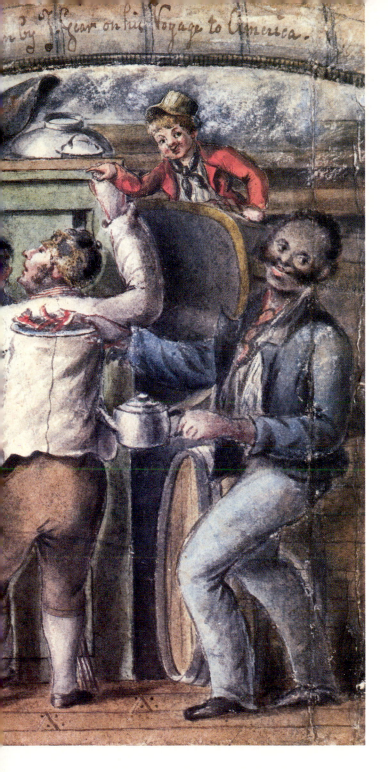

Hamburg to New York. Pitifully few—by a German report, only 89 out of 542—survived this disaster, one of the worst on the Atlantic.

Anna Oppitt mit ihren 2 Tochtern von Groß-Ziegenfeld reißten
nach America, als sie auf dem Wasser fuhren, kam auf dem Schiff
Feuer aus, so daß sie sich verloren schätzten, sie nahmen aber ihre
Zuflucht zu den 14 hl. Nothhelfern, und augenblicklich war
das Feuer gelöscht und sie blieben am Leben.
Geschehe den 6 July 1845.

an acre of good land in the Illinois." That sum, spent in Liverpool or Le Havre or Antwerp, would be an acre lost.

Fortunately for them, the Remeeus family waited only four days in Antwerp before sailing. During that time Johannes fixed up his family's "berth," a space about six feet square, hanging coarse wallpaper and curtains. He volunteered his woodworking skills when the ship's carpenter left after a quarrel with the captain ("the cause of which we did not learn because we could not understand their language"). He obtained, from the crew, standard provisions that included green peas, navy beans, rice, salt, and ham.

Then the family enjoyed a pleasant crossing of just under two months. They had some privacy, generally fair weather and winds, and a healthy diet supplemented by fresh fish that the crew caught. The passengers whiled away the voyage playing games and singing; they wrote letters; women got on with their sewing. Devout travelers turned to the Bible or to prayer, for reassurance, while more worldly individuals looked for flirtations or other distractions.

Miracle rescue at sea appears in this Bavarian tablet dedicated to the "14 Holy Helpers"—saints revered by German Catholics—who saved a woman and her daughters from a fire on July 6, 1845. At harborside, the Archangel Raphael, a patron saint of travel, escorts the faithful in their venture to the New World (above). Financed by devout German laymen, St. Raphael societies rendered assistance on both sides of the Atlantic by the 1880s.

Carnivals of sea life awed wide-eyed peasants and farmers. Johannes Remeeus spotted sharks and yellow turtles near the ship. A Norwegian recalled a "remarkable view" of whales—"I think they numbered into the thousands; they sported with each other on the quiet surface of the sea at sunrise; at times they threw their whole body out of the water. . . ." On still another ship, an old Irishman—"looking straight off from the bows, as if he expected to see New York city every minute"—would sometimes see porpoises playing in the bow wave; then he would shout to his friends, "Look, look, ye divils! look at the great pigs of the s'a!"

Diversions varied according to the nationality of those on board. A Scotswoman, Isabella McKinnon, on a ship out of Greenock for New York, mentioned the music of bagpipes in her diary, and a night of dancing. Germans celebrated their saint's days with music and wine, and ended one party with a toast "to the captain, the officers of the ship, and in fact everybody and everything." Johannes Remeeus noted in his journal one day: "July 4. Declaration of Independence, which is celebrated by everybody American. So did we. Early in the morning flags were run up, and at 8 the crew fired salutes." German and Dutch passengers added small-arms fire, and pork from the ship's stores was distributed for a feast.

Did they think of it as a start toward becoming American? What, after all, would the Americans really be like? The guidebooks usually included answers of a sort. An early example praised the American females—"affable, intelligent, and well bred"—and stressed their "frank and engaging manners." Social subordination in the United States was bluntly dismissed: "there is no such thing." The American character inspired this comment: "They seem to have little sympathy, because their social system does not compel them to suffer."

In the 1830s European novelists were beginning to write blood-and-war-whoop tales of the western frontier. Cheap paperbacks recounted the dirty doings of knife-fighters and brawlers, river pirates and land speculators, and the desperate battles between ferocious Indians and heartless Yankees. Emigrants who read these unnerving best-sellers would be forewarned of the worst. Usually the hero shared the nationality of the author—and the virtues of the European homeland.

Awaiting their confrontation with the Americans, whatever they might be like, emigrants found fellow passengers strange enough. Dutch matrons gossiped about the treatment a newborn baby received from German parents—in Holland it would have "far more elaborate attention." Minor differences led to quarrels, especially with travelers of other nationalities, for nerves frayed quickly in the crowded steerage.

Until mid-century, sailing ships would carry cargo from America

"*Is this a time for sleep?*"—So an 1883 cartoon challenges medical science. Robert Koch isolated the cholera bacterium in that year, but physicians had known for decades that it spread by fouled water and poor sanitation—conditions still found on crowded emigrant ships. Hardly new to American ports, fear of diseases had haunted colonial authorities. As early as 1647, Massachusetts had imposed a quarantine on all inbound ships from the West Indies. In 1796 New York required compulsory inspection, and three years later approved a hospital on Staten Island to isolate sick immigrants. Cholera epidemics in 1832 and 1849 intensified local fear of it. An attack on the hospital in 1856 (opposite), one of many, followed a yellow fever scare.

"Belted round by wharves as Indian isles by coral reefs," Herman Melville wrote in 1850 of New York City, arrival point for 70 percent of all immigrants in the late 19th century. The state's center for them, Castle Garden, the offshore circular structure at left, quickly won praise for its information center, labor market, money exchange, and security. A ban by the Supreme Court on a head tax that supported it, and a devastating fire, led to its demise in 1890; it had processed an estimated eight million since 1855.

to Europe, where the holds would be hastily converted for passengers on the return trip. Herman Melville, who signed on as a sailor for such a voyage in 1839, compared the steerage bunks, "rapidly knocked together with coarse planks," to dog kennels. A bunk would usually be all of 18 inches wide, with 3 feet of headroom. Faint glimmers of light would filter down through open hatchways, each sheltered by the little structure called a "booby hatch."

In such quarters a young woman without a protector—father, husband, or brother—braved nasty indignities. Irishwomen, famous for their modesty, were often at risk; from 1880 to 1900 they undertook the voyage in larger numbers than did their countrymen. (In all other ethnic groups, male emigrants outnumbered females.) When the sexes were not separated—that is, most of the time—such women might be molested by other passengers. Separation exposed them to the greater danger of predation by the crew, who tended to be the dregs of their trade; the better sailors chose better, cleaner ships.

O urs is one of the worst trades in the world for seamen, we get very bad sailors indeed," remarked a Liverpool broker who specialized in the emigrant traffic; "in fact, we get a class of men who go more to pilfer from the steerage passengers than for the purpose of going to sea." Novelist Nathaniel Hawthorne, who served as American consul in Liverpool from 1853 to 1857, complained of the predominance, on U.S. ships, of "a very poor class" of foreign sailors. Still, American ships and American skippers—whose character was carefully checked by American insurers—generally enjoyed a better reputation than did their European counterparts.

Captains were too busy to see to the well-being of passengers, who fended for themselves. Only when weather permitted could they go on deck to the "galley," a single large fire or range. There, a perennial chaos prevailed. The only travelers who could depend on regular meals were "the richer passengers who can bribe the cooks with half a crown now and then, the pretty women who can coax them with smiles, or . . . strong men who can elbow their way with their broad shoulders." A Yorkshire woman described a "small fire surrounded by half-a-dozen sturdy rustics, as busy boiling, roasting, and frying, as if their lives depended upon a single meal." She soon gave up trying to prepare punctual meals, and used the fire whenever she could; between the rolling of the ship and the uncouthness of her rivals, "your fortune would be better than mine if you got your meal prepared without being scalded." A sailor might have to quench the fire at any moment if it threatened to spread in a freshening wind, whatever the irritation of the hungry passengers. On more than one occasion, a large wave drowned the fire—and washed the stove overboard.

Seasickness, inevitably, afflicted many. Isabella McKinnon wrote on April 15, 1852: "Sick still. 12:00 o'clock. Took nothing the last two days except a little brandy and Laudnum." A German on a small ship was grateful for his mother's homemade *Zwieback:* "Had it not been for this twice baked bread, mother, who did not leave her bunk during the entire voyage, could not have survived." A Scotsman wrote in 1816 that he had "continued vomiting for thirty-two days," after which he "recovered every day."

Of all the shortages a ship suffered, lack of drinking water was most dangerous. Leaky casks were one source of trouble. Dishonest rations—such as "gallon" jugs that held three quarts—were another. Passengers trying to live on salted beef or herring would suffer special torments of thirst; and the fresh water doled out for drinking and cooking was the only supply they could use for washing, seawater excepted.

On many vessels, as Melville explained, the emigrants in steerage

were "cut off from the most indispensable conveniences of a civilized dwelling. This forces them in storm time to such extremities that no wonder fevers and plagues are the result." The preventive measures of the time were of little help. One of the guidebooks had suggested, for instance, a few bottles of vinegar "to sprinkle on the floor." From another tract: "The smell of soap is a great enemy to all fevers."

Most ships, especially the smaller ones, carried no physician. One reassuring guidebook noted that "the captains of the better class of ships are quite good medical men." But not all the officers. "If anybody is ill," said one passenger, "the mate goes to him and gives him what he thinks will do him good, and then laughs if it produces a more powerful effect than the one intended." Even if ships happened to have surgeons, they were often "nothing but apothecaries." In steerage, dysentery and cholera would spread quickly, as would "ship fever"—typhus, an infection transmitted by lice, but then considered a result of starvation.

Melville described such an episode, when rainstorms kept the emigrants below, food could not be cooked, and "malignant fever" broke out. The dark steerage was like "a crowded jail. . . . In every corner, the females were huddled together, weeping and lamenting; children were asking bread from their mothers, who had none to give." Old men leaned against the water casks, gasping for breath. Four died, then seven, then four, then six—day after day. A newborn's first cries sounded almost simultaneously with the splash of its father's body into the deep.

Shipboard mortality rates hovered around one percent in normal years, but sometimes soared much higher. The toll of death and illness seemed to vary, as well, according to the ships' flags—in reality, according to conditions in the passengers' homeland. From 1842 through 1848, roughly 9 per 1,000 passengers on German ships arrived sick in New York, 10 per 1,000 on American ships, and 30 per 1,000 on British vessels. Beyond quantifying, however, was the misery of the notorious "coffin ships" of the Irish famine. Desperate people tried to escape starvation in ships too old, too rotten, too small, and too ill-supplied for the journey; in this crisis emigrant ships under sail actually risked the North Atlantic in winter.

One monument of several at Grosse Île, Quebec, memorializes 5,424 persons who, "flying from Pestilence and Famine in Ireland in the year 1847 found in America but a Grave." Because the Canadian voyage was shorter, and cheaper, it had always attracted the poorest emigrants, and so many famine victims reached Quebec. Now, partly because of a change in American attitudes, captains steered for American ports only when ice blocked the St. Lawrence. The seaboard states

Runners set upon their vulnerable countrymen the moment they left Castle Garden, using the varied ploys revealed in the cartoon (opposite) from Puck, a satiric weekly started in 1877. Then they quickly conned the greenhorns out of their possessions, sold them overpriced railroad tickets, or lured them to boardinghouses where owners swindled them out of their meager resources. A menace in every port, runners found abundant prey in New York. Castle Garden assured newcomers initial protection at least. "Nobody cares for my grief or distress, / Friendless am I in the new world today," ran the lyrics of Charlie Baker's ballad "Only An Emigrant" (above), from 1879.

had begun to qualify their welcome. By this time, Massachusetts and New York had enacted laws to deal with sick or destitute newcomers. Each captain had to pay a dollar or so per passenger, to help the state support sick aliens; and aliens who seemed likely to become paupers had to post a substantial bond, or be turned away. Officials usually let the sick and the aged go ashore, bond or no bond. One, required to explain his disobedience, said, "My only plea is humanity."

Compassion led the State of New York, in 1855, to aid the newcomers in an official manner. Its great harbor became the only American port to offer them any kind of protection from its "foul brood of villains" when Castle Garden, an old stone fort at Manhattan's tip, was turned into a receiving center. Health inspectors would detain the sick at the quarantine station on Staten Island, while the rest went on to make their landing.

Fewer passengers arrived ill as steamships shortened the voyage; scurvy became rare. Nevertheless, conditions in steerage could be as disgusting as in the days of sail. As ships grew larger and engines stronger, owners and captains were more willing to accept the dangers of early spring and late autumn, even of winter crossings, when the finest ships would pitch and wallow in the gales.

But finally, emigrants stepped ashore and became immigrants, bearing visions bounded only by the limits of their imagination. Melville thought that "if they can get here, they have God's right to come." There was the beginning. Beyond lay the brave new world that would be made and successively remade by them.

Seeking America's promise of good jobs, immigrant men line Castle Garden's labor exchange as a clerk posts newly announced openings (left). Females also looked to the exchange for work, among them the Irish, whom housewives carefully screened for live-in domestics (opposite). Women—typically single and under 35—accounted for more than half the immigrants from Ireland between 1880 and 1900, a ratio unlike any other ethnic group's. In America they saw an escape from a life of drudgery in a strict, male-dominated society with few opportunities for marriage or for careers. As servants receiving free room and board, they could save most of their earnings for contributions to their church or to bring sisters and aunts across the ocean. Before the turn of the century, however, the ambitious "Bridgets" had begun to abandon their aprons. Like other women with some education, they might become salesclerks—or enjoy higher status as schoolteachers and nurses.

New Jersey. By railroad, wagon, or steamer, newcomers could continue their journeys westward to—they hoped—a prosperous future.

LEADING BUSINESS HOUSES FARGO

WEST WARD EMPIRE THE TAKES ITS WAY

DAKOTA LAND OF GOLDEN GRAIN

New World

OLD World
FAMINE GERMANY
FAMINE RUSSIA
FAMINE IN IRELAND
FAMINE IN EGYPT
FAMINE IN INDIA

TO AMERICA THE LAND OF FREE HOMES

TO DAKOTA Homesteads, Pre-Emptions, Tree Claims FREE

U.S. LIQUID PAINT CO.

No.1 HARD WHEAT

COPYRIGHTED AUGUST 1888 BY E.A. Colby.

Promise of a Young Land

Dakota Territory boasts of her riches in an 1888 poster; banners of business names proclaim the sophistication of Fargo. Such advertisements blared the merits of other regions as they competed for immigrant labor and settlers.

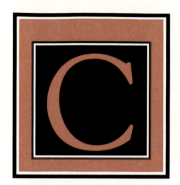

rossing Lake Erie by steamboat in 1841, a Swede named Gustaf Unonius takes note of the national distinctions he observes in his fellow passengers. He watches three Chippewa Indians, "a banked fire" burning in their eyes. He encounters the westward-bound American frontiersman who has dispossessed them, a representative of "the most mobile and roving people on earth"; the Yankee carries little more than the clothes he wears. There sits the Englishman, who "would take even his well-anchored island if he could only get it loose from its anchorage," but instead presides placidly over an old mirror and some unbroken china. Pale and aloof, he differs sharply from his Irish bunkmate, a florid, kinetic type "who thinks that everything concerns him and who concerns himself with everything." *His* array of burlap bundles inevitably contains a long-handled spade and "one or two bottles of whiskey." A German farmer? "The Americans look at him as though he were a recent arrival from another planet," with all his possessions—from plows to broken tobacco pipes—crammed onto a creaky old wagon not worth its freight cost. Probably he has "not the faintest idea of the country where he is going."

Perhaps, but like the rest of Unonius's motley cast, the German had hitched his future to the star-like promise of the American interior. Perhaps he guarded in his hunting bag a crinkled letter from a sister or cousin in Illinois, for whom that promise had come true. By 1841, personal networks stretching across the ocean were already drawing reinforcements to new immigrant communities both in the East and in the frontier areas. But the location of those settlements was largely the result of larger, impersonal forces.

Whether buffeted or becalmed by Atlantic westerlies, immigrants were often wafted into a particular harbor on the winds of trade. The northern German who debarked at Baltimore, stiffened his rubbery sea legs, and lit a pungent pipeful was smoking tobacco grown on a nearby Tidewater plantation—but purchased in Bremen, where he had embarked. In a sense, he was simply ballast for the westward leg of the early 19th century's main tobacco route. Likewise, the peasant woman from the Palatinate, bewildered amid the rough hustle of New Orleans's wharves, proved the New Orleans-Le Havre nexus of the cotton trade. Such commercial ties etched important traditions of ethnic settlement into the American grain. Tobacco gave Baltimore and the lands along the newly graveled National Road to Ohio a lasting German imprint, already clear by the 1830s. Germans traveling northward from New Orleans gave the Upper Mississippi Valley so strong a Teutonic accent

1850

Canadians (45,000)

Irish (115,000)

Irish (345,000)
Germans (120,000)
British (115,000)

Irish (150,000)
Germans (80,000)

Germans (110,000)

Scandinavians (10,000)

Based on 1850 census figures, arrows identify the states with the largest numbers of foreign-born from the immigrant groups shown on the chart below.

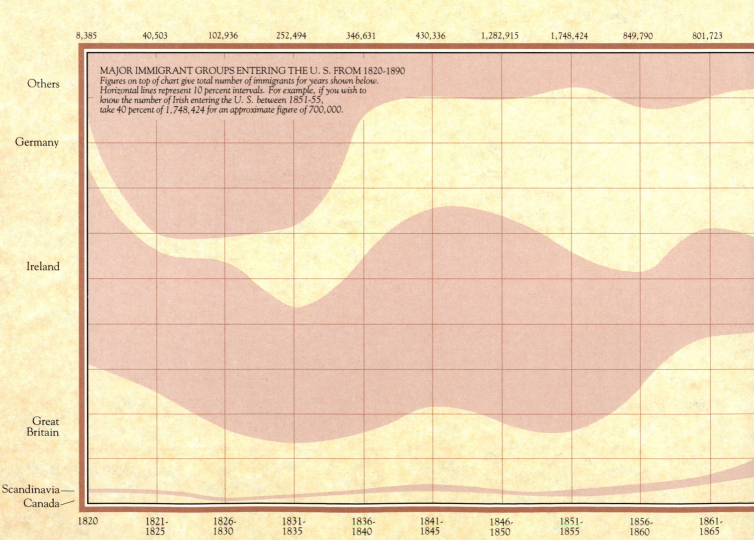

| 8,385 | 40,503 | 102,936 | 252,494 | 346,631 | 430,336 | 1,282,915 | 1,748,424 | 849,790 | 801,723 |

MAJOR IMMIGRANT GROUPS ENTERING THE U. S. FROM 1820-1890
Figures on top of chart give total number of immigrants for years shown below. Horizontal lines represent 10 percent intervals. For example, if you wish to know the number of Irish entering the U. S. between 1851-55, take 40 percent of 1,748,424 for an approximate figure of 700,000.

Others

Germany

Ireland

Great
Britain

Scandinavia
Canada

| 1820 | 1821-1825 | 1826-1830 | 1831-1835 | 1836-1840 | 1841-1845 | 1846-1850 | 1851-1855 | 1856-1860 | 1861-1865 |

The Rising Tide

From a trickle of only 8,385 arrivals in 1820—the first year that immigration was recorded—the flow of people into the United States would grow to a torrent of 455,302 in 1890. (For a graph of immigration from 1821 through 1980, see pages 294-295). By 1820 the American population had more than doubled (to 9.6 million) since the 1790 census, mainly by natural increase. The 70 years charted here would see generally rising immigration: 15 million newcomers would help the population reach 63 million by 1890. The nation had room for them.

By 1850 the contiguous United States had nearly reached present-day boundaries, having added Texas and large portions of Mexico in the 1840s.

Arrows on the map indicate the states that registered the greatest number of foreign-born in the five major groups charted below. Census-takers found most of these people in the Northeast. Railroads had not yet spanned the continent; the South, with its slave labor and its stunted industries, offered little opportunity.

Except for the short-lived Alien Act of 1798, the young nation welcomed its newcomers; it even encouraged contract labor during the Civil War. In 1875, however, a federal law barred convicts and prostitutes; in 1882 the first general Immigration Act excluded other undesirables, among them persons who might become public charges.

For these 70 years, immigration data are inconsistent and incomplete. Land arrivals were not routinely counted before 1908. Until 1850, only eastern and Gulf ports were monitored. It is difficult to ascertain totals for West Coast arrivals, or figures for Canadians and other aliens entering from Canada. Border changes in Europe also confuse the records. The Ottoman Empire lost Romania, Bulgaria, and Serbia, which became independent. And after the Franco-Prussian War, Alsatians were counted not as French but as Germans.

Germans form the largest incoming group in this era, totaling 4.5 million. Their influx rose in the 1850s, reached an all-time high in 1882. Often skilled farmers or craftsmen, they fit Bismarck's description: "There are two kinds of emigrants—those who emigrate because they *still* have money enough . . . and those who *now* have money enough."

Some came via New Orleans to Illinois and Missouri, helping to give St. Louis a German character. In 1850, 8,191 were counted in Texas. A number went to Wisconsin. Milwaukee in 1850 had 7,271 Germans out of 20,061 residents. Though more Germans stayed in the populous East, it was in other regions that they—and other immigrants—had greater impact. In Wisconsin, for instance, 35 percent of the population was foreign-born; in Massachusetts, only 16 percent.

Famine drove the Irish—the second largest group in this period—across the sea. Ulster Protestants ("Scotch-Irish") continued to come in, but after the mid-1840s the vast majority of Irish were from the Roman Catholic south. The Irish total passed 3 million in 1883.

Immigration from Great Britain tended to run about 20 percent of the overall total, while before 1840 and after 1875, the groups charted as "others" made up a larger percentage.

Over the years, many Canadians settled in New York State, but others crossed into the North Central region in search of good farmland. Enlarged U.S. borders put some Mexicans in the odd position of being counted as American-born, although they had been born under a foreign flag and had never budged from their birthplace.

Only a handful of Chinese had entered by 1850, but their numbers rose rapidly. The flow peaked in 1882 at nearly 40,000—and then was halted abruptly in that same year by the Chinese Exclusion Act. For the first time a law barred a whole national group from the United States, foreshadowing an era of restricted immigration.

1,513,101   1,726,796   1,085,395   2,975,683   2,270,930

| 1866-1870 | 1871-1875 | 1876-1880 | 1881-1885 | 1886-1890 |

by mid-century that Abraham Lincoln thought it made good political sense to purchase a German-language newspaper.

The rich Irish brogue now heard in New England was a by-product of New Brunswick's timber trade with the British Isles, often an occasion of a cheap passage for impoverished Irishmen. Eager to escape British rule altogether, the newcomer boarded a Canadian gypsum trader to Boston or a smaller port; or, penniless, he simply hefted his load onto his wiry frame and set off afoot for the States.

Still, no other harbor ranked with New York as passenger ships came into service at mid-century. By the eve of the Civil War, nearly half of New York's population was foreign-born. The Irish predominated, followed by the Germans who would soon overtake them; then came the British, and representatives of smaller nations. Scandinavians appeared less frequently, preferring to travel via Quebec. New York's occasional contingent of sunburnt Swedes distinguished itself by the snappy military manner in which it marched along, with little Swedish and American flags held aloft. Otherwise, Swedes were known vaguely as "Jenny Lind men," after their wildly popular countrywoman.

On tour in 1850, the "Swedish Nightingale" had made her American debut at Castle Garden while it was still a public amusement center. The old fortress survived brazen mob assaults in 1855, when the runners were shut out of the new immigrant center; at night, blazing rockets whistled through the darkness toward its circular walls. By 1874, Castle Garden was so well known in Europe that, as the *New York Times* reported, "few emigrants can be induced to sail for any other destination." They could send telegrams, buy railroad tickets, meet employers on fair terms. They could slake their hunger with large sandwiches, 13 cents apiece, or slices of pie for 10; a dime also bought a bottle of beer and a nickel paid for a cup of coffee.

Immigrant Gothic: Straightforward and severe, Norwegian settlers in Wisconsin (above) mirror the pose of a "Volga German" couple in Kansas (opposite). Norwegians began immigrating as early as 1825; "Volga Germans" and "Black Sea Germans"—German-speaking descendants of 18th-century emigrants to Russia's steppes—started coming to the U.S. during the 1870s. Both groups flocked westward in tens of thousands, drawn by cheap and fertile land. Russia's ethnic Germans saw America as their refuge from growing persecution and loss of privileges granted them a century before by Tsarina Catherine the Great.

Outside the reassuring depot, the newcomers found that New York's streets were not, as many had heard, paved with gold, but layered ankle-deep in refuse and the mire created by livestock, including the city's 10,000 scavenging swine. But if silver still jangled in his pocket, the stranger could enter a bookseller's, buy a copy of *The Wealth and Biography of the Wealthy Citizens of the City of New York,* and take heart in the success stories of other immigrants, men like the German-born John Jacob Astor, whose daily income was reported in 1846 to be $5,760. America was possibility: "It is the dream of a high fever made real," gasped a Swiss immigrant. It was a contagion to match emigration fever in Europe.

The symptom was mobility, physical as well as social. As the

Norwegian novelist Knut Hamsun wrote, "every day is moving day. . . .
The population is only half-settled." Stephen Vincent Benét placed his
poet's finger on the pulse of the era and diagnosed "unassuaged and rest-
less hearts." With a historian's insight Frederick Jackson Turner identified another condition: "perennial rebirth."

The signposts pointed west, where expanses of fertile land so vast
as to defy fantasy awaited settlement. As the pioneer armies advanced
across the continent, however, "out west" became "back east," the
frontier retreated beyond the setting sun, and the pioneers uprooted
themselves again to go seek it. Still, by 1860 the frontier of settlement

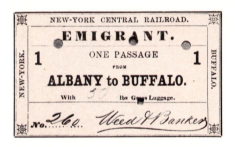

Like many of its rivals, the New York Central offered reduced fares (above) for immigrants. Such favors helped generate business on new lines, attracted needed laborers, and encouraged settlement along the right-of-way. Railroads quickly became land companies as well as transporters, for they held vast western tracts given them by the federal government. Whenever they sold a parcel of land to a settler, they made a profit—and often they won a lifetime customer for their rail services. Not surprisingly, brochures advertising such lands appeared in eastern port cities and overseas; handbooks of every description also besieged new immigrants. Fifty cents guaranteed the gullible a piece of another perennial American dream (opposite). From cabins on Cherry Creek in 1859 grew Denver City; thousands of goldseekers passed through—and some of them struck it rich in the Rockies.

had barely reached the Great Plains, and between St. Louis and Sacramento the only community of significant size was the Mormon settlement at the Great Salt Lake.

Frontiersmen and pioneer farmers were, more often than not, native-born Americans, who had more of the skills and resources and habits needed for wilderness life than did most foreigners. (The Americans tended to move westward in familiar latitudes and climates; New Englanders settled Ohio's Western Reserve district, and many Southerners wound up in "the Texies.") When Americans decided to move on, the most venturesome immigrants went too: east of the Appalachians in the 1820s and '30s; in Missouri, Illinois, and Wisconsin by the '40s; in eastern Iowa and Wisconsin during the '50s and '60s; and on the prairies and high plains by the 1870s.

But two out of every five immigrants registered at Castle Garden declared New York their final destination, and the majority of 19th-century immigrants went no farther than the eastern seaboard states. Those with specialized industrial skills congregated in the centers of their trades. Welsh coal miners headed for the anthracite fields of eastern Pennsylvania, and Welsh stonecutters for the slate quarries of Vermont, New York, and Pennsylvania. English textile workers boarded coastal steamers for New England, where mills whirred with the clatter of looms and the hum of spindles.

Many immigrants were paralyzed by poverty at their port of arrival. Others had to let their longing for the land languish until they could finance the inland journey—often by digging the canals or laying the rails that would carry them west.

By 1840 the trip from New York to Chicago cost about $14 for an adult. The inland trek was long, circuitous, and not without danger. Until about 1850, most westering immigrants went by Hudson River paddle steamers from New York to Albany, where they boarded Erie Canal boats for Buffalo; then they continued on Great Lakes steamers to Chicago or Milwaukee. In 1850, a Norwegian group spent "ten hard and long days" on the Erie Canal, while Gustaf Unonius's barge one night collided with another so violently "that I feared it was being crushed like an egg shell." On the lakes, steamboats ran the risks of sudden storms, fog, ill-charted hazards, and fire. When the *G. P. Griffith* burned on Lake Erie in 1850, most of the 326 on board were lost—among whom were many aliens. Boiler explosions were an even greater threat on river steamers when captains raced with rivals.

In first class, riverboat passengers enjoyed glimmering chandeliers, cut-glass stemware, well-polished spittoons, and the attentions of black servants in livery. But most immigrants were "penned up like cattle" near the boiler rooms, where the heat seared them and crowding spread contagion. A Memphis paper reported that "nearly every boat buried from 15 to 20 between this place and New Orleans." Conditions were especially bad in 1849, when cholera raged along the Mississippi.

By the 1850s, railroads were the preferred, if most costly, means of westbound travel. Special immigrant trains—which reportedly "stretched to the length of a monstrous serpent"—offered cheaper and slower service than their regular counterparts, which also pulled cut-rate "Immigrant Cars." These might be screeching, springless boxcars with hard benches or none at all. More than transportation, the expanding rail networks opened vast new areas to development.

"Here in America it is the railroads that build up the whole country," wrote a Norwegian in Springfield, Illinois, in 1855. "Because of them the farmers get wider markets and higher prices for their products. They seem to put new life into everything. Even the old apple woman sets off at a dogtrot when she hears the whistle, to sell her apples to the passengers. Every ten miles along the railways there are stations which soon grow up into towns. 'Soon,' did I say? I should have said 'immediately'. . . ." He sketched the process for his kinsmen in Norway.

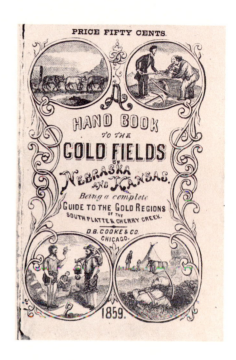

The company builds a depot. A speculator buys the hundred acres around it, lays out lots, and makes "many hundred per cent" at an auction. Day after day, someone new steps off the train, sees an opportunity, and decides to stay—a wagonmaker, a blacksmith, a doctor, a lawyer. A "velvet-frocked" German hurdy-gurdy man turns up; he sells his music box and trained monkey to start a restaurant, serving sausages and whiskey to the railroad crews. Soon he is "murdering the English language" and becoming a capitalist. "Within a few years the town is very large," its farms and commerce flourishing.

Late in the century, Jacob Dolwig, from Hungary, was able to travel by rail all the way from Baltimore to his final destination of Dickinson, North Dakota. On the second morning out of Chicago, he awoke to see some horses in deep snow and a few ash trees, spare sketches of civilization. More typical, especially in the 1840s, were experiences like those of the Norwegian Lars Davidson Reque. From Chicago, he walked the hundred miles to the Koshkonong area of Wisconsin, selected a promising parcel of eighty acres, trudged another fifty miles to pay $100 for it at Milwaukee's land office, and then walked a hundred miles back to Chicago to seek employment for the winter. Before he could afford to begin working his own land, Reque had to spend two years laboring at other jobs.

Once on the land, most immigrants found things strange and alarming. Arriving in the dead of night at the fast-growing settlement

Wisconsin's woodlands lured thousands of Finns, Norwegians, and other northern Europeans in the 1800s. Many worked for logging companies in winter, applying old-country skills while earning cash to buy farms. As usual, the best lands went first; cutover areas—full of stumps— fell to latecomers. Even with stump-pulling devices, families might toil for months to clear a few acres. Boulders left by long-departed glaciers littered the region, bedeviling settlers' attempts to put their plots to the plow. Still, many persisted, enduring a year or two in a shack before erecting a permanent home, typically of log construction. Above the log walls of frontier tradition, Germans might close the gables with vertical board-and-batten siding (opposite); Scandinavians often used logs up to the roof line.

of Holland, Michigan, Engbertus Van der Veen suffered true shock: "The moaning sounds of the western pine, the night birds' shrill, weird cries, the hoots of the owls, the squeaking of birds and croaks of the insects throughout the woods made a painful impression on us who had come from Amsterdam, and filled us with dismay." Still, some residents were fortunate enough to see the first welcome slants of morning daylight through the openings of a log shanty—in 1847 Michigan's first Dutch settlers had slept on the cold, bare ground, and kept drenching rains at bay by stretching cloth canopies over high branches.

To the southwest, their countrymen at Pella, Iowa, made their first shelters out of prairie sod and roofed them with sticks, branches, and mats of tough grass from nearby sloughs. Rainfall soaked the roofs and walls, and turned living quarters into mudbaths. Fires brought a bit

of relief from the cold and damp—and then snakes came slithering out of the walls toward the warmth.

In spring, building four walls of any kind took second priority to the hasty planting of crops that would see the family through its first winter. When Per Hansa, the hero of Ole Rölvaag's novel *Giants in the Earth*, first dug his spade into the Dakota sod, he saw to both needs simultaneously: "Field for planting on the one hand, sods for a house on the other—that was the way to plow!" For him, as for every real-life prairie farmer, the going was slow, for the sod, "which had been slumbering there undisturbed for countless ages, was tough of fibre and would not give up its hold on the earth without a struggle."

To the east, the clearing of woodlands was more backbreaking still. In Wisconsin, even some of the Germans simply "let the stumps

Westward-bound covered wagons carried traders and homesteaders, native and foreign-born, through floods, storms, and quicksands on the overland trails. Plains Indians raided them for trade goods and livestock; wagon masters formed ever-larger trains for safety—as in the picture below. Various details, such as the absence of women and children, lead experts to suspect that this photograph comes from the filming of a silent movie, on location in the West in the 1920s— one of many re-creations of an epic.

"Nebraska marble"—sod—provided building material for many a homesteader. Fresh flowers and obvious pride of ownership brighten one soddy's grim facade (above). A joker's sign in Norwegian identifies a dollar-a-meal sod "Hotel of Short Rations" near Appleton, Minnesota, in the late 1800s. Thick earthen walls gave excellent insulation from hot summers and freezing winters; whitewashing the interiors eased the hardship of housecleaning a home built of dirt. Many settlers began with rudimentary dugouts carved into riverbanks or hillsides and simply roofed over with turf (right, lower).

Clustered before their prized possessions, English-born David Hilton and family create a portrait of Plains prosperity at Weissert, Nebraska, in 1889. The pump organ makes a luxurious display. Basic assets fill the background: land, livestock, a corn planter, a wagon, a cultivator. Not long before, the roof of the family dugout simply had caved in; a frame house quickly replaced it. Hilton had to make a journey of 120 miles round trip to buy lumber—not unusual in an almost treeless region.

stand in their fields." Time, like energy and money, had to be expended prudently. In Iowa at mid-century, many had to postpone as luxuries the most basic alternatives to aching human muscle—a span of horses cost about $90, a team of sturdy oxen (with yoke) $40, and a good wagon about $70. The new mechanical reapers cost about $100.

Prosperous and poverty-stricken farmers alike were scourged by the brutalities of nature. Droughts turned fields to tinder, and prairie fires raged like sunsets "blood-red in hue." Clouds of locusts drifted in like snow in June. Or a spring flood might dash a last hope just as velvety new grass carpeted the land. Sickness might claim immigrants who, already weakened by an arduous journey, were worn down further by the harsh new climate and circumstances. Reports like those of an American clergyman, who found in one rural household "a dead man lying upon a bench out of doors, and ten sick ones indoors," were not rare.

Still, most survivors stayed on and counted themselves lucky. They had the tenacity of an Ole Knudsen Trovatten, who "in no circumstances" would return to his homeland: "Though I have been sick almost half a year and have a family to take care of, still I have achieved much more than a worker can in Norway." Prosperity did come to the majority, but slowly, and in tiny increments—the purchase of a cow or pig, the clearing of another acre, a basket of golden squash, or the news that a community now had only one pauper to support. Prosperity was also measured in the growing numbers of immigrant farmers who, once well-established, pulled up stakes and marched on west with their American counterparts.

In some respects, the experiences of the immigrant and the native-born differed little in rural America. Milking, helping a mare deliver a foal, slaughtering a pig—chores were chores. Yet the physical transition itself, for Europeans accustomed to cramped conviviality, left many an immigrant lonely and homesick in the new land. Under the Homestead Act in 1862, a grant of 160 acres was a godsend; but, to a sensitive woman in Nebraska, the terrain itself "seemed to overwhelm the little beginnings of human society that struggled in its sombre wastes." For Per Hansa's brooding wife, Beret, the "formless prairie had no heart that beat, no waves that sang, no soul that could be touched." Gone were the quirky graces of nature that had led the eye, comfortingly, across the green-blue spectrum of forest, meadow, crag, and cove, and then back to the whitewashed village of a Norwegian girlhood.

Obsessed, Beret envisioned the prairie horizon circled by a magic ring, within which no living thing could penetrate. But that very isolation was a boon to thousands of immigrants who organized their own

Utopias

tark yet detailed, the images created by Olof Krans record life in Illinois' Bishop Hill colony. Founded by Swedes whose anti-Lutheran convictions put them at odds with the state church, Bishop Hill was one of many utopias that flourished in the fertile soil of America.

Settlers drawn by visions of a promised land arrived on the *Mayflower*—and on later ships. Even their orthodoxy encouraged the spread of different faiths: Banished from the Massachusetts Bay Colony in 1635 for "newe & dangerous opinions," Roger Williams founded the colony of Rhode Island, where "no man should be molested for his conscience."

The American Revolution, with its creed of liberty, and the Constitution's separation of church and state, confirmed the ideal of tolerance and fanned the flames of "America fever" in the hearts of many Europeans.

In a petition to President Jefferson in 1805, members of a German group called the Society of Harmony wrote: "having been persecuted & punished in many manner for sake of the Truth which they perceived and confessed, they was necessitated to look for a place, where is liberty of Conscience. . . ." The history of the United States told them "America would be such a place." So it was.

Religious utopias blossomed in the early 19th century. Many were settled by German sectarians, and most remained on the religious and geographic fringe of American society. Some groups, including the Hutterites and

From "Pile Driving," by Olof Krans, c. 1896

"Corn Planting," by Olof Krans, c. 1896

Amana Inspirationists, sought isolation. Seeing danger in exposure to worldly evils, these sects desired only to be left in peace. Others, like the Moravians, established both new colonies and churches within existing communities. And, like the Quakers, a few groups lived in—but not by—the framework of the popular culture.

Distinguished by points of creed and place of settlement, many utopian communities shared a way of life based on agriculture, rejection of private property ("communism"), and—to a lesser degree—a belief in celibacy. Both the Hutterites and the Rappites based their adherence to communism on the Bible. For the Inspirationists, communism was a way to provide adequate employment; for the Shakers, it was a means of withdrawing from the world and achieving a life without sin.

An evangelical zeal also characterized several religious utopias. More often than not, however, attempts at conversion were unsuccessful. Sometimes they even backfired—as in the case of a Bishop Hill missionary who, instead of converting the Shakers, was himself converted to celibacy, a practice briefly adopted at Bishop Hill.

Celibate or not, most utopias eventually succumbed to internal dissension, economic woes, or the death of a leader. Only a few have survived with their traditional way of life intact. The Hutterites, the largest true communal group in the Western world, have embraced the benefits of technology while clinging tenaciously to their religious beliefs. The Old Order Amish virtually shun the modern world.

Yet even the less successful sects have often left their mark on American life. The Inspirationists founded the appliance company that gave the world the Amana Radarange microwave oven. The common clothespin, the buzz saw, and a timeless furniture design recall the ingenuity of the Shakers. And in the restored buildings of Bishop Hill, where people of the vicinity demonstrate the crafts of their forefathers, the paintings of Olof Krans bring the world of American utopias to life once more.

GRANGERS VERSUS HOPPERS — KANSAS 1874, '75.

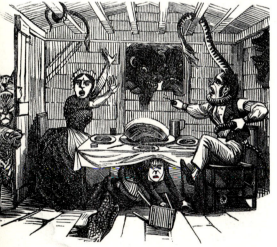

colonies and utopian communities of all sorts. For them, America's great empty spaces were buffers, circles of protection, within which they could re-create old lifeways or boldly experiment with new ones, untroubled by outside interference or worldly distractions.

Some religious groups sought seclusion through fear of aggressive American zealots, but outright persecution forced the largest community into isolation. Joseph Smith founded the Church of Jesus Christ of Latter-day Saints, or Mormon Church, in rural New York in 1830. By the 1850s, when his much-tried followers had found refuge in the valley of the Great Salt Lake, overseas missionaries were winning tens of thousands of converts—mostly Britons and Scandinavians—for their new Zion. Superb organization distinguished Mormon-directed travel. Church officials chartered ships for the faithful, instructed them in their new language when necessary, and sent them west to Deseret in covered wagons led by experienced plainsmen.

If the ordered influx of European converts helped give the Mormons numbers and strength, things went otherwise in the celebrated Harmony Society settlements in Pennsylvania and Indiana. Few

newcomers joined the communities of the German pietist George Rapp after 1807. In that year celibacy became a professed ideal and general practice; matrimony was strongly discouraged. Some of the young gave up membership in order to marry, while scandalmongers repeated a rumor (baseless) that Rapp had castrated his own son. But generally such groups fared well, blending ironclad religious dogma—usually imported—with business acumen of the sort that Americans praise as "American style." Until it was literally extinguished by old age, the Harmony Society thrived on its industries, selling hats and saddles and textiles, and on its shrewd speculations in railroads and real estate.

Another well-known group of German pietists, the Community of True Inspiration, settled down in Iowa, at Amana. It owned assets listed at two million dollars when, after nearly a century of holding all goods in common, it reorganized in 1932, separating a secular corporation from the Amana Church Society. And in a similarly enterprising vein, the Swedish "Jansonists" of Bishop Hill, Illinois, dispatched a delegation to California in 1849 to prospect for gold in the name of God.

More often than not, however, these heavens on earth were

castles in the sky that dispersed like cloud puffs on the cold winds of discord. But while they lasted, there was room in 19th-century America for every conceivable utopian dream. Every prominent citizen, said Ralph Waldo Emerson, had "a draft of a new community in his waistcoat pocket." While some of these were strictly home-grown ventures, scores were the work of newcomers. Swiss immigrants founded "New Helvetia" in Missouri, Norwegians a "New Norway" called Oleana in Pennsylvania, and the French a commune inspired by a popular novel. In the 1840s *Voyage en Icarie* left its readers eager to turn fiction into fact. The author, an exile named Étienne Cabet, had been influenced by the British socialist Robert Owen; his "Community of Equality," New Harmony, had acquired its land in Indiana from the Rappites.

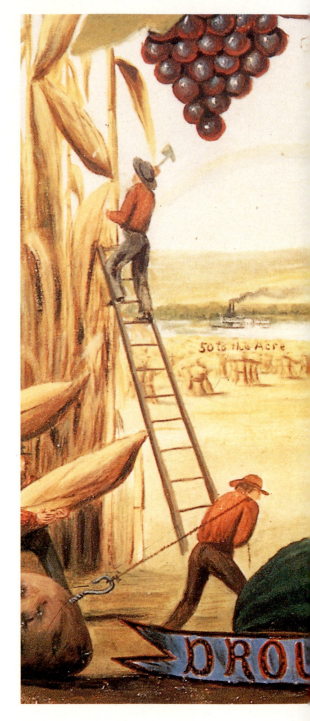

Not socialism, but rather the transplanting of England's class system, motivated several hundred younger sons of the landed gentry to attempt their own genteel versions of Utopia. In remote Rugby, Tennessee, a visitor noted that "pretty British faces appear at the windows, smart young Oxonians meet you, and the good dress and manners of the men must impress their American brethren." These young gentlemen, who had planned to run livestock, did not take to ditch-digging or tree-felling. Instead, they played tennis and cricket, or donned boots, spurs, bowie knives, and pistols for a swagger from the sawmill to the post office.

Likewise, some of their young compatriots at Victoria, Kansas, developed a fondness for the saloons of Hays City—Wild Bill Hickok's town. After a few unlucky years, their land was repossessed by the Kansas Pacific Railroad and sold to an industrious group of Volga Germans.

Earlier, a set of German princelings and noblemen, the *Mainzer Adelsverein,* had attempted to establish a German domain deep in the rawhide Republic of Texas. They may have hoped for a new feudal realm, a buffer state with a crowned head, but their stated purpose was philanthropic. To direct the project they sent Prince Carl of Solms-Braunfels, age 33, whose manners reminded even fellow Germans of medieval pomp. In July 1844, with jeweled sword and three retainers, he reached Texas. He welcomed his first party of 285 settlers on the coast that winter, and decorated a live oak with lighted candles for them on Christmas Eve. Learning that his peers had bought a very remote tract between the San Saba River and the Colorado, he acquired a beautiful site—with a clouded title—near San Antonio. By April 1845 the colonists of New Braunfels were building log cottages, fencing land, and blaming all difficulties on His Serene Highness. In May, the prince left for home—"laughed out of the country," said local tradition.

THY KANSAS

Denying realities of drought, Henry Worrall's 1869 image of his state flaunts gigantic melons and grapes, man-size ears of corn, pumpkins as big as carriages, 50 shocks of wheat per acre. This painting helped propel Worrall to local and, eventually, to national fame. Kansans didn't care that early maps had labeled the area the "Great American Desert" or that Daniel Webster once dismissed it as a "region of savages and wild beasts"; they had high hopes for the deep, rich soil that would make it part of the granary of the world.

By 1846, with Texas the newest state in the Union, hundreds of new recruits were stranded for months on the coast: Their Highnesses' company was bankrupt. Some of the newcomers managed to get home, some enlisted for the Americans' war against Mexico, some struggled inland to New Braunfels and up an Indian trail to the outpost called Fredericksburg. Disease hounded the settlers, who had to rely on salt beef, ground-up acorns for bread and coffee, and plants like wild thistle. But the dreaded Indian attacks never took place, and a survivor reported that after the famine periods the young people "lived a gaysome life," amusing themselves with fandangos.

Only a decade later, an astute observer, Frederick Law Olmsted, traveled through Texas and reported that its German settlers were thriving. Except for necessary business, they seldom mingled with Americans, each regarding the other with "unfeigned curiosity" and some contempt. Olmsted encountered the typical "Forty-Eighter," or refugee from a liberal revolt: a man "in blue flannel shirt and pendant beard," a "Latin farmer," a scholar who quoted Tacitus. In his rough cabin were "Madonnas upon log-walls; coffee in tin cups upon Dresden saucers; barrels for seats, to hear a Beethoven's symphony on the grand piano; . . . a book-case half filled with classics, half with sweet potatoes." That New Braunfels and other settlements survived to give south-central Texas a lasting German imprint owed little to the pretensions of noblemen but much to the German immigrants' tenacious pride in their own traditions, wherever they went.

Shiny metal promises efficiency in the fields—a wooden-beam plow for heavy work (left), a "stubble plow" (right)— at the small town of Argyle in Lafayette County, Wisconsin, in the 1880s. Potential customers assess design and price. Scandinavians favored the state from its early years; its Koshkonong region became the most successful initial "colony" of Norwegians, producing wheat. Tobacco served as a cash crop. Its quick prosperity helped make the state a way station for parties of Norse immigrants. Here they garnered information and aid, before moving on to establish other Norwegian outposts that eventually leapfrogged across Iowa, Minnesota, the Dakotas, and beyond.

I n Wisconsin, as Gustaf Unonius found, Germans had "their own schools and their own justices of peace and other municipal officers. . . . Here I traveled several miles without finding anyone who knew English, though they had lived in this country several years." In New York and New Orleans, and especially in the cities of the Midwest, "Little Germanies" flourished. In Hermann, Missouri, streets were named for Schiller, Gutenberg, and Mozart. Residents of Cincinnati, remarked a visitor at mid-century, "live here as in their old Germany." For many years services were conducted in German at St. Peter's Evangelical Protestant Church (organized in 1832). In 1837 an Italian count noticed "peasants dressed in black velvet with red vests and big silver buttons." In the early 1860s men were still wearing the "blue worsted pantaloons," wool jackets, and low-crowned hats of Bavaria. Their fair-haired wives sat knitting in the recessed doorways of their homes, "their squat, stout figures" looking even bulkier "in the stuffed woollen petticoats of German fashion."

Cincinnati's "Over the Rhine," like (Continued on page 114)

The Blacks

"O nobody knows who I am, who I am, Till the Judgment morning." No music rings with greater power from the American past than the spirituals; no strangers found a harsher fate here than the black victims of the Atlantic slave trade. Of millions ripped from their African homelands, some 275,000 reached Britain's 13 mainland colonies, perhaps 70,000 the 13 states. About 28,000 more entered Louisiana before 1803. And after 1808, when the United States made the importing of slaves a crime, perhaps a thousand a year were slipped onto American soil.

In the tobacco fields of Maryland and Virginia, blacks and whites worked side by side under compulsion before the 1660s; but thereafter the ratio of white indentures to black slaves declined. In northern as well as southern colonies, the laws defining slavery grew more sweeping, more severe.

"How is it," snorted an English Tory in 1775, "that we hear the loudest yelps for liberty among the drivers of negroes?" From George Washington, Thomas Jefferson, James Madison. . . .

To many leaders of the Revolution and the nation it created, slavery seemed a shameful, short-term necessity: an inherited evil.

Cotton, and in 1793 Eli Whitney's gin for separating fiber from seed, fixed slavery's place in southern life. By 1790, slavery was fading out of New England and the mid-Atlantic states; by 1800, cotton was replacing rice on Georgia plantations. Soon the planters were eagerly seeking new lands for cotton, moving inland and along the Gulf coast. If cotton sold for ten cents a pound, ran a rule of thumb at mid-century, a sound black field hand was worth $1,000.

Slaves broke new ground, planted the seed, chopped weeds with the hoe, picked the white bolls—200 pounds a good day's work. On a small farm the owner's family and slaves might share the tasks; on a big property, the white overseer and black drivers managed the work and swung the lash. *"Black man beat me—white man cheat me. . . ."*

Whipping punished all sorts of offenses: dawdling, malingering, running off to evade irksome jobs like pulling corn leaves for fodder. One slave woman suffered fifty lashes for slipping food to a poor white neighbor who was old and sick. *"De blood came twinklin' down. . . ."* A little boy in Maryland grew up to remember an overseer who liked long hickory whips; the child found one of these lying around, "picked it up, and boy-like, was using it for a horse" when the overseer came by "and flogged me most cruelly."

No sane owner wanted idle cruelty. In the 1850s a Virginia tobacco planter hired Irishmen to risk fever and snakebite draining a swamp, remarking that "a negro's life is too valuable" for such work. But value itself created cruelty whenever a sale separated members of a family. Charles Ball, who never forgot how his mother was dragged away from him, grew up to be sold away from his own wife and children; although he escaped once to rejoin them, he was kidnapped and enslaved again.

". . . I wonder where my mudder den. . . . My fader gone to unknown land. . . ." "Sometimes I feel like a mudderless chile. . . ."

Day after day a traveler from Sweden, Fredrika Bremer, thought with amazement, "These children do not belong to their parents. . . ." The mother's owner had title to them, and could sell them at will. In a Richmond slave pen Miss Bremer saw "a pretty little white boy of about seven" —apparently white, but the son of a slave, to be sold for $350.

"God forgive us," wrote a lady of South Carolina, "but ours is a *monstrous* system. . . . our men live all in one house with their wives and their concubines. . . ." A young lady might have her half-sister for a personal maid; a gentleman might free his mistress or their son.

Free "persons of color" faced social barriers even on free soil, and legal restrictions as well. Still, freedom was worth the earning, for skilled slaves who could make money enough to buy themselves—or worth the taking, for "self-stealers" who ran away.

Some fugitives made their way north to free soil. Some hid in coastal

swamps like the Great Dismal. Some, in Florida and southern Georgia, joined the Seminole Indians and fought with them in a war that lasted from 1835 to 1842, a war that involved U.S. troops as well as local militia and stirred the ever-present dread of a general slave rebellion.

Black and white bondsmen had planned a revolt in Virginia as early as 1663. Black slaves fought the authorities in New York City in 1712. A thousand slaves menaced Richmond in 1800; more than four hundred rebelled in Louisiana in 1811.

Such uprisings inevitably inspired new measures to keep the slaves in subjection; but Nat Turner's rebellion in 1831 marked a change. He and his followers in Southampton County, Virginia, killed some 60 whites before state and federal forces crushed the revolt. A new fear, and new ruthlessness, spread through the South after that. White southerners showed a new grimness in defending their "peculiar institution." In public, at least, they praised it as a positive good, not only permitted by God but also divinely ordained.

"Jesus mount de milk-white horse, halelu, halelu. Say 'you cheat my Fader children,'. . . Say 'you cheat 'em out of glory,' halelu, halelu. . . . ''

While other nations abolished slavery, and American abolitionists denounced it, the slaves endured it and survived it. Combining ancestral tradition with present circumstance, they shaped a new culture for themselves. They enjoyed whatever they could: a barbecue when the sugarcane had been cut; a corn-shucking party; a wedding celebration; Christmas holidays; an extra ration of molasses.

"Pharoah's army got drownded, Oh, Mary, don't you weep!"

Slavery disintegrated as the Confederacy crumbled in 1865. "I felt like it be Heaven here on earth to git freedom," a black Texan declared. To marry—legally. To learn to read—legally. To vote, to hold high public office—at least during Reconstruction.

But drudgery and trouble outlived the old order. A family of sharecroppers might work the sweltering cotton fields in freedom, and never get out of debt. A black farmer on his own land might contend with drought and boll weevils and conclude, as one said long after the Civil War, that "all God's dangers ain't a white man." Still, white men could mean danger with or without the law; and black chain gangs worked on southern roads within living memory.

Prejudice flourished outside the South as well as in it: *"I've been 'buked and I've been scorned. . . ."*

Yet blacks have overcome great obstacles in the United States. From Bunker Hill to Khe Sanh, they have fought in the nation's wars. And their experience, like that of unwelcome aliens, has put American ideals to the test. The challenge echoes in the old refrain *"Didn't my Lord deliver Daniel? An' why not every man?"* It emerges bluntly in the words of David Walker, a free black from North Carolina who quoted the Declaration of Independence on the equality of all men and asked, in 1829: "AMERICANS!!! Do you understand your own language?"

Plantation slave cabins near the Georgia-Florida border, c. 1864 (top)
Work team in closely planted upland rice, Georgia, c. 1855

For immigrant Norwegians, their own Lutheran church ranked as a necessity of life. Opposite: dedication day at East Blue Mounds Evangelical Lutheran Church in Wisconsin, August 1875. Pastors traveled on circuit to hold Sunday services for rural congregations. America's freedom, however, encouraged many to challenge the orthodoxies of the Church of Norway; new synods formed, split, and merged. Pastor Peter A. Rasmussen of Lisbon, Illinois (above, with his family), helped form the liberal United Norwegian Lutheran Church by a merger in 1890.

the other Little Germanies, had its breweries (26 in the city in 1880) and its numerous *Bierhallen*, where even the family's youngest apple-cheeked member gurgled its foamy lager amid the rattle of dice and dominoes. Beer halls often doubled as clubhouses or headquarters for innumerable organizations: musical, theatrical, and literary clubs; charitable societies; gymnastic organizations, the *Turnvereine*, started by liberals in Germany to promote both mental and physical culture; compatriot groups—Palatines, Bavarians, or German Swiss. New York's third annual Steuben festival in 1861 counted 35 singing societies alone. Everywhere, reported a Swedish woman traveling at mid-century, the gregarious Germans stood in sharp contrast to the Anglo-Americans who seemed to "have no other pleasure than 'business.'"

Tradition was reinforced by the ease with which many German immigrants transferred their own craft and business skills to the New World. Some built fortunes on inventions ranging from air brakes to typesetting machines. More likely, the immigrant thrived as Americans acquired a taste for frankfurters, sauerkraut, potato salad, rye bread, and fine beers. And if the German gentile fed Americans, German Jews, like Levi Strauss, were likely to clothe them or to answer the widening demand for new and appealing goods. Many German Jews exchanged a peddler's pack for a country emporium, which in turn gave way to the modern American department store.

Scandinavians, arriving in much smaller numbers and concentrated in rural areas, escaped the attention given to German immigrants at the time. But they also formed tight-knit communities, maintained their own churches and newspapers, and rarely married outsiders. On the other hand, British immigrants—including English-speaking Canadians—neither clustered in particular regions nor suffered from linguistic barriers. Like the Germans, though, many of the British newcomers brought highly valued skills that allowed them to pursue their old occupations in a new setting.

Thousands of skilled British workers in the 1890s thought little of shuttling back and forth across the Atlantic on the ebb and flow of wages and opportunities. While some followed the broad swings of boom and depression, others were migrants who would "go out for the run in the summer season in the United States" and go back in October, pockets bulging. One Lancashire bricklayer, whose family "lived 'ome," reported that "I goes 'ome every year and takes five 'undred dollars with me." Ever-lower Atlantic fares, noted another Englishman, made Macclesfield silk weavers speak of Paterson, New Jersey, "as if it were only a run of half an hour by train."

Off on a Sunday school picnic—but not, of course, on the Lord's Day—a 1903 parade float full of Welsh-Americans represents the Caersalem Church of Wild Rose, Wisconsin. Sunday schools in Wales and America greatly enhanced literacy rates, for often they gave the poor elementary lessons not available otherwise. Primarily Methodist, Congregationalist, or Baptist, immigrant Welshmen also found their way into other churches, including the Latter-day Saints, who welcomed several thousand to Utah in the mid-1800s. Regardless of denominational differences, Welsh congregations traditionally sponsor gymanfa ganu—assemblies for hymn singing—and make choral music a regular part of almost every religious or social event. A Welsh immigrant, John Parry, served as the first director of the group that became the Mormon Tabernacle Choir.

But most who came stayed, for, as one workingman put it, "In America, you get pies and puddings." In return, America received the skills it needed to rival—and then surpass—British industrial production. In 1864, a single shipload of America-bound emigrants included iron puddlers, roughers, rollers, finishers, blast-furnace men; turners, fitters, planers; dyers, bleachers, and calico-printers. Wherever a new gingham mill, tinplate works, pottery, or mine opened, British immigrants quickly became foremen and superintendents.

Virtually the entire labor force of some British industries crossed the Atlantic. To see Cornish miners, a visitor to England was told in 1881, "you must go to Pennsylvania, to Lake Superior, to Nevada; you'll find very few of them in Cornwall." Lawrence, Massachusetts, a worsted center, became the "Bradford of America," and the Connecticut carpet village of Thompsonville an outpost of Kilmarnock. A Lancashire dialect writer, visiting Massachusetts, met so many home-county lads in Fall River's mills that "I soon forgeet wheere I wur, an' fancied I're i' England, an' wur th' only Yankee i' the company."

Except in centers like these, the British quickly blended into the dominant Anglo-American culture. Welsh colliers might awe their American coworkers with the echoing harmonies of hymns rehearsed a mile underground, and Scottish housewives might baffle a small-town grocer with requests for finnan haddies or Glasgow peasemeal; but to Americans, British immigrants hardly seemed like foreigners. Except for Welsh churchgoers, who disdained English as the tongue of everyday business and worldly bargains and wanted to hear sermons intoned in their haunting *hwyl*, the British were not set apart from America's Protestant majority by religious belief or devotional practice. Nor, of course, was language a problem.

To most of these newcomers, America was simply a "Greater Britain" where few felt the call to citizenship or political organization. Thus their transition into American life differed from that of any other immigrant group, but most radically from the traumas suffered by the Irish. The English workingman might exchange Preston for Fall River easily enough, but to the Irishman used to the yielding peat underfoot, even the hard, slippery cobblestones of Boston inflicted a new kind of pain. His old, damp shanty at least stood amid a spellbound emerald landscape. Boston's teeming cellars admitted no light. But the same misty panorama he eulogized, once in America, was also the symbol of want and oppression that left him with a bitter aversion to rural life.

In an era when open spaces beckoned insistently to other immigrants, it struck one observer as a paradox that "a people who

hungered and thirsted for land in Ireland should have been content when they reached the New World . . . to sink into the condition of a miserable town tenantry. . . ." Content or not, as America's least skilled and least schooled newcomers, they struggled for a toehold on the bottom rung of the economic ladder. Paddy the day laborer provided the brawn of urban construction and industry while his blue-eyed Bridget replaced, as a domestic servant, the strong-headed American girl who "would rather want bread than *serve* to gain it." For the men, inadequate pay was earned by grueling work, as 15-hour days—with no breaks to gossip, smoke, or rest—replaced the peasant routine with its seasons of leisure and interludes of idleness and sport.

Ironically, the very poverty that immobilized hundreds of thousands of the Irish in eastern seaports drove others westward to dig canals and tunnels and lay the tracks of the nation's new transportation network. Such work was brutal, and native-born Americans and better-off

GARIBALDI GUARD!

PATRIOTI ITALIANI!
HONVEDEK!
AMIS DE LA LIBERTE!
DEUTSCHE FREIHEITS KÆMPFER!

APPEAL!

The aid of every man is required for the service of his **ADOPTED COUNTRY!** A Regiment of Riflemen, Bersaglieri, Honvedek, Chasseurs, or Scharfschutzen, is now formed under the name of the **GARIBALDI GUARD**, and encamped near Washington. This Regiment will be increased by order of Government to 1150.

Wanted at once,
250 ABLE-BODIED MEN!

Italians, Hungarians, Germans, and French, Patriots of all Nations,

AROUSE! AROUSE! AROUSE!

The Families of our Soldiers shall be cared for.

PER ORDER, **Col. F. G. D'UTASSY,**
Lieut. Col. A. REPETTI,
Quartermaster, CHAS. B. NORTON. Maj. GEO. E. WARING, Jr.

Headquarters, Irving Building, 594 & 596 Broadway.

BAKER & GODWIN, PRINTERS, PRINTING-HOUSE SQUARE, OPPOSITE CITY HALL, NEW YORK.

Recruiting poster, 1861

The Civil War

Southern guns bombarded Fort Sumter in April 1861; President Lincoln called for volunteers to serve the Union—and men from many lands came forward. Patriots of the Garibaldi Guard (later the 39th New York) included Spaniards and Portuguese, Cossacks, sepoys, Englishmen, Turks, Croats, and Bavarians.

Imperfect federal records show about 2,500,000 men enrolled. Roughly a fifth, or more than 500,000, were foreign born, resident aliens as well as naturalized citizens.

Of these some 200,000 were German; often they formed regiments of their own. "They know too well, from experience in their dear fatherland," wrote one of their leaders, "what it is to have a country torn asunder. . . ."

More than 144,000 Irishmen joined the fight. A priest declared, "This is the first country the Irishman ever had that he could call his own." New York's famous Irish Brigade won its battle honors at heavy cost, and its banner earned the grimmest of compliments from a wary Rebel: "There comes that damned green flag again."

"Oh, God, what a pity!" cried Irish-born Georgians, recognizing the New Yorkers in a hopeless charge at Fredericksburg. Southerners boasted of "pure Anglo-Saxon blood," but men of other origins fought among them.

Officers by profession went South as well as North. Englishmen came, admiring "the noble, peerless Lee." The Prince de Polignac—"I have been militaire all my life"—commanded Texans who called him a "frog-eating Frenchman," and coped with terms like "ze 'lay-out' or ze 'shebang.'"

But for every immigrant who was living in a slave state, eight had preferred free soil. The eleven embattled states of the Confederacy, with nearly 5,500,000 whites and 3,500,000 blacks, held fewer than 250,000 foreign born. A clerk might note a recruit from "Cannady" or "Wayles," "Pauland" or "Yermany." Inadequate records indicate that tens of thousands from abroad fought for Southern Independence.

In 1864, young Maj. Gen. Patrick Cleburne, C.S.A., from Ireland and Arkansas, suggested the unthinkable: Enroll fit young slaves; promise them freedom when peace had been won. By the end of March 1865, his plan had been approved; but his cause, and his life, had been lost.

Inevitably, numbers had favored the Union, with its 22,400,000 people. The Emancipation Proclamation, and the enlistment of 186,000 black troops, had transformed the struggle. Soon the Fourteenth Amendment would define American citizenship.

Victory came from the staunchness of a free population and the unity of a varied one. The Union ranks included Dutch cavalry from Michigan and Swedes from Bishop Hill in Illinois; Yankees, Hoosiers, Jayhawks; Polish signals officers; men who had fought Indians on the frontier or Habsburg rule in Hungary; men from city gangs like the notorious Dead Rabbits. The language of command might be Norwegian in the 15th Wisconsin (shredded at Chickamauga in 1863). The ideal was American, and above nationality. At war's end, one of the Swiss sharpshooters in the Army of the Potomac summed it up: "It is beautiful to fight for an idea that is to bring freedom to all men. . . ."

Regimental color, battle-worn (top)
Officers of the Irish Brigade at Mass in camp in northern Virginia, 1861

119

German sausage and beer flavor the "American" end of Cincinnati's Vine Street where it intersects 5th; northern Vine threads the "Over-the-Rhine" district where signs as well as products remained German in 1887—and for thirty years afterward. More than five million German-speaking immigrants reached America during the 19th century. Most settled in mid-Atlantic and midwestern states, about half as farmers and half as urban dwellers. A city that attracted them would soon contain its "Little Germany," where English might seem a foreign language.

Other Americans soon developed a taste for the Wienerwurst (wiener), hamburgers, and lager bier—a light alternative to the heavy ales then dominating the country. Dozens of German brewers, not only Joseph Schlitz, made Milwaukee beers famous; "beer gardens" flourished in many German communities, offering a relaxed and family-oriented alternative to the stand-up Yankee bar. German-Americans in business succeeded with goods ranging from Heinz pickles and Harnischfeger cranes to Bausch & Lomb optics, Studebaker cars, Pfizer pharmaceuticals, and Levi Strauss blue jeans.

immigrants refused to do it. But for many desperate Irishmen, it offered a chance—of sorts. The same Irish newspaper that warned its readers to "do anything, in fact, in preference to railroading" was likely to print dozens of bold-lettered want ads for that work. "Good wages" on the Ohio canals ran to $13 a month; the best wages on the National Road, to $1.50 a day.

As traditional mores cracked like tenement walls, old vices— drinking and brawling—and new ones like prostitution bedeviled the residents of the "Little Dublins." By 1849, Boston had 1,200 groggeries. A slum "grocery" in New York was "a rotten, crazy-looking wooden tenement with leaking casks and damaged fruit strewn about it, and filled with five or six half-drunken, wholly-brutal men, and youths. . . ." Drunkenness strengthened the Irish reputation for violence. So did the cities' roisterous "fire laddies" who fought rival volunteers with "stones, trumpets and pistols" even at the scene of a blaze. Moreover, the Irish reacted with violence to exploitation. The notorious Molly Maguires, Irishmen who terrorized Pennsylvania's anthracite fields in the 1860s and '70s, killed foremen and vandalized equipment— in the tradition of older secret societies in Ireland that killed the agents of English landlords and officials, and destroyed their property.

Impoverished immigrants were arriving while the American states were liberalizing or dropping the old requirements that a man must own property to qualify as a voter. Thus the Irish laborer, once naturalized, could vote—and, in some cities, vote decisively. The classic Irish political machine began to take shape. New York's "Society of Saint Tammany," incorporated in 1789 as a fraternal order, had Irish leaders in the 1850s—though its most infamous boss, William Marcy Tweed, was native born. Outrageously corrupt more often than not, political machines met basic needs of otherwise helpless immigrants. Votes were exchanged for help, and that help included jobs (as on police forces) and charity. Machines marshaled thousands of loyal voters by speeding their naturalization through corrupt judges, and, often, by employing less-than-delicate forms of political persuasion.

As the Irish gained political muscle, hostility toward them grew. The noisy cartoon Paddy in red fireman's shirt was overtaken by the jut-jawed, slope-browed brute of Thomas Nast, the German-born artist whose pen savaged the Tweed Ring in the early 1870s. But even more threatening than the image of the Irishman as political tough was that of the newcomer as priest-ridden communicant of an alien religion.

Insignificant in numbers until the Irish influx, Roman Catholics had by 1850 become the nation's largest Christian denomination.

Catholics were less than 6 percent of the population, outnumbered roughly 17 to 1. Yet their rise greatly dismayed some Protestants. Many of Rome's adherents were German, but most—and notably their leaders in America—were Irish. Their efforts to establish a separate, publicly financed school system fanned anti-Catholic sentiment into outbreaks of violence and furthered doubts about the immigrants' commitment to "Americanism." Did they not owe ultimate obedience to the Pope, and was he not a temporal prince in Rome? As early as 1834, the inventor Samuel F. B. Morse argued that Jesuit priests were directing Catholic immigrants in a conspiracy to overthrow the government. Two years later, the editor of an anti-Catholic newspaper avowed that a papal military invasion was imminent. Meanwhile, books like Maria Monk's *Awful Disclosures* purported to tell, in lurid detail, of priests as seducers and of orgies in convents.

Nativist, or anti-immigrant, hostility focused on the Roman Catholic Church. It encompassed, however, a broad range of other issues. Germans were suspected of revolutionary tendencies because the Forty-Eighters were a small but very articulate group of reformers, including abolitionists like Carl Schurz. As "lager-beer loafers" or "grog-shop rowdies," Germans and Irish alike were seen as foes of temperance. Moreover, both tended to ignore the strict conventions of the Puritan Sabbath. Immigrants of most nationalities were accused of clannishness, and of pauperism and crime out of all proportion to their numbers.

Nativist feeling at mid-century coalesced around the party usually called Know-Nothing—from its members' answers to questions from outsiders: "I don't know" or "I know nothing." The slogan "America for the Americans" covered their goals: restricting immigration, barring the foreign-born (especially Catholics) from public office, and lengthening the naturalization process (to, perhaps, 21 years). On a brief wave of popularity, the Know-Nothings swept 43 Congressmen and 5 Senators into office in 1855; they elected a governor in Massachusetts. But when the "American Party" ran Millard Fillmore for President in 1856, he went down to a resounding defeat. As Horace Greeley of the *New York Tribune* remarked, the party had "as many elements of persistence as an anti-cholera or anti-potato-rot party would have."

In retrospect, the Know-Nothing party suggests a feverish effort to unify a nation increasingly divided over tariffs, slavery, and the very nature of the Union—issues beside which immigration paled. In 1861, newcomer and native-born alike were brutally swept into the maelstrom of the Civil War, and the issue of immigrant loyalty was buried

Three thousand bodies move as one during a wand exercise performed in 1892 by Milwaukee's Turners, or gymnasts. Founded in Berlin in 1811, the organizations called Turnvereine pioneered the use of devices like the parallel bars and vaulting horse. They stressed not only health and physical development, but also liberal politics, good citizenship, and a convivial spirit. Their members often mixed with Freie Gemeinden, or free-thinkers' groups, which favored humanist philosophies.

under the battleground turf. Like their comrades at arms, immigrants served the section where they lived, mainly the North.

In essentials, their war experiences differed little from their American fellows'. Whether they dreamed of mutton chops or sauerbraten, they ate hardtack; they exchanged homespun or red flannels for woolen blue or gray. Sons of one fatherland fought each other. And for families at home on a windy prairie or in a stifling slum, thoughts turned from the land of their fathers to the land where their children fought and died on battlegrounds whose names they could not pronounce.

For the immigrant, as for the nation, the Civil War was an end and a beginning. War and Reconstruction left nativism in eclipse. The war brought a new sense of equality to "foreigners" who had marched to the same tragic beat as Americans. The Union, preserved, embraced those who had survived its struggle. War had stimulated the economy, and the spacious West would beckon for decades yet. But by 1890, when the Census Office declared that an American frontier no longer existed, these older immigrants would join the native-born in facing issues of race and labor posed by a newer set of immigrants.

Christmas in America owes much of its merriment to immigrant traditions. The Christmas tree, which originated in 17th-century Germany, has thrived overseas. Below: Alexander and Tina Krueger, parents of twins Jennie and Edgar, trim the tree on Christmas Eve in 1901. Today's image of Santa stems from the artistry of German-born Thomas Nast, famed as a political cartoonist. His Republican elephant and Democratic donkey still cut their editorial capers.

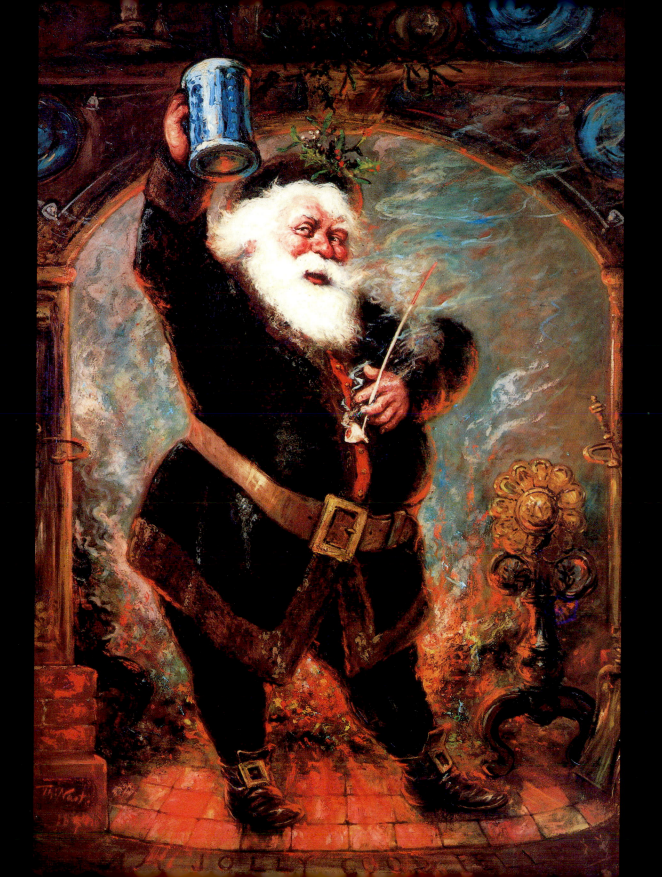

innovation that has endured in America. Mrs. Carl Schurz founded the first one in the U.S. in Watertown, Wisconsin, in 1856.

Iron Rails, Golden Mountain

Temporarily snowbound, a work party clears the tracks in an 1871 lithograph. By the mid-1800s a network of rails was spreading over the United States. Railroads helped open the frontier to settlement—and provided employment for many thousands of jobless immigrants.

rocker's pets," they were called. But Charles Crocker, a backer and chief overseer of the Central Pacific Railroad's works, cared not a bit for the taunts of his Irish rust-eaters—or anyone else—when he began hiring Chinese laborers in 1865. White manpower, the kind employers preferred, was in desperately short supply, diverted by the call to arms or the shout of "Eureka!" in the goldfields. The few white recruits who did straggle in—diehard grubstakers to a man—leaned on their picks when the boss rode away and shouldered their shovels on payday. Crocker was about ready to swallow his loss, "take a clean shirt, and get out." After nearly two years, the railhead was inching along into the Sierra Nevada only 50 miles east of the Sacramento starting point and, worse still, the rival Union Pacific was beginning its sprint across the Nebraska Territory in a race to capture new markets and control the mountain west.

The Central Pacific management even considered importing 5,000 Rebel prisoners (the Civil War's end foiled the plan) and peons from Mexico (rejected as too lazy). Diligent beyond a doubt were some 40,000 Chinese already in California. But "rice-eating weaklings"? A skeptical construction boss argued that the lowly Chinese, who rarely weighed more than 110 pounds, were hardly the stuff of transcontinental railroads. Crocker, who seldom weighed less than 250, countered that the ancestors of these delicate "Celestials" had erected a wall which, as an engineering marvel, outdid even the Central Pacific. He proved his point at Cape Horn.

This "cape" was a wall of rock 2,700 feet high, rising steeply from the American River and largely innocent of even a toehold. But the Chinese wove large wicker baskets, marked them with bright symbols to ward off evil spirits, and at the sound of the sunrise whistle marched silently off to the ridgetop. From one end of their bamboo carrying poles hung discarded kegs filled with strong tea; from the other, their woven baskets. Fortified by the contents of the former, they entrusted their lives to the latter. Lowered in the baskets hundreds of feet down the cliff, they chipped and chiseled small nooks out of the rock, inserted charges of black powder, then nimbly scampered up the ropes, pulling their baskets out of harm's way as the fuses crackled and flashed. Years later, a writer who rounded the Horn by train remarked that the sight from his car—down 1,300 feet to the faint green filament of the river— was "not good for nervous people."

At Cape Horn, it took 300 Chinese ten broiling days to "clear and grub" one mile of right-of-way through exploded rock. At the crest of

Advertisement for the Illinois Central Railroad contrasts a gleaming 1882 locomotive with earlier modes of travel; the map indicates the railway's routes in midwestern states. Always short of men to grade land and lay track, railroads competed with one another for newly arrived immigrants. Distributed in New York City in 1853, the handbill above attracted immigrants encouraged by the prospects of high wages and good living conditions. Thousands of Irishmen as well as Scandinavians, Poles, and Germans signed on with high hopes; some found reality a disappointment.

the Sierra, it took thousands more two savage winters and the summer between to bore 15 tunnels, 10 of them at least a thousand feet long, through solid stone—at an uncounted cost of deaths in avalanches and blasting accidents. In their home provinces near Canton, they had never seen snow; here it starched their blue pajamas to stiffness over numbed flesh. Near Donner Pass they worked 73 feet underground for weeks on end. And beyond, at the edge of the Great Salt Lake Desert, they teamed up, for once, with an Irish crew to lay a record 10 miles, 56 feet of track in 12 hours.

At Promontory, Utah, on May 10, 1869—when the rival rails were joined with great fanfare—the Chinese finished the job. But there and elsewhere, Crocker's Asians were excluded from the festivities. At San Francisco's grand celebration, the keynote speaker attributed the railroad's existence to "the commingled blood of the four greatest nationalities of modern days"—the French, Germans, English, and Irish of America. And at a centennial observance in 1969, Secretary of Transportation John A. Volpe echoed the sentiment: "Who else but Americans," he intoned, "could drill ten tunnels in mountains thirty feet deep in snow? Who else but Americans . . . ?"

Manual labor and the sweat of the brow built the growing nation's railroads. On the Northern Pacific, an 1885 work party—of obvious ethnic mix—takes a break (opposite). Using horse-drawn wagons to bring up supplies from the railhead a mile or so behind them, crews for the St. Paul, Minneapolis, and Manitoba Railway (below) lay track across the Dakota Territory in record time. Bosses pressed them hard, for only completed track could start returning profits to the company's investors.

Rickety web of wood spans a chasm in the Cascade Range of Washington, where men of the Northern Pacific pose for a photograph with visiting wives and children. "It will shake the nerves of the stoutest hearts when they see what is expected to uphold a train in motion," reported a San Francisco newspaper. Such temporary trestles carried the trains until tunnels and bridges could be built.

Frustrated by the rugged terrain and the chronic scarcity of manpower, Charles Crocker of the Central Pacific Railroad began hiring Chinese immigrants in March 1865. They proved industrious and uncomplaining. Reported Crocker's associate Leland Stanford: "More prudent and economical, they are content with less wages"—about $30 a month, paid in gold. Pleased with their diligence, Crocker contracted to import laborers directly from China, where peasants were anxious to flee a land devastated by flood, famine, and political upheaval. By 1869, when the Central Pacific and Union Pacific met at Promontory, Utah, to complete the first transcontinental rail route, Chinese made up 90 percent of the Central Pacific's labor force.

"People from all parts of the world are here, and every language seems to be spoken, but the babel resolves itself into one great motive 'Gold, Gold!' . . ." wrote a young fortune-seeker in San Francisco at the height of the gold rush. With the famous discovery at Sutter's mill in 1848, gold fever spread quickly, and adventurers from around the globe poured into San Francisco. Within one year this village of 800 people burgeoned into a city of 25,000. Forty-niner Frank Marryat sketched the ramshackle boomtown in the winter of 1849 (opposite, upper) noting that "the mud was unfathomable." By 1851 (opposite, lower) the city had a more orderly appearance, and by 1855 a cosmopolitan elegance prevailed.

"On entering one of these saloons the eye is dazzled almost by the brilliancy of chandeliers and mirrors," wrote Marryat. "The crowd of Mexicans, Miners, Niggers, and Irish . . . look dirtier . . . from contrast with the brilliant decorations." San Francisco supported a population of widely differing cultural and racial backgrounds; many groups—notably Indians and Mexicans—felt the sting of discrimination. Persecution, however, would bear hardest on the Chinese.

No one but Americans, in this tenacious myth of the frontier, had the virility to turn mountains to molehills. Only as long as the Chinese stuck to "women's work"—laundering, cooking, domestic service— were they accepted. For them, penetrating the Sierra's fastness proved far easier than breaching the great wall of bigotry around the "Golden Mountain" itself.

The name they gave America dated their exodus from crowded, war-torn southeastern China, an Asian Ireland, to the gold rush of 1849. Imperial edict and Confucian tradition alike forbade emigration. Even more fearsome was the prospect of life among white "ghosts" and "green-eyed foreign devils" who roared with "the voice of the tiger or the buffalo." But, as the travelers to Golden Mountain would explain, "to starve and to be buried at sea are the same."

Those who survived the 7,000-mile voyage usually paused in San Francisco only long enough to purchase miner's boots. At first, they aroused mere wonder. "They were queer-lookin' chicks, and no mistake," declared a crusty old-timer; they had shaven heads and glossy plaits, like "long tails to their heads," and hats "very like beehives"; the women wore trousers "with enough material in one leg to make a pair" for a denim-clad Westerner. Some wished them well. A reporter in 1850 hoped they would "get dust enough to build pagodas of gold."

Few did. American miners forced them away from rich lodes to worn-out claims. Some simply weighed the odds, gave up on mining, and began dishing up crisp-fried fare or scrubbing tattered flannels for womenless men in the camps. But as gold strikes petered out, "John Chinaman" became a whipping boy for assailants primed with rotgut and frustration. A trail of scattered rice; a tent slashed near Chili

"Very useful, quiet, good citizens . . . deserving the respect of all," wrote the editor of San Francisco's Alta California when Chinese immigrants first arrived. This sentiment changed radically when they ventured into the goldfields. As anti-Chinese feelings flared into mob violence and murder, many Chinese turned to other occupations. Their fishing camps sprang up along the West Coast, and picturesque junks— "decidedly foreign" in appearance— became a familiar sight (opposite). Using fine-mesh nets imported from China (above, left), the fishermen pulled in huge catches of shrimp, squid, and other seafood, which they sorted in baskets (above, right), then sold in Chinatown markets (right) or dried for export to China. White fishermen—mainly Italian, Dalmatian, and Greek immigrants— complained; and California made fine-mesh nets illegal in 1876. Discriminatory laws and taxes plagued the Chinese in nearly every employment they chose. The situation worsened during the postwar depression of the mid-1870s. The Workingmen's Party, founded by a fiery Irishman named Denis Kearney, raised the angry cry "The Chinese must go!"

141

BE JUST—EVEN TO JOHN CHINAMAN.

Gulch; a state official's diary boasting of "a great time, Chinamen tails cut off"—as racism focused on the Chinese, it found support in the law's long arm.

In pre-Civil War California—a free state as of 1850—no black or Indian could testify in any case to which a white was party. In 1854, Orientals were barred also, after the state's highest court overturned the conviction of a white citizen for murder. His victim, and the only witnesses, were Chinese. In that same year, the Chinese were held ineligible for citizenship on racial grounds. Already, anti-foreigner ordinances in the mining districts were modeled on anti-black measures; already, the "heathen Chinee," with his stage-sweeping queue, was a comic stereotype like the minstrels' black-faced "Sambo."

After the Civil War another issue came into ironic focus. As workers, the Chinese seemed to some "slave-like," supposedly dominated by powerful labor contractors. Moreover, these workers seemed able to live on lower wages than their white counterparts. The families they supported in far-off China were invisible. The Chinese "spend nothing," wrote a Norwegian law clerk, "and when they have earned something, they go back home."

Far more Chinese arrived than went home even before 1868, when the Burlingame Treaty gave Chinese and Americans the right to live and travel freely in each other's countries. Word of jobs in California's new factories had reached Canton's seamy wharves. Moreover, the burgeoning population of the Golden State wanted more vegetables and fruits, which the Chinese picked; more seafood, which they harvested; more restaurants and laundries, which they established; more land, which they reclaimed; more roads, rails, buildings, and transit systems, which they built. Wealthy Californians insisted upon having the diligent Chinese for house servants—which at least one newly hired immigrant, Lee Chew, found amazing: "I did not know how to do anything, and I did not understand what the lady said to me."

Even as thousands of Chinese were coming from Hong Kong, their usual port of departure, the new transcontinental railroad was bringing waves of demobilized Civil War veterans and fortune-seekers to California. As long as jobs held out, there was little unrest. But the railroad also brought cheap goods from eastern factories. To compete, California manufacturers had to slash costs—and they lowered wages.

Usually the Chinese accepted lower pay. White workers rarely did. And as postwar recession yielded to depression in 1873, and low pay to unemployment, "anti-coolie" leagues sprang up to combat "this menacing migration of the savage, vicious, idol-worshiping and barbarous race." When a series of harassing statutes and ordinances was found unconstitutional, *ad hoc* legalities prevailed. Lee Chew, who became a laundryman, recalled: "Sometimes we were taken before Magistrates and fined for losing shirts that we had never seen."

To him, it was "the jealousy of laboring men of other nationalities—especially the Irish—that raised all the outcry against the Chinese." In singling out the Irish, he hit upon a perennial irony: the attack by a recently arrived immigrant group on an even newer one. By the fall of 1877, immigrant members of a new, anti-Chinese organization, the Workingmen's Party, crowded San Francisco's sandlots nightly to scream their support as their leader, Denis Kearney, exhorted them by the light of huge bonfires to "drive every greasy-faced coolie from the land." Born in Ireland and recently naturalized, Kearney was a

"Be just—even to John Chinaman," implores the benevolent judge (with top hat) as a multi-ethnic class in 1893 jeers the dreaded "yellow peril" out of school. Their victim carries his ironing board, iron—and opium pipe. The caption (not shown) continues: "You allowed that boy to come into your school, it would be inhuman to throw him out now—it will be sufficient in the future to keep his brothers out!" As anti-Chinese attitudes spread across the country, legislators decided to appease voters on this issue. In 1882 Congress passed the Chinese Exclusion Act, barring Chinese laborers from the United States for ten years (courts had already ruled Chinese ineligible for naturalization). In 1892 Congress renewed the ban for ten more years, and in 1902 extended it indefinitely. Not until 1943 were these laws repealed. The saying "not a Chinaman's chance" reflects the plight of the Chinese in 19th-century America.

WE, THE UNDERSIGNED, Citizens and Residents of the City of Los Angeles, County of Los Angeles, and State of California, not of Chinese birth or extraction, do hereby certify that QUAN SAM, whose photograph is hereunto attached,

is a Chinese Merchant of good standing and is a member of a Chinese General Merchandise and Grocery Firm doing business in this City at No.22 Plaza Street, under the style and name of QUONG TSUE LUNG & CO., and that we have known the said QUAN SAM as a Merchant with the above mentioned Firm for more than one year past, and know that he has performed no manual labor, except what was necessary in his business as a Merchant, for at least one year last past.

The said QUAN SAM wishes to visit his Native Land (China) and being desirous of again returning to the United States to continue his business, to facilitate his landing upon his return we have made the above statements, for we know the said QUAN SAM is a bona fide Merchant and is well know to many business men of Los Angeles. He was registered as a Merchant on the 6th day of March,1894: Certificate #93117.

M Way Teller ....(SEAL).

Alphonse Paradis ....325 N. Los Angeles........(SEAL).

Anderson ....(SEAL).

Subscribed and sworn to before me this ...16th...day of October, A.D.1900.

Barton Darlington.

NOTARY PUBLIC in and for Los Angeles Co. State of California.

self-made man who secretly disdained the workingmen who worshiped him. His call for "Judge Lynch" would scatter listeners in search of Chinese victims. And during a Thanksgiving parade, the rough-and-tumble "Irish Boys of the Second Ward" carried signs of warning: "Discharge your Chinamen and you will find no more Hoodlums."

Neither rival politicians nor capitalists like Crocker would risk favoring the Chinese, though a few Christian missionaries defended them. In 1879, Californians approved a new constitution with many anti-Chinese provisions, and a referendum showed voters favoring total exclusion of the Chinese by a margin of 134,268 to 10,820.

For the first time in the nation's history, in 1882, a federal law checked immigration of a specific ethnic group. Ignoring the Burlingame Treaty, it banned the entry of Chinese laborers for ten years. The Geary Act of 1892 extended the exclusion for another ten. In 1902 the ban was made "permanent." Only in 1943, when China had become a wartime ally, were these laws repealed.

Resentment of these unwelcome aliens produced its worst outbreaks in 1885 and 1886. The Chinese in Eureka, California, were given 24 hours to leave town—and shown a makeshift gallows for emphasis. In Washington Territory, men of Tacoma packed the local Chinese into Portland-bound boxcars in a cold, drenching storm. In Wyoming's coalfields, a fight between white and Chinese miners—the latter hired as strikebreakers—touched off a massacre. A Winchester-toting mob chased the Chinese from the town of Rock Springs, shot at those who fled into the sagebrush hills, and threw the wounded into burning buildings. At least 28 Chinese died. Federal officials apologized to Chinese diplomats and paid an indemnity, while lamely pointing out that the attackers had been not Americans but European immigrants.

Only within the larger Chinatowns—only behind the handsome blue facades where carved lions stood guard, or in hidden alleys pungent with garbage and sweet jasmine—did the Chinese find a measure of security. Family-name and benevolent associations—the latter known as the Chinese Six Companies—acted as job brokers, banks, or undertakers; the tongs, secret societies like the Chamber of Far-Reaching Virtue, feuded and furthered the vices of a generation of lonely men, unable to bring their families from China or to find Chinese brides.

Some of those for whom life in America was "more miserable than owning only a flute in the marketplace of Wu"—a byword for wretchedness—returned to China. Others couldn't muster the fare or the courage to face their families empty-handed; moreover, China remained in turmoil. And still, the dream of the Golden Mountain held

Exclusionary laws imposed limits on the rights of prosperous Chinese residents. Merchants, for example, wishing to return home to visit their families, needed special documents (left) to re-enter the United States. Racial discrimination spoke bluntly in the popular culture. Above, the title page of sheet music shows a stereotyped portrayal of "The Heathen Chinee." The lyrics—pirated from a satirical poem by Bret Harte—tell how a Chinese gambler outcheats two white cardsharps. "We are ruined by Chinese cheap labor," sighs loser Bill Nye.

fast for a continuing trickle of new arrivals who endured months or years of detention in San Francisco, hopeful of squeezing through the needle's eye of legal loopholes.

> *The dragon out of water is humiliated by ants;*
> *The fierce tiger who is caged is baited by a child.*

Thus one anonymous detainee described the plight of his people in America, carving his calligraphy into a wall at the immigration center on Angel Island, in San Francisco Bay. Another alien sojourner—he was Robert Louis Stevenson—perceived, in his outrage at the Chinese predicament, its broader implications: "It seems, after all, that no country is bound to submit to immigration any more than to invasion. . . . Yet we may regret the free tradition of the republic, which loved to depict herself with open arms, welcoming all unfortunates." For the Chinese experience had set an important precedent, a counterweight to that "free tradition" on the scales of justice and in the hearts of Americans.

Dressed in embroidered silk robes, a Chinese woman and her children pose outside their cabin in Olympia, Washington, in 1896. Few Chinese women emigrated to the United States. Confucian tradition dictated a woman's role as that of producing heirs and serving her husband's parents.

Leaving wives behind, husbands came to the U.S. to earn money, fully intending to return to their homeland. By 1890 the male-female ratio among Chinese in America ran as high as 27 to 1. These "bachelor societies" tended to band together in urban ghettos, or Chinatowns, to foster a feeling of community and for protection from hostile white "ghosts." Living in close quarters, men crowd Ross Alley (opposite) in San Francisco's Chinatown. Seeing little need to adopt American culture, they retained their traditional dress, hairstyle (shaved head with a single plait called a queue), foods, and customs. Often, if a member of a Chinese family association died, the group would send his bones back to China for burial with his ancestors.

Through Ellis Island

They came and they came—the second great wave—notably from southern and eastern Europe. In this dramatic mural artist Ben Shahn chose to include Charles Steinmetz (with spectacles), his own mother, and later arrival Albert Einstein—symbols of immigrant genius and humanity.

he day of the emigrants' arrival in New York was the nearest earthly likeness to the final Day of Judgment, when we have to prove our fitness to enter Heaven." Who among the newcomers could imagine their meeting with the Man at the Gate? For they spoke of the State in personal terms, and of the uniformed American in tones of shuddering respect due to Tsar, King, or Sultan and his appointed emissaries. Omnipotent, the Man would decide who was "clearly and beyond doubt entitled to land" and who would be barred. As the ship glided into Upper New York Bay in the early hours of Easter Monday, 1913, the pearly lights of Brooklyn Bridge arched into the heavens. Below, in the ship's sleepless hold, darkness likewise gave shape and sheen to the private visions of a hundred minds' eyes.

When the engines stopped, the anchor chains groaned and clattered. Some passengers wept. "For many this sound was like the bones of Europe rattling one last time, and they felt that they were finally released." Other sounds still echoed: the lilt of an Italian blessing on "you who can leave this hopeless land"; the thunder of hoofbeats and rampaging Cossacks nearing the *shtetl*—the little Jewish village—on Easters past. Now, in the harbor, dawn would slowly unveil the Statue of Liberty: "She was beautiful with the sunshine so bright. Beautiful colors, the greenish-like water—and so big, and everybody was crying." One Russian informed another that the Statue bestrode the tomb of Columbus. But for others, there was sheer awe.

"We just gazed on it. We couldn't really grasp the meaning of it, but it was a very penetrating feeling to see that symbol of freedom."

She was, to one traveler, "a celestial figure," and to another, "this new divinity." But the Lady with the Torch stood in counterpoise to the unseen Man at the Gate, the law. By 1900, a resurgence of nationwide nativism, focused on the "Slav, Latin and Asiatic races, historically down-trodden, atavistic, and stagnant"—and presently surging toward America—had given rise to a series of federal restrictions. The change was decisive: Never again would immigration be widely perceived as desirable, as necessary to the country's prosperity. Still, the newcomers prayed that the Man would bless them just as the Lady seemed to.

Immigrants arriving in the 1890s and later also took a number of decidedly worldly steps to ensure that the Man would smile on them. Few knew the legal particulars—for instance, that as far back as 1882, the year of the Chinese Exclusion Act, another law barred all newcomers likely to become public charges. But their hands traveled to the

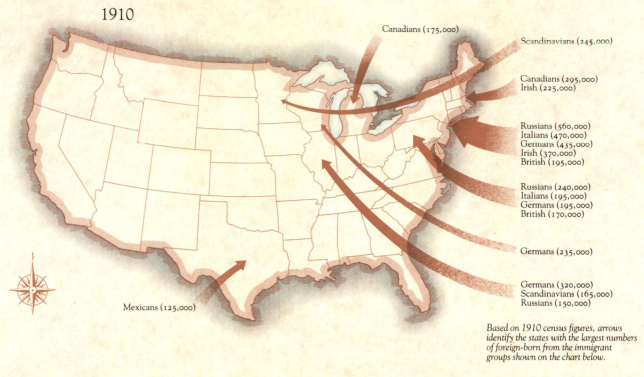

1910

Canadians (175,000)

Scandinavians (245,000)

Canadians (295,000)
Irish (225,000)

Russians (560,000)
Italians (470,000)
Germans (435,000)
Irish (370,000)
British (195,000)

Russians (240,000)
Italians (195,000)
Germans (195,000)
British (170,000)

Germans (235,000)

Germans (320,000)
Scandinavians (165,000)
Russians (150,000)

Mexicans (125,000)

*Based on 1910 census figures, arrows
identify the states with the largest numbers
of foreign-born from the immigrant
groups shown on the chart below.*

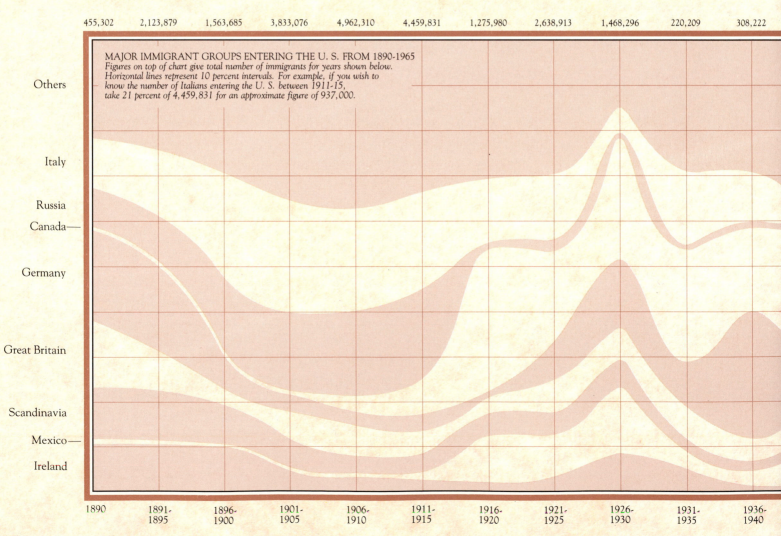

| 455,302 | 2,123,879 | 1,563,685 | 3,833,076 | 4,962,310 | 4,459,831 | 1,275,980 | 2,638,913 | 1,468,296 | 220,209 | 308,222 |

MAJOR IMMIGRANT GROUPS ENTERING THE U. S. FROM 1890-1965
*Figures on top of chart give total number of immigrants for years shown below.
Horizontal lines represent 10 percent intervals. For example, if you wish to
know the number of Italians entering the U. S. between 1911-15,
take 21 percent of 4,459,831 for an approximate figure of 937,000.*

Others

Italy

Russia

Canada—

Germany

Great Britain

Scandinavia

Mexico—

Ireland

| 1890 | 1891-1895 | 1896-1900 | 1901-1905 | 1906-1910 | 1911-1915 | 1916-1920 | 1921-1925 | 1926-1930 | 1931-1935 | 1936-1940 |

A Broadening Torrent

If the tide of immigration had run high in 1850, the 25 years before World War I brought the flow to a flood. Records show 16,942,781 arrivals from 1891 through 1915, exceeding the total for the previous 70 years and including a wider variety of peoples. The 1,285,349 aliens of 1907 mark the all-time high for a single year.

By the 1890s immigration from prosperous western Europe was dropping—dramatically, from Germany and Britain. Meanwhile, it was rising from Italy, Russia, and other parts of eastern Europe. Wars reshaped the Balkans. Social and economic change in these regions was provoking emigration, made possible by cheap transportation. The 75 years covered in the chart would bring two world wars, a worldwide depression—and major shifts in U.S. immigration policy.

The map at left shows the states with the largest numbers of foreign-born newcomers from the charted groups. They are still concentrated in the Northeast and North Central regions, with Scandinavians appearing in Minnesota and Mexicans in the Southwest, especially in Texas.

Generally, 60 to 80 percent of all immigrants came from eight main groups. Other peoples arrived in significant but elusive numbers. The label "Turk" might cover any subjects of the Ottoman Sultan; various terms referred to the estimated 2.5 million Poles.

Because of the 1815 partition of Poland, Polish-speakers might be tallied as Germans, Austro-Hungarians, or Russians. The "Russians" in Illinois in 1910 may have included Poles, who were coming to industrial cities like Chicago in the 1880s and '90s "*za chlebem*—for bread"—to earn money enough to buy land at home.

These new immigrants stirred mistrust and fear. In 1891 the Secretary of the Treasury wrote that they "do not readily assimilate with our people and are not in sympathy with our institutions." A movement to control their numbers gained momentum.

For the first time, in 1921, a law limited the number of admissions. The Immigration Act of 1924 set quotas based on national origins. Minimal quotas were assigned to new nations formed after World War I. Barriers against Asians remained. New World nations escaped these limits—partly because of Monroe Doctrine principles, partly because of unpatrollable borders, partly because few Central and South Americans had yet come. A few other special categories were exempted. The spirit of the 1924 law would guide overall policy till 1965.

Immigration across American borders had always fluctuated with economic conditions, and Mexicans and Canadians were counted with some consistency after 1908. They formed a greater fraction of the total when European immigration was cut. Until 1952, a number of West Indians came under the British quota. Generally well educated, they offered competition to black Americans moving from the rural south to northern cities. Although U.S. citizens since 1917, Puerto Ricans did not reach the mainland in large numbers until the late 1940s.

Despite the quota system, the nation's ethnic balance continued to change—if slowly. Southern and eastern Europeans consistently filled their quotas; northern nations only half filled theirs. The Great Depression, however, reduced immigration far below permitted levels—in 1933, to only 23,068, the lowest since 1831.

To help refugees and stateless exiles after World War II, the Displaced Persons Acts of 1948 and 1950 allowed "mortgaging" of future quotas. Later laws admitted nonquota refugees from such countries as Hungary, Yugoslavia, Cuba, and Indonesia. The Internal Security Act of 1950 and the Immigration and Nationality (McCarran-Walter) Act of 1952 tightened restrictions on ideological grounds. For many, the open door had become a strait and narrow gate.

170,952   864,087   1,087,638   1,427,841   1,450,312

1941-1945   1946-1950   1951-1955   1956-1960   1961-1965

frayed coat linings where the slender stash, which the Man would demand to see, was stored. Sons of Erin, anticipating a query about job intentions, rehearsed their reply: "Jine the perlicemen." On the other hand, one could not admit to having a job already lined up, as the Foran Act of 1885 had outlawed the importation of contract labor. That concept was especially difficult for the Italians, heirs to a long tradition of hiring out as seasonal labor in neighboring European lands.

"Remember," repeated an intrepid Sicilian to the swarthy *paesani* assembled on deck, "you have got no work and you paid your own way."

Few had to fear the 1891 law's ban on polygamists. But the same law, placing immigration wholly under federal control, also contained a provision that excluded "persons suffering from a loathsome or dangerous contagious disease." Especially feared was trachoma, a highly communicable eye affliction, often unnoticed in early stages. Preparing to debark, passengers asked each other whether they looked "sick in the eyes." One mother, knowing that her infant did, was gorging it in a desperate effort to make it sleep through the examination. Other mothers worried about other ailments. Would the ragged child with the angry sty be torn from its family and sent back to Europe? Was seasickness a loathsome disease?

Hands quested deep in pockets, where callused fingertips traced

"Mountains! Look at them!" "Why don't they have snow on them?" Italian boys, standing tiptoe, craned their necks to watch New York's skyline—then dominated by the 47-story Singer Tower. Edward Corsi, one of the newcomers in 1907, remembered, "Soon we were permitted to pass through America's Gateway"—Ellis Island, where he later became commissioner. For most immigrants the island meant only an anxious pause. ". . . everybody was . . . looking at Manhattan," recalled one. "And I must admit, that sight I don't think I will ever forget."

the crowns embossed on cold metal. The coins, withdrawn, were counted for the hundredth time, and a couple were set aside to "pay something to the American inspector and American doctor." How could it be otherwise? The currency of everyday life in southern and eastern Europe was extortion in many guises. Everywhere, it was high taxation: often a crushing burden, particularly for a Slovak farmhand who earned the equivalent of 25 cents a day during the flax harvest and perhaps half that at other times. In newly unified Italy, it was the heavy tax levied on the mules and donkeys of the poor *contadini*, while the cows and horses of the *latifondisti*—the great landowners—went untaxed. In Hungary, extortion was the bribe to dodge military service and secure a forged passport; in Russia, it was the exorbitant cost of the genuine article. The cost of life was higher for ethnic minorities in the Slavic lands, and dearest for some five million Jews confined to Russia's western area called the Pale of Settlement. "If a Jew and a Gentile kept store side by side," wrote author Mary Antin of her childhood village, "the Gentile could content himself with smaller profits. He did not have to buy permission to travel in the interests of his business. . . . He was saved the expense of hushing inciters of pogroms. Police favor was retailed at a lower price to him than to the Jew. . . . What his shield is to the soldier in battle, that was the ruble to the Jew in the Pale."

In 1890 Congress designated low-lying, three-acre Ellis Island in Upper New York Bay as an immigration station. Engineers dredged a channel around it; ballast from incoming ships contributed landfill. The station opened in 1892, but burned to the ground in 1897. Fireproof structures—planned to process half a million new arrivals a year—opened in late 1900, and had greeted some six million by the end of 1910. Despite periodic expansion (opposite), the station's facilities remained painfully inadequate (except during the immigration lull of World War I) until 1924. Then Congress tightened quotas and U.S. consuls overseas began to screen applicants.

For the Jews, the insatiable outstretched palm inevitably clenched to an iron fist. During the 19th century, more than 600 anti-Jewish laws were instituted in Russia. In the 1880s and '90s, waves of officially sanctioned violence bloodied many communities. Children of Moses, boys as young as eight or nine with "helpless, pitiful eyes," were forced into military service for as long as 25 years.

"We didn't want to give our lives to the Russian army, so some boys would damage their own bodies. They would puncture their eardrums or give themselves a hernia. They would chop off a finger. The one that pulls the trigger."

Discriminatory laws also afflicted national groups submerged under foreign occupation. In Slovakia and Transylvania, the Magyar ruling class forbade the public use of local languages and monopolized official positions. The "Iron Chancellor" Otto von Bismarck, founder of the German Empire, sought to eradicate Polish culture in areas held by Prussia, placing the parochial schools there under state control. In the Russian-occupied portion of Poland, a would-be emigrant who wanted "to give my children some education at least," lamented that "here in Ostrowo there is no school but a Russian elementary one." Everywhere, for those not born to wealth and rank, there were "few of the privileges of citizenship but many of its burdens."

The forces that had uprooted millions of "old" European emigrants now stirred the much larger "new" emigration from these other lands. As the locus of change shifted south and eastward, however, the impact was far more dramatic to peoples who had seen little change over the centuries. The railroad arrived; but Nicholas Gerros, a Macedonian Greek who emigrated in 1912, recalled that "when I went to get my passport . . . was the first time I saw a wagon with wheels." Metalworks were built; but in the wattle huts of Romanian peasants, "you probably do not perceive a single thing in which iron has been employed." Population growth was more marked and sustained than in western Europe; but in Polish Galicia, 81 percent of all farms were by the turn of the century already too small to support a family. In Italy, infestations of olive flies and vineyard phylloxera wiped out countless tired, tiny holdings. Said one departing Italian peasant, "If America did not exist, we would have to invent it for the sake of our survival."

Shipping agents, "America letters" containing prepaid passages, and the reappearance of townsmen in American "store clothes" sped the process, as in the past. So did the new steamships: vessels boasting 25-knot cruising speeds and space enough for as many as 3,000 hapless souls. Transatlantic fares dropped to $12, and the crossing to ten days or less. "Now people feel more confident about going to New York than to Rome," reported a provincial prefect in 1894. As the voyage

154

became routine, more and more men ventured forth without families; so did unescorted girls, teenage steerage passengers like Bessie and Rose Yellin, whose lovely singing voices earned the captain's attention and recitals in the first-class dining salon.

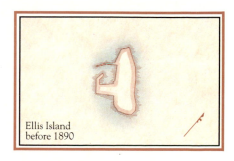

Ellis Island before 1890

An extra $20, in 1905, bought the status of cabin class "pet, to be coddled, fed on delicacies, guarded against draughts." That same $20 exempted a passenger, once at New York, from the thousand-and-one scrutinies endured by steerage travelers. Cabin class inspections were usually a cursory shipboard formality. Canny travelers knew this: Women of uncertain reputation, sickly children, banditti, and other "excludables" took advantage of it. Assistant Surgeon General H. D. Geddings, for another, knew the stratagem. "There are numerous instances," he reported sternly in 1906, "of rejected steerage passengers showing up in the first cabin of another line in from 21 to 28 days." Those who didn't already know found out when the ship docked in Manhattan, the cabin class set was released, and the steerage passengers found themselves subjected to seemingly endless delays.

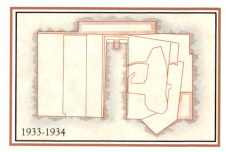

1890-1892

"And so there was this slight feeling among many of us that, isn't it strange that here we are coming to a country where there is complete equality, but not quite so for the newly arrived immigrants."

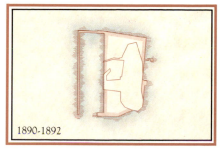

1896-1908

Even the steerage passengers were often lined up according to the appearance of class. Steamship companies, financially responsible for transporting deportees back to Europe, were conscious of their reputation; debarkation processions were led by the most prosperous-looking and "respectable" passengers. One of them had donned her best, rust-brown suit and matching hat for the occasion: "The captain came and pulled me and Sarah by the sleeve and in an ugly way told us to be sure to stay in front of the line when the inspectors came." No matter that she had fared poorly on the voyage and grown so thin that "my clothes fell off of me and I had to pin them with safety pins so to hold them up." Behind trailed the "mountain women with handkerchiefs on their heads." Behind John Bull's daughters in faded silk, or travelers "in caps so green that the wearer could only be Irish," came the more alien-looking in *their* best: Russians in matted sheepskins; Greeks in white kilts; "sober-minded Amazons" mocking "modern modes of scanty skirts by wearing sixteen of them at a time."

1919-1924

Whatever the dress, badges and labels of various kinds were soon affixed to it. In America, it seemed, everyone wore special markings. A man who wore nautical insignia gave them one badge, a bill of lading. Later, a man who wore gold-thread eagles would give them another, with numbers that corresponded to their place on the ship's manifest.

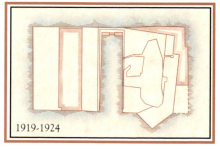

1933-1934

Tickets and vaccination cards sprouted from the caps, hats, or teeth of immigrants whose hands were full of baggage and babies. Some men in uniform gave them nothing but a rough shove. "Hurry up!" these men shouted in a dozen languages.

They hurried, and then waited—sometimes for hours, aboard barges. At last the motley crowd grew solemn as all eyes sought Ellis Island, a half-mile across the water, a half-hour ride warped into an eternity by apprehension.

Some confused it with New York's old immigration station at the tip of Manhattan and called it Castle Garden, or *Castn Gare*, or *Kasselgarda;* among Italians *Batteria*—the Battery. "Ellis Island was," recalled an Austrian Jew, "like what they call a *Kesselgarden*. . . . It was turmoil." It was, first of all, the place of judgment—mingling, as the awesome often does, the momentous and the banal, the weighty and the whimsical. The island where the hopes of 12 million people soared or plunged could not have been, in its natural state, a less imposing three acres of slush, sand, and oyster shells. In colonial times, it was the occasional haunt of fishermen who netted the "fat shad . . . lean shad and fat herring" that Samuel Ellis, the island's last private owner, advertised in his Manhattan market. After independence, Ellis Island's strategic location was deemed "infinitely precious" and a coastal battery and magazine were built. But life there was so uneventful, even during the War of 1812, that the only action most artillerists saw was the execution of a soldier who had tried to murder an officer. In 1890 the military installation was abandoned.

That same year, Treasury Secretary William Windom scouted the island as a possible site for an immigration depot to replace Castle Garden—a new Bureau of Immigration would soon be placed under his jurisdiction. He was not impressed by what he could see from 150 yards offshore, which was as close as his revenue cutter could get in the shallow waters. But his first choice, Bedloe's Island, was ruled out by the protests of the New York *World* (the island would be converted "into a Babel"), the Statue's influential sponsor Senator William Evarts, and Bartholdi himself ("a monstrous plan and a downright desecration"). So a deep channel was dredged around Ellis Island, its area was doubled with landfill, and new facilities rose alongside the ramshackle old military structures. Buff-painted Georgia pine, "picturesque" towers, and blue slate roof combined handsomely in the main building.

Commissioner John B. Weber graciously offered a ten-dollar gold piece to young Annie Moore from County Cork, the first newcomer to pass through its portals in 1892. Five years later, a mysterious

Steerage passengers, transported from the pier by barge, crowd the deck as they approach Ellis Island. They face medical screening, then interrogation by inspectors who check them against ship's manifest 23. A wrong answer, physical or mental infirmity, or lack of money for self-support while seeking employment means detention, more questioning, and possible deportation. Most will pass the tests. Later, on the ferry Ellis Island (bottom), newly admitted immigrants leave for Manhattan. "Success had melted most of us. . . . That is what it feels like to have passed the Last Day and still believe in Heaven, to pass Ellis Island and still believe in America."

married strangers by prearrangement. Women traveling alone were detained until someone arrived to assume responsibility for them.

midnight blaze reduced the station to charred rubble. No lives were lost, but thousands of immigration records were. During the reconstruction, a temporary center operated on the Battery. Ellis Island's new facility, opened in 1900, was, noted the *New York Times*, "absolutely fireproof." The new main building was also more imposing than its piney predecessor. It was "a conglomeration of several styles of architecture, the predominating style being that of the French Renaissance." Distinctly American, stern-eyed limestone eagles surveyed the newcomers from aeries high above soaring archways. Reported the *Times*: "It is estimated that 5000 persons can be thoroughly examined with perfect ease" each day. Immigration had fallen off in the 1890s in response to a nationwide depression; officials concluded that no more than half a million immigrants would ever again reach New York in any one year.

But in the decade beginning with 1901, more than 6.7 million arrived, of whom some 6 million were shunted to Ellis Island. The busiest year of all at Ellis was 1907 (866,660) and April 17 was its busiest day (11,747 newcomers). At such times, immigrants were often "compelled to remain on board ship for two or three days." Among them were those who arrived on the morning of May 2, 1907, when there were "eleven ships on the list, with 16,209 passengers, while during the day four more arrived making the total number of passengers 21,755."

Haunted face tinged with hope, an elderly grandmother waits for relatives to claim her. A son may have immigrated first, struggled to establish himself, and saved to pay his mother's passage. Whatever trials await, there are no regrets for those fleeing poverty, chronic hardship, or official hostility and popular violence. "Am I not despised? . . . urged to leave?" wrote a Russian Jew. "Can I even think that some consider me a human being capable of thinking and feeling like others? Do I not rise daily with the fear lest the hungry mob attack me? . . . It is impossible . . . that a Jew should regret leaving. . . ."

Numbers alone presented an overwhelming challenge to the staff. The processing of most immigrants was hasty; "not over two minutes can be devoted to each of them," reported Commissioner William Williams in 1909. An efficiency-conscious Wall Street lawyer, Williams begged Washington for more personnel, for "to accomplish even this inadequate inspection the inspectors must work nine hours almost continuously." Stenographers fell ill from "working days and days in succession, some of them 30 days, without any rest." There were never enough interpreters. One of them was a future mayor of New York: The young Fiorello La Guardia spoke Croatian, Italian, and German. He later recalled that "for two years we worked seven days a week."

If "roughness, cursing, intimidation and a mild form of blackmail" sometimes prevailed, the workload partly accounted for it. The Reverend Edward Steiner, who studied immigration at the century's turn by traveling with immigrants, pointed out another factor: "the new spirit had not yet come into politics and the spoils still belonged to the victors who made full use of the privilege."

At Ellis Island the most attractive of the spoils went to the private concessionaires: to the bakers who supplied the island with seven tons

of bread a day; to railroad and steamship ticket sellers who took in as much as $560,000 a week. Profits soared when immigrants were served an unvarying diet of prunes on rye bread; when they exchanged a 20-mark German piece worth $4.75 in 1904 for a handful of "new pennies, whose brightness was well calculated to deceive any newcomer."

When, after a major scandal in 1901, President Theodore Roosevelt urged Williams to accept "the most interesting office in my gift," he was referring to the need "to get this office straight." During his two terms, the diminutive Williams proved up to the task of weeding out graft. But the greatest challenge for him, and for his successors, was to administer the complex laws to the letter, but with compassion—with a surgeon's precision and a saint's touch. Williams, for one, thought the quality of current immigrants "inferior on the whole to the old." He

sought through the law to keep their number to a minimum. But he papered the walls with an explicit notice: "Immigrants shall be treated with kindness and civility by everyone. . . ."

"What I remember most about Ellis Island was that for the first time in my life I did not see any religious pictures on the walls."

Immigrants had little time to notice anything when they first entered the main building. In detachments of 30, the number of names on one manifest sheet, they were quick-marched over to a wide, steep staircase. Williams thought the stairway an inconvenience. So, certainly, did the immigrants themselves, who had to negotiate it with an unwieldy featherbed and pillow, a big wicker basket, a bulging sack fashioned of an old red or blue bandanna, perhaps a small trunk that "becomes ragged around the edges and tears and cuts."

For the medical inspectors looking on from above, however, the immigrants' struggles on the crowded staircase comprised the first part of their examination. Official Victor Safford compared the procedure to evaluating a used car on a test drive, for "the wise man who really wants to find out all he can about an automobile, or an immigrant, will want to see both in action." Thus the faulty heart, like the sputtering engine, was found out; the immigrant who gasped his way up the stairs had the letter **H** chalked on his coat.

"*And on some of the people those men put chalk marks on their back. Of course, the people themselves did not know it, but the people in back of them could see it and were worried and wondering what it was all about.*"

Like the used-car buyer, "the medical examiners must ever be on the alert for deception," reported one observer; "the child strapped to its mother's back, and who appears old enough to walk alone, may be unable to walk because of infantile paralysis." And, noted Safford, "no horseman would think of buying a horse until he had seen how the horse stands." Called to halt, the immigrant was eyed from head to toe. More chalk marks asked for detailed examination: **B** for back, **L** for lameness, and so on. A high collar would only temporarily conceal a

"Then we slowly filed up to a doctor who turned our eyelids inside out with a metal instrument," checking for trachoma. (Use of the buttonhook, wiped on a towel between victims, may have done more to spread the blinding disease than to contain it.) Medical inspectors chalked letters on the clothes of two out of ten—**E** for eyes, **H** for heart, **S** for senility, **X** for mental deficiency—and detained them for further examination. Below: Timed with a stopwatch, a woman takes a test given suspected mental defectives.

167

goiter **(G)**. "Pompadours are always a suspicious sign"—and elaborately coiffed individuals often received a chalked **Sc** for any of several contagious scalp ailments, especially the common disease favus. Tuberculosis, the so-called Jewish disease, had a tragically high incidence. Lice, not loathsome enough for a chalk mark, were commonplace; one official recalled how he would find "something crawling over my neck," usually on the left side because "the alien always stood on my left."

Matrons looked for prostitutes; the feared "eye men" flipped back eyelids with buttonhooks and looked for trachoma, whose victims were usually deported. In the stringent mental examination, doctors looked for retardation, and especially for "psychopathic organization." Its multitudinous symptoms, outlined by the Surgeon General, included "facetiousness," "apparent shrewdness," "smiling," "tremor of tongue," "preoccupation," "biting nails," "unusual decoration worn on the clothing," and "other eccentricities." Sometimes "racial considerations" explained the oddity. "If an Englishman reacts to questions in the manner of an Irishman, his lack of mental balance would be suspected. The converse is also true. If the Italian responded to questions as the Russian Finn responds, the former would in all probability be suffering with a depressive psychosis."

Not surprisingly, "from 50 to 100 per cent" of the immigrants were subjected to questioning. Some were asked their names; others, to add small sums on the spot. Those who received a chalk **X** were led away for closer observation. That yielded detailed notes: "Insane. Loves America and wishes to defend America." "Says she is prophet of the earth." "Heart beats rapidly when talking with strangers." "Can sew garments but can not cut them out." "Crying and weeping because her little 21-year-old daughter is alone." "He fell in love with a young lady on board ship. She did not reciprocate."

Most of those delayed for further testing were eventually released. But whether they were taken for an hour's psychiatric interview, for a month in Ellis Island's hospital, or for deportation, it seemed the nightmarish realization of their worst fears about the place of judgment. They were often "set aside in a cage," recalled an official, "like a segregated animal." Their families, separated from them "without a minute's warning," became frantic. One mother, whose child had contracted scarlet fever, "attacked the attendants, beating and scratching them, and then tried to throw herself into the bay because she thought her child was being taken from her forever." Or the mother might be taken away and the child left. One little girl, about five, cried: *"Mitter, mitter, ich will zu meiner mitter gehen*—Mother, mother, I want to go to my mother." But she had to stay alone and uncomforted, among "rough-looking men."

Stephen Graham, an English writer who traveled in steerage with Russian passengers, thought Ellis Island's procedures in general a product of "the mechanical obsession of the American people. This ranging and guiding and hurrying and sifting was like nothing so much as the screening of coal in a great breaker tower." The hub of such activity was the vast Registry Room, to which immigrants proceeded if the doctors cleared them. Under its vaulted ceiling, 58 feet high, waited thousands of people, more than the home village had inhabitants. More convoluted than the twisting alleys of the old village was the maze of open passageways created by cold pipe-railing. Above hung immense illuminated American flags. Below, "future Americans were kept moving along like puppets on conveyor-belts" toward the immigration inspector, another figure of dread, rumored to be intent on tripping them up.

He "sat bureaucratically," wrote Louis Adamic from Carniola, "very much in the manner of officials in the Old Country—behind a great desk, which stood upon a high platform." There, under a portrait

Boards of Special Inquiry, made up of three inspectors, decided exclusion cases. One out of six such detainees was deported. The law barred those with physical deformities or mental deficiencies (opposite) as likely to become public charges. Encouraging careful judgments, President Theodore Roosevelt wrote to immigration officials: ". . . but we must remember that so to send him back is often to inflict a punishment upon him only less severe than death itself. . . ." Some preferred death: over the years several hundred committed suicide at Ellis Island.

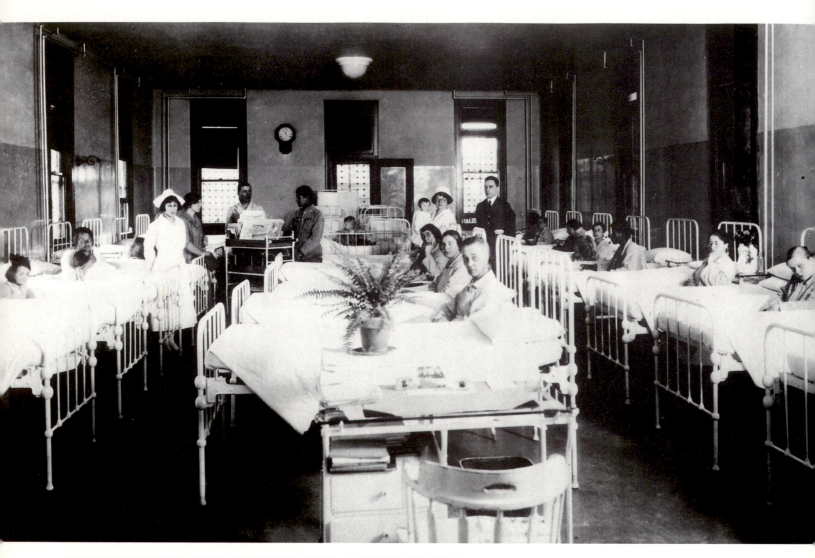

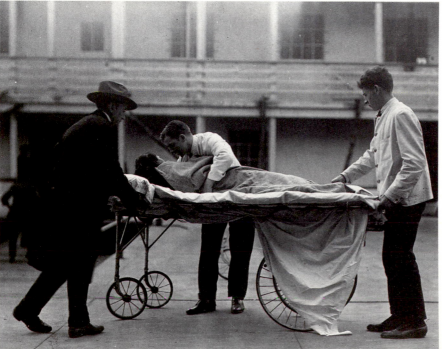

Ellis Island had contagious-disease wards, a psychopathic pavilion, and a general hospital. Immigrants ill on arrival were taken there immediately. Families often waited while a child recovered from diphtheria or measles. The medical staff had its hands full. Patients from far corners of the earth brought "a rare variety of diseases"—and notions. One man pleaded that his wife, detained in the hospital, be spared a bath because "she is very weak and cannot stand them, for she has never taken them."

of George Washington and an American flag, he spoke a "dreadful botch of Slavic languages." Most of the examiners had interpreters, but Slavic-speaking employees were in greater demand than supply. Other interpreters might struggle with a bewildering variety of Italian dialects. Or they might try a regional variation on Yiddish, and be told by the immigrant that "I do not understand your English."

The questions themselves seemed straightforward, even familiar; the inspectors worked from information compiled at the port of embarkation by steamship company officials. "What is your name?" A Hagop Nersesian, a Yeorgos Avgerakis, an Antek Milkowski might pass into America with names intact. Many, however, didn't. Names were often misspelled or altered on the manifests; immigrants sometimes shortened their own names or Americanized them. Portnovsky became Porter; Schmidt, Smith. But only too frequently the officials "helped" the immigrants. Thus Mr. Goldstein became Mr. Gold when an immigration officer demanded, "What good is Stein to you?"

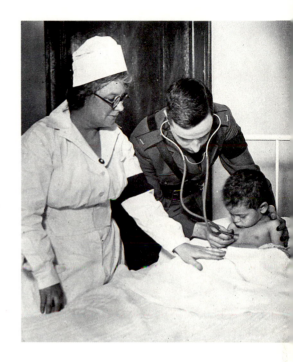

Marital status? Where born? Where last resided? "Where are you going?" was sometimes problematic. It took ingenuity to decipher "Szekenevno Pillsburs" as Second Avenue, Pittsburgh, or "Kellisland, where stones are and big sea" as a Pole's description of Kelley's Island, Ohio, in Lake Erie. Another newcomer answered clearly: "Springfield." But which Springfield? "The cheapest one."

Was the immigrant a legitimate child? An anarchist? A prostitute? An imbecile? Ever been convicted of a crime involving "moral turpitude"? Who had paid for his passage? Himself (whether or not this was true). Where was he going? To the brother he hadn't seen in ten years; to the friend pounding track in Montana—but never, never should he say "To the *padrone* with the jobs." To the husband she searched for in the crowd; to the daughters she didn't mention "because they lived so far off," somewhere in Brooklyn; to Father Henry, who "takes them over to his Mission." For their own safety, women were rarely allowed to leave the island unaccompanied, but many were considered well-escorted after they were married to men who came for them, or to men with whom they had traveled.

How much money was the immigrant carrying? The hand went to the pocket and hesitated there. The affluent few thought it unwise to show too much; one man carrying $3,000 had been detained for having "too much money and no one to go to." Many more immigrants faced the opposite problem. At some times, at least $25 was the price of admission to America.

"And I can assure you that a certain $25 were passed along from one passenger to another to help those out who didn't have it. And this had to be done with a quick motion of the hand. . . ."

Suddenly, it was over, for at least four of every five. They were out of limbo, released from purgatory, free to go their way. The rest received yet another badge: a white one—temporarily detained while awaiting relatives or money; a yellow one—to appear before a Board of Special Inquiry, as were those suspected of being contract laborers or potential public charges; a grayish linen one—under 15 and unaccompanied. It was the detainees who renamed Ellis Island the "Isle of Tears." It was for them a place of monstrous uncertainty. It was also, found incoming Commissioner Henry H. Curran in 1923, a place where often "there were bedbugs but no beds," a place where people slept on wire contraptions "that would make a sardine sick." Carbolene, a potent disinfectant, freshened the air for a few minutes daily. Curran had "seen many jails, some pretty bad," but none "as bad as the dormitories at Ellis Island."

Representatives of immigrant aid societies tried to help the detained. They cheered them, or made inquiries and arrangements for them; they distributed inspirational tracts. One detainee treasured her *Guide to Stoicism.* Another read his Bible day after day, "because I thought that would help me get into America." For many, "there was absolutely nothing else to do." They waited: for the relatives, for the money, for the illness to run its course. Thousands of "mail order brides" waited for fiancés, who sometimes failed to appear. (The large number of female detainees brought Ellis Island a reputation as a marriage market, and many letters, like one from a lonely Pole in San Francisco: "I am Sober and yus no tobako dont gambel, wery loving and hepi dysposition, pley flut. I can mak one good woman heppi if one wold wish to kome.")

As trying as detention might be, aspects of it could serve as an introduction to American life. An Italian child who had never seen running water was suddenly made to take a daily shower. The father of author Michael Gold was impressed even by naked bedsprings: "I was such a greenhorn that I had never seen a spring before. I thought it was wonderful, and bounced up and down on it for fun." All night long, he and a friend practiced the "new funny" language to a squeaky metallic accompaniment. "Potato! he would yell at me. Tomato! I would answer, and laugh. Match! he would say. All right! I would answer. Match! all right! go to hell! potato! until everyone was angry at us. . . ."

Anger had other sources in the mixture of ethnic groups. Louis

Inflow of new arrivals strained all the island's facilities. "There are so many detained here. You have crossed the ocean, endured hardships and danger. . . . You have found the doors closed," Father J. Moretto told more than 2,000 at dinner during the Christmas holidays in 1910. ". . . those who will finally get in . . . must live to be a credit to your country and the land of your adoption." There were 723 waiting for deportation, more than a thousand for hearings. Immigrant aid societies decorated the dining hall and brought presents—socks or stockings for men and women, toys and cake for children. One mother and her daughters forgot their gifts on learning that an order to deport them was revoked; they were free to join husband and father.

Adamic listened all night to "snores and dream-monologues in perhaps a dozen different languages." At dawn he was awakened by the Muslim prayers of his bunkmate, a Turk, one of those feared and hated as cruel raiders and overlords by Balkan Slavs like Adamic. Another man complained—"as any self-respecting Englishman" would—about the "dastardly treatment in putting 4 English ladies and 16 English gentlemen in that common room." They were surrounded by Italians who "were eating garlic, and you can imagine how offensive it was."

In the mess hall, it was impossible "to suit the palates of sixty different national tastes." All would eat kosher roast beef and Italian bread; but oatmeal was wasted on Italians, Scandinavians disliked spaghetti, and 30 Muslim dervishes, from religious scruple, ate nothing but boiled eggs. Everyone else sampled such American specialties as ice cream ("I didn't know if it was kosher but I ate it"), bananas (skin and all the first time), and corn-on-the-cob (barnyard fodder in Europe).

Some of those detained first encountered the American tradition of due process when called before a Board of Special Inquiry. The immigrant was given an interpreter, and could introduce witnesses. The

Gravely, a very young man carries his baggage. Admitted immigrants were quickly sorted out by destination—two out of three traveled beyond New York. To stem abuses, the government arranged for money exchange and other services. "The railroads all have agents on the spot," so that no immigrant need go through the city unprotected. "Baggage is checked at a special rate . . . and food is sold under large signs, 'Provisions cheaper here than on the railroads,' in five languages. . . ."

votes of two of the three examiners would decide a case, but the immigrant could appeal an unfavorable ruling and engage a lawyer—often a compatriot, frequently a shyster. Or the applicant might call in a medical specialist for a second opinion, as did one elderly woman certified to be of low intelligence. She hadn't been able to work the jigsaw puzzles the doctors gave her, but now she promised that "if they would let her have some meat she would make a delicious soup for them," and bake "bread finer than they served on Ellis Island." She was admitted, as were five of every six immigrants whose cases came before a board.

Why should I fear the fires of Hell? I have been through Ellis Island." Often the elderly did not fare so well as the confident cook, nor did suspected contract laborers, many of whom La Guardia considered "only borderline cases." The forthright Italian who produced a letter from a relative promising him work was deported. So was a suntanned Serbian peasant who had "passed the dreaded dead line—is over fifty years of age, not too well built, used up by the hardships of his native country. . . ."

Edward Steiner thought the "most melancholy of all" the detained were the Jews, who often had strong family ties in America already and who, if deported, could expect persecution. He described the deportation hearing of two Russian Jews, a father—"a pitiable looking object"—and his "stalwart" son. The father was a tailor, the son a student. The old man had another son in America with a wife and four children. "Ask them whether they are willing to be separated; the father to go back and the son to remain here?" said the examiner.

"They look at each other; no emotion as yet visible, the question came too suddenly. Then something in the background of their feelings moves, and the father, used to self-denial through his life, says quietly, without pathos and yet tragically, 'Of course.' And the son says, after casting his eyes to the ground, ashamed to look his father in the face, 'Of course.' And, 'The one shall be taken and the other left,' for this was their judgment day."

In 1914, the number of deportations rose to two percent (16,588 people) of that year's total arrivals; usually, it hovered around one percent. Over the years, several hundred excludables chose suicide over deportation. The heartbreak, by most accounts, was shared by the Man at the Gate. Still, thought Steiner, one might envy him who could answer the immigrants' cries "and give the children to their fathers and the wives to their husbands; who may unite those who have been divided by long years and a wide sea. . . . But what if he cannot answer the cry of the children?"

Finally processed and sorted, each "like a hurrying, bumping, wandering piece of coal being mechanically guided to the sack of its type and size," immigrants board the ferry to New York. "Let no one believe that landing . . . is a pleasant experience," wrote a survivor of the ordeal about 1906. But for those admitted, that is past. Ahead is the freedom of a wide new land and the opportunity to realize a dream. ". . . finally we saw our father. . . . it was seven years since I saw him. . . . And I said, 'Well, thank God, we are in America.'"

The Station

Echoes of happiness and grief, despair and triumph haunt the halls of Ellis Island's empty buildings. Here stood the "kissing post" where families were reunited. And here was the "stairway of separation." From it, one passage led to the railroad ferry; another, to the boat for Manhattan; a third, to detention and possible deportation.

"For some people . . . it was a joy . . . if nothing was wrong with them, they just went with their families." For those not admitted, there was heartbreak and desolation. For everyone, there was confusion.

When the station opened in 1892, it was run by the largely inexperienced staff of the new Bureau of Immigration under Treasury jurisdiction. Almost immediately the facility was overcrowded. "The complaints about rude or brusque treatment by officials are probably most valid from this period," points out historian Alberto Meloni, himself an immigrant of more recent times. "The first inspectors came from the Customs Service, and weren't trained to deal with immigrants as such." Nor did early administrators strictly regulate concessionaires, who often cheated the new arrivals.

Fire destroyed most of the station in 1897, and the island closed for three years while the masonry-and-ironwork replacement buildings were under construction. The immigration center reopened in 1900; and in 1903 the Bureau of Immigration was transferred to the new Department of Commerce and Labor. President Theodore Roosevelt, aware of recurring abuses at Ellis Island, chose his commissioners with special care. William Williams made merit the basis for contracts. His successor, English-born Robert Watchorn, continued and expanded reforms. Corrupt money-changers were ousted, and American Express was brought in to assure an honest exchange of currency. In the great Registry Room, benches were installed.

One after another, commissioners worked to humanize the system and stem discourtesy to newcomers. Interpreters did their best, in 36 tongues—among them, Albanian, Armenian, Bulgarian, Flemish, Lithuanian, Persian, Ruthenian, and Syrian Arabic.

Still, sheer numbers almost overwhelmed the station in those early years. One official recalled a Sunday morning in 1907 when there were 1,700 detained women and children "in one room with a normal capacity of six hundred. How they were packed in!"

In 1914, World War I swept over Europe. Submarines cruised the Atlantic; passenger ships were sunk or held in port, and arrivals at Ellis Island began to dwindle. Deportees often waited for months to be returned. Commissioner Frederic C. Howe introduced movies and concerts, a playground, benches on the lawn; he let out-of-work immigrants from New York City sleep in empty dormitories.

Meanwhile a surfeit of cheap labor, fear of involvement in the war, and anti-German emotions combined to intensify a mood of distaste for aliens. In 1916 German saboteurs blew up munitions at Black Tom Wharf on the New Jersey shore, and the explosion badly damaged several of Ellis Island's buildings. Amazingly, the only serious injury on Ellis was to a cat.

It was the extensive repair work after the explosion that gave the Registry Room its ceiling of interlocking glazed ceramic tile.

In 1917, the United States entered the war. Ellis Island's buildings held German and Austrian internees for a time, then became a military hospital.

After the war, refugees poured in until Congress established a quota system that sharply limited immigration. In 1924 federal law finally provided that consuls abroad should inspect and screen would-be immigrants. Thereafter only a few persons were sent on arrival to Ellis for questioning or medical treatment. The island was "like a deserted village."

In the depths of the Great Depression of the 1930s, with America suffering massive unemployment, more people left the country than entered. Many, unable to find work, left voluntarily; but others were given no choice. Deportation regulations—"inexorable and in many cases inhuman," according to Commissioner Edward Corsi—forced hundreds of "men and women of honest behavior . . . back to the countries they came from, penniless. . . ."

World War II closed the shipping lanes again. After October 1939 the Coast Guard used Ellis Island to lodge and train recruits. After December 1941 the Federal Bureau of Investigation delivered hundreds of enemy aliens—Germans, Italians, and Japanese—for internment; they played poker "day and night," commented one.

Long-standing concern over national security and fear of subversion, combined with the desire of the Department of Labor to rid itself of immigration responsibilities, had prompted yet another change for federal immigration personnel. In 1940 their work came under the Department of Justice, which still administers INS—the

Immigration and Naturalization Service. A decade later, the Internal Security Act caused another spate of detentions and expulsions.

In late 1954 Ellis Island closed its doors. A few months later it was declared surplus property. It was offered for sale, but no bids proved acceptable. Its future was debated from time to time, inconclusively. Various uses of the facilities for social services and to provide special programs for minorities were proposed but were never carried through. Thieves pilfered the station for scrap metal; vines grew through broken windows. In 1964 a lone Doberman watchdog lived on the island; a human guard helped patrol by day.

President Lyndon B. Johnson, on May 11, 1965, proclaimed the island a part of the Statue of Liberty National Monument, noting that millions of steerage immigrants had "entered into the very fiber of American life" through Ellis Island. Congress authorized—but long failed to appropriate—funds to restore the station.

Now, after years of neglect and decay, restoration has finally begun.

But even in its deteriorated condition, the center remains impressive. One student of American immigration visited the island well aware of its statistics and its controversies, but unprepared for the impact of its dignity and architectural beauty. "When you go there," he said, "when you walk through the Great Hall and the hospitals, when you see what was provided for these newcomers, these strangers—you know that someone genuinely cared."

Polish visitors appear as ghostly images in a time-lapse photograph of a tower stairwell in the main building (above). A fish-eye lens records the Registry Room (opposite).

From its site near the New Jersey shoreline it commands a dramatic view of lower Manhattan and the New York skyline.

The Shock of the Great City

Strange faces, swarming into crowded cities, alienated the natives. In this acid sketch the noble visage of welcome sours at the sight of more European "garbage." The Secretary of the Treasury, soon to take charge of immigration, ponders the problem.

hristopher Columbus himself was not more shocked by the New World than were some of his compatriots who rediscovered it 400 years later. Stepping ashore, they heard a din like the ocean's roar: "Waves of people pounded the streets, their faces like foam." Simple countryfolk beheld a bizarre landscape of cloud-raking peaks of masonry; they saw beardless natives, "almost like women." There were monsters enough to populate a medieval map. The elevated railway shrieked and hissed and lurched through space, its "green and red fiery eyes staring ahead and plunging into the darkness." Buses and trolleys careened like juggernauts through the streets. And the streets "exploded like fireworks."

It was "all wild, all inconceivable." It was New York, "this unimaginable city." It was also—to a lesser extent—Chicago, Boston, Philadelphia, and other places planned for a preindustrial America and now exploding with new multitudes. Gone, by the late 19th century, was most of the cheap land that had guaranteed equity in America. Gone, with the abundant land, was the lure of rural life. "Like a lighted candle to the moth," the city glimmered. Irish and German immigrants had come first, and with them, Americans uprooted by agricultural depression in the 1870s. Close behind, the "new immigrants" poured in.

Some, like their Irish predecessors, felt no pull toward a rural existence, for which they harbored bitter memories. Others suppressed agrarian longings to follow the jobs, largely unskilled, into urban America. The shock of the new land was magnified in the city setting. So was human struggle—massed, stacked, and multiplied. When Danish-born journalist Jacob Riis wrote in 1890 that "the arched gateway leads no longer to a shady bower . . . but to a dark and nameless alley," his unblinking gaze was trained on a swatch of Manhattan, but he might as well have been referring to America's transformation from an agrarian to an urban nation. The gateway might have been Ellis Island itself.

In 1900, one-third of Greater New York's 3,500,000 residents were foreign-born. Riis, their tireless chronicler, observed that "a map of the city, colored to designate nationalities, would show more stripes than on the skin of a zebra, and more colors than any rainbow." He noted the older ethnic areas: green for Manhattan's West Side Irish districts, a long blue swath for the German East Side. "Be dad! it's for all the wurrld loike Corrk," exclaimed an Irish greenhorn; *"Ganz wie Berlin,"* cried the German. New York or New Cork? Whichever, the metropolis boasted 275,000 Irish-born as against Dublin's 373,000, and had Germans enough—324,000—for a respectable city in the fatherland.

By 1910 its 340,000 Italians outnumbered Genoa's 272,000. Riis found Italy's vivid scarlet "forcing its way northward" along Mulberry Street in Lower Manhattan, erupting again in Harlem, and stippling parts of the Lower West Side. "Many Italians hardly know they are outside their native land," remarked a visitor, "because here they have everything Italian. . . ." Likewise, Riis's gray splotch—the Lower East Side, below 14th Street—was like "Jerusalem in its palmiest days." There was no need, advised an uptown New Yorker, to board a steamship for Europe in order to see a Jewish ghetto. Instead, visitors often arrived via tour bus for a short outing to the exotic neighborhood. Sometimes the bus would be chased by a ragtag gang of boys who "pelted rocks, garbage, dead cats and stale vegetables at the frightened sightseers."

Tourists in Chinatown did not have to contend with rowdy children; nor did they see women there. Only "silence, a sullen stare, an air of distrust greeted the too curious visitor" to the narrow strip between Little Italy and the Jewish blocks. Other smaller ethnic groups were also wedged in amid more populous peoples. The "sombre hue" of the Bohemian contrasted with the German blue, the French "purple" with the Italian red, and "dots and dashes of color here and there" would indicate Finns, Hungarians, Swiss, Poles, and Arabs—some of the tints

"The crush and the stench were enough to suffocate one." A newcomer recoiled at Orchard Street (below) on New York's Lower East Side. Nearby in Hester Street a visitor heard pushcart peddlers blending Yiddish, Hebrew, even a bit of English: "Gutes frucht! Metziehs! Drei pennies die whole lot—Good fruit! Bargains! Three pennies a whole lot." Immigrants squeezed in, to a density of 330,000 to the square mile. "Was this the America we had sought?" asked one. Or only "a circle that we had traveled, with a Jewish ghetto at its beginning and its end"?

"spreading rapidly like a splash of ink on a sheet of blotting paper."

In the flux that typified such neighborhoods, newcomers often displaced older residents. Longtime black inhabitants of the old "Africa" district, a narrow strip on the West Side, retreated uptown to Harlem beyond the advancing Italian front. Down around Mulberry Street, the Italian succeeded "the contentious Irishman or the order-loving German" who had prospered and moved on. He was found more willing than either to submit to extortion at the hands of his landlord—often a "picturesquely autocratic" Irishman who had purchased his former abode "with the profits of his saloon." At the same time, Italians and Jews, each overrunning their districts "to the point of suffocation," were disputing "every foot of available space in the back alleys of Mulberry Street."

In other cities, the situation was similar. One of Boston's "little Dublins" became "little Syria" and then Chinatown. In a part of Milwaukee, Prussia yielded to Poland, and "Fritz" to "Ignatz." There, a visitor read "no names but those that end with a sneeze." In James T. Farrell's novel *Studs Lonigan,* Old Man O'Brien complains of the Jewish influx in Chicago: "Pretty soon a man will be afraid to wear a shamrock on St. Patrick's day, because there are so many noodle-soup drinkers around." Ethnic progression was equally dramatic, and contentious, in smaller industrial cities. The French-Canadians of Lawrence, Massachusetts, objected to their new Italian neighbors, the Welsh of Johnstown, Pennsylvania, to the Slovaks who were moving in.

Even in ethnically homogeneous neighborhoods, there were well-defined sub-boundaries and regional antagonisms. Northern Italians in New Haven, Connecticut, protested that "We don't want no Dago here" when southern Italians began to arrive. Much larger, Chicago had at least 17 distinct Italian groups, clustered according to *campanilismo*—the traditional bonds shared by those within earshot of the same church bell. In New York, Neapolitans and Genoese, Piedmontese and Ligurians all eyed each other warily. *"Campobassiani mangia patani, cide pidocchi e suona campane*—People from Campobasso are potato eaters, lice killers and bell ringers." The old taunt was perpetuated in America, where "Siciliani" or "Calabrese" might be substituted for Campobassiani.

Likewise, the Russian Jew, or *Litvak,* thought the Austrian *Galitzianer* "had no taste, took cream with herrings." The latter retorted that the former was backward and uncouth. Block by block ("Rivington Street was only a suburb of Minsk") and synagogue by storefront synagogue (New York had several hundred by 1910), Jews played out their own version of campanilismo, as did every other new ethnic group with more than a few hundred members.

Severed from home, village, region, and country, immigrants returned by steps to each after they crossed the ocean. They proceeded to the ethnic neighborhood, to the blocks where the *paesani* or *landsleit* clustered, and finally, to the dark and crowded room where the relatives waited. "Every tenement home was a Plymouth Rock like ours," recalled author Michael Gold. Life in the city almost always took root in such a place. But the tenement home was a sudden contradiction of America's promise. The notorious dumbbell tenements—named for their shape—appeared in the 1880s. They used every possible bit of land, "built through from one street to the other with a somewhat narrower building connecting them." Between buildings, there was "a damp foul-smelling place, supposed to do duty as an airshaft; had the

Against the hoofbeats' clatter, children dance to the hurdy-gurdy on the sidewalks of New York. As ever with young dancers, girls swing in with smiling gusto—and the boys look trapped. "The streets were ours," wrote Irving Howe of his East Side childhood. "We would roam through the city tasting the delights of freedom." For parents, child's play might have a different taste. Orthodox Jews railed against ballplaying as an abomination of the goyim—gentiles—for sports-minded boys seemed allergic to piety. In time, the hurdy-gurdy, usually cranked by an Italian with a begging monkey, came under interdict. Mayor Fiorello La Guardia, himself the son of an Italian musician, banned organ-grinders for causing street jams. He did so gladly, resenting an ethnic stereotype, remembering all his life the taunt of his youth: "A dago with a monkey! Hey, Fiorello, you're a dago too."

Like gaudy flowers, parasols bloom in
the summer sun. With timely wares and
zero overhead the East Side peddlers
and their packs created moving malls for
bargain hunters: Five cents keeps the sun
away . . . latest styles, lady . . . take your
pick. Need an upholsterer? Here's one,
a walking advertisement, displaying his
work—in miniature. Only a penny buys
a new whip. Who would dare raise
children without one? Chroniclers of
the bustling immigrant streets recorded

the "Hurry and push . . . the . . . whole-
souled, almost religious passion for
business," and the astonishing variety:
"collah buttons, 'lastic, matches,
hankeches" . . . "the yolk or the white
of an egg, or a chicken leg or wing."
Around the bakeries of Hester and
Rivington Streets the hawkers cried,
"Buy, Jews . . . buy, wives . . . buy,
girls . . . buy fresh cakes, buy little white
loaves and eat them in good health." Lack
of work, or a hatred of work in the foul

sweatshops and factories, drove many
into street trade. Some prospered, saving
enough to stock a store or pay for the
passage of loved ones still in the old country.
Others saw peddling as an unbearable
last resort. Author Michael Gold
remembered his father after one day out
with a banana cart: "His face was gray;
he looked older by ten years; a man who
had touched bottom."

foul fiend designed these great barracks they could not have been more villainously arranged to avoid any chance of ventilation. . . ."

The design was as inimical to sunlight as to fresh air. Windows were a luxury. A little girl described her home as "a place so dark it seemed as if there weren't no sky." How much darkness was legally allowable? Jacob Riis interpreted a city ordinance: "If the sink in the hall could be made out . . . and if a baby could be seen on the stairs, the hall was light; if, on the other hand, the baby's shrieks were the first warning that it was being trampled upon, the hall was dark." The baby's lullaby was the squeaky corridor pump—if the water ran, and if the tot beat the odds on infant mortality.

Tenement residents enjoyed little privacy. In the crowding, tragedies, quarrels, cockroaches—and a single courtyard privy or hallway water closet—were shared by all. Still, there was always a hearty welcome for the greenhorns; "the hospitality was taken for granted until the new family rented its own flat." That event was often postponed indefinitely. In the meantime, life exploded onto balconies, fire escapes, and rooftops. There were "countless beds, with tangled sheets and blankets"—or one bed, its use assigned on a nightly basis to the married couples. In addition, many families made ends meet by taking in boarders. "A star boarder," recalled one tenement dweller, "slept on a folding bed. But I knew a printer who every night unscrewed a door, put it on two chairs; he couldn't pay as much as the one who had the bed." If the printer's fortunes fell even further, he could still find shelter in the police stations—until 1896. Then, Police Commissioner Theodore Roosevelt visited one, "turned alternately red and white with anger" at its conditions, and ordered such lodgings closed.

Crowded around the table on their first night in the new land, still smelling of Ellis Island disinfectant, the newcomers would "ask endless questions about America." Already, they perceived its bizarre, disconcerting effect on relatives who had arrived only a few months before they did. Here was the formerly pious uncle: Now his hands flapped like laundry in a gale as he shouted about "business" and "jobs." There was a young cousin whose cheeks had once been "like red oranges," now ashen as the sky. How was one to carve a niche for oneself—or merely survive—in this urban maelstrom? A popular guidebook advised the newcomers: "Do not take a moment's rest. Run, do, work and keep your own good in mind."

If work was an American obsession, toil was the price, for most immigrants, of a precarious foothold in America. His parents, wrote

Shawled women buying crusty loaves of pane out of the wicker paniera on Mulberry Street . . . wheels of grainy Parmesan stacked high in a store festooned with prosciutto, pepperoni, salami, sausage links, garlic, provolone cheeses, the dried cod called baccalà. All proclaim the distinctive enclave of Little Italy, spreading west beyond the Bowery from the Jewish East Side. A boy who ventured across the divide discovered exotic vegetables he had never tasted and the fare forbidden by his faith: a pig's head in a butcher shop, clams and oysters on a pushcart.

Even amid their cramped tenements the Italians found room for the delight of growing things; they hurried to new construction sites, digging fresh soil for their bean vines, geraniums, morning glories. Within the quarter, people from the same hometown in the old country clustered together in "villages," sharing a patron saint whose day became a holiday. Neighbors who cared, the nearby church and school, the tavern down the street, the shimmering aromas of the kitchens— a subtle web of community cushioned the passage of laboring folk into the frenzied world of "la Mecca del dollaro."

Children of the abyss known as Gotham Court hold still for a muckraker's camera. This "cradle" of New York tenements, reported Jacob Riis, "tested the power of sanitary law" for 40 years. When cholera broke out, mortality here spurted to 195 per thousand, more than ten times the epidemic rate of the "clean" wards uptown. During one three-year period death took nearly half the 138 babies born in this festering trough. Summer turned tenements into ovens; an eight-day heat wave in 1896 killed 420 residents. Amid the huddled masses prostitutes plied their trade, and sweatshops flourished. Kitchens and bedrooms did double duty as workrooms, morning till night, seven days a week.

The whole family turned to, even post-toddlers such as these, at right, producing artificial flowers. Thus "kindergartens are robbed to provide baby slaves," wrote the reformer John Spargo. "What can four-year-old babies do? A hundred things, when they are driven to it." The Society for the Prevention of Cruelty to Children found little beggars who had been sold in Italy, shipped to New York, and sent out on the streets. Often they had been mutilated by their masters to enhance their appeal.

author Mario Puzo, "knew little more economic security than those ancient Roman slaves who might have been their ancestors." Security had to wait. Survival was the immediate challenge, the daily demand.

Lacking even the rudiments of English, newcomers found their chances for employment sharply limited. Italians frequently became construction laborers. English-speaking *padroni* found them jobs, handled their affairs, and bossed them at the sites. Many others, however, were confined by barriers of custom to the economy of their own neighborhoods. For the unskilled, a pushcart or a peddler's pack provided a start: "You need no more than to know the names of a few items in English and to have been blessed by heaven with a special gift—shamelessness, so that you don't become depressed when you are turned away or are taunted by strangers." With that and a ten-cent daily rental payment, thousands of pushcart entrepreneurs were in business, knotting the streets into a commercial gridlock.

In Little Italy, the "carts made two rows of booths in the roadways; on the sidewalks, ash barrels served for counters." Colorful mounds of fragrant cheeses, coiled sausages, bulging tomatoes, juicy watermelons —"*Freschi* and good!"—were arranged as meticulously as a painter's still life. Nearby, dry goods—from secondhand stockings to lace —were, like everything else, sold in penny fractions. On the Lower East Side, where competition was even more intense, bandannas and tin cups went for two cents, peaches a penny a quart, spectacles— "warranted to suit the eye"—for 35 cents. (Streetcorner photographers also kept boxes of eyeglasses as props for their many customers who desired the scholarly look.) Meanwhile, reported the *New York Tribune*, bargain-hunters from uptown discovered that a real steal—15 cents for a handkerchief, "without the slightest haggling"—also brought

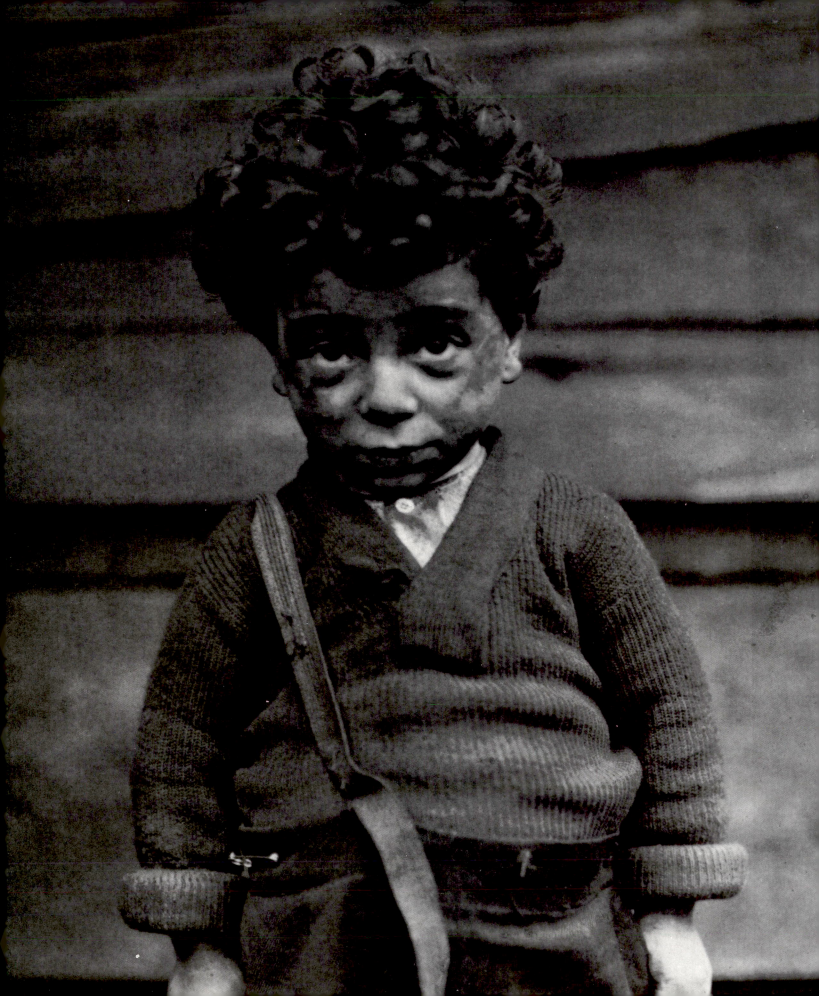

Napping alfresco, a young girl escapes the stifling innards of a Little Italy tenement. Amid an ash-clogged kitchen in Chicago's immigrant slums, a woman bends to her washtub. Not far away, young-old eyes peer out of a face in want of a scrubbing. To answer such needs, to inspire hope and self-respect, Jane Addams founded her "settlement" called Hull-House.

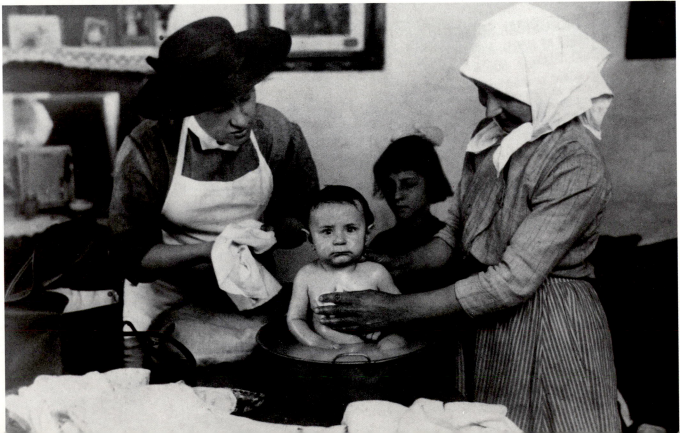

"blessings on your head and gives you a fine sense of superiority."

Sightseers and local residents alike jammed the streets of Jewish neighborhoods on Thursdays and Fridays, when Sabbath preparations produced an unparalleled display of free enterprise. Housewives now haggled for the finer commodities. Crowds coagulated around the fishmonger, whose wet, glistening goods—"big fish and little fish, light fish and dark fish, bluefish and whitefish, fresh fish and fish not quite so fresh"—were the *"pièce de résistance* of the Friday evening meal." At the mysteriously named Pig Market, everything *but* the forbidden pork was sold. The Pig Market's real mystery, though, was the ubiquitous suspender peddler. Nobody ever seemed to buy his dangling wares, but he kept on crying "Suspenehs!" ceaselessly. Peddlers in general were known by their distinctive calls. Glaziers wailed out "a depressed sort of tune." Even more plaintive was the wail of "I cash clothes!" from a limping old-clothes trader with derby hats stacked high on his head.

Recalled Michael Gold: "In my ears still ring the lamentations of the lonely old Jews without money: 'I cash clothes, I cash clothes, my God, why hast Thou forsaken me?'"

A picture of health, if not happiness, displays "perfect" babies at the East Side's University Settlement. In such centers and in the public schools, girls received "the first simple instruction," wrote Jane Addams, "in the care of little children—that skillful care which every tenement-house baby requires if he is to be pulled through his second summer." The baby opposite endures a bathing demonstration by a visiting nurse in Chicago. The young socialite Eleanor Roosevelt taught calisthenics and dance at a New York settlement house. She left after her marriage—her mother-in-law worried lest she bring slum diseases home.

Gold's own father, in desperation, resorted to peddling. His bananas "became a symbol to him of defeat, of utter hopelessness." The poor, selling to the poor, usually remained impoverished. A vigorous few saved enough to start a petty business. But many, including the noted reformer Jane Addams of Chicago, thought the peddler's license at least a "ransom" that let the unskilled man seek his livelihood in the open air. The main alternative—especially for the skilled Jewish immigrant—was the claustrophobic twilight world of the sweatshops.

New York, by 1900, was the center of the nation's garment industry. Its thousands of sweatshops were its high-rise factories, or more likely, the tenement rooms where a "cockroach contractor" or "sweater" employed "helpers" to turn cut cloth into finished garments. In the factories, the work day was legally limited to ten hours, the work week to six days, and the minimum age to 14. But in the tenement, no such rules applied. Day and night, weekday and weekend, childhood and adulthood, workplace and home ran together seamlessly, "each day and each night like a wind-driven sail." In a single stuffy, dark room, as many as a dozen people—basters, pressers, finishers, fitters—toiled "from they can see till bed-time."

"The faces, hands, and arms to the elbows of everyone," wrote Jacob Riis, "are black with the color of the cloth on which they are working." But when Riis, with his camera, would enter such a sweatshop, workers seldom even paused. Machines whirred on, children snipped threads with little scissors, pressers rocked over their hissing irons in July. All knew that winter, the slow season, would soon arrive, and that job competition could drive them back to the pushcarts even sooner. In the meantime, the contractor strove for a 5-cent profit on each dozen pairs of knee pants he delivered to the manufacturer for 70 cents. That could mean earnings of as much as 20 dollars a week for him, and perhaps half of that for his workers.

Close equivalents to the Lower East Side sweatshops took hold in other ethnic neighborhoods. Many Bohemians were cigar-makers. In one Czech-speaking household, Riis found a husband and wife working "at the bench from six in the morning till nine at night." Together, they stripped the tobacco leaves; then the husband shaped the filler and the wife rolled the wrapper around it. "For a thousand they received $3.75, and can turn out together three thousand cigars a week." Often the Bohemians were skilled artisans, but as one cigar-making blacksmith lamented, he could not practice his trade because he knew no "Engliska." He would be lucky if he didn't become incapacitated by lung disease, considering his constant exposure to tobacco fumes.

Young voters rally round the flag at the Beach Street Industrial School in New York, passing a test in democracy with colors flying. School leaders let the students vote on a proposed new exercise called "saluting the flag"—scheduling the canvass for the eve of Election Day. The children took the ballots home— a reminder to any new citizens of their own duties at the polls—then returned to vote. The results: a landslide for Old Glory. Industrial schools, observed Jacob Riis, set themselves "squarely in the gap between the tenement and the public school." Run by welfare societies, the trade schools taught skills in demand on the job market. Public, industrial, and parochial schools speeded the process of Americanization. Pupils first recited the Pledge of Allegiance in 1892—just after a magazine published it to honor the 400th anniversary of Columbus's discovery of America.

Little Italy's sweatshop specialty, artificial flowers, brought four to eight cents per gross. There, the meager family income would be threatened if a mother, weakened by child-bearing and toil, succumbed to tuberculosis, or if the white hearse came for a small coffin. But despite its human toll, the tenement sweatshop did have one advantage. It tended to hold the family together just as a multitude of forces—poverty, emotional stress, and so forth—conspired to pull it apart. The padrone might appear with the promise of a job for the father on a distant railway project or construction site. And sometimes the father would simply never return.

The circumstances varied among ethnic groups, but the effects remained similar in the whirling centrifuge of urban life. In New York, the *Jewish Daily Forward* was filled with plaintive personals: "I am looking for my husband, David Silecki, the butcher from Pruzani. . . ." "My dear husband, Barney, I beg you to come home." In Chicago, Jane Addams noted that "four fifths of the children brought into Juvenile Court . . . are the children of foreigners. The Germans are the greatest offenders, Polish next. . . ." *(Continued on page 206)*

At "Uncle Sam's Lodging-House," the proprietor confronts an obstreperous boarder: "Look here, you, everybody else is quiet and peaceable, and you're all the time a-kicking up a row." From *Puck*, c. 1880

The Machines

 artoon bosses," notes a student of big-city political machines, "are unmistakably Irish." In life not all were—although there were more than a few, and rascally too. But did ever there breathe a lout as rank as the Irish pol of caricature? Not a hint of the smiling eyes, the lilting voices that put talk to music.

"The average Catholic Irishman of the first generation, as represented in this Assembly, is a low, venal, corrupt and unintelligent brute." This, written in 1882, is from the legislative diary of 24-year-old Theodore Roosevelt, a New York Assemblyman who rode the tide of reform to the bully pulpit of the White House.

Irish who were riled by the preachments of reformers found the perfect spokesman in Mr. Dooley, Finley Peter Dunne's fictional saloonkeeper. Doo-

ley was blessed with an Irish wit and realism: "To give a man an office jus' because he's honest," said he to his friend Hennessy, "is like ilicting him because . . . he don't bate his wife. . . . A man ought to be honest to start with and afther that he ought to be crafty."

Hennessy was soon convinced: "I don't like a rayformer."

"Or anny other raypublican," concluded Mr. Dooley.

Such pro-Democratic sentiments had been noted since Jefferson's time:

in 1800 the Yankee Federalist Uriah Tracy called the Irish "the most God-provoking Democrats this side of Hell." Small wonder. Tracy's party tended to sympathize with the English—under whose rule in Ireland no Roman Catholic need apply to a university, try to vote, seek public office, or covet the hand of a Protestant lass.

Life under such governance had propelled the Irish—barred from the politics of the establishment—into political agitation. Before the mid-19th century most of them had learned the English language—an important edge for those who ventured to America. But, largely unskilled, they faced a bleak existence as manual laborers in the growing cities. For three dollars a week they worked six 15-hour days. A newspaper took note of the powers at work in the Republic: "waterpower, steam-power, and Irish-power. The last works hardest of all."

Politics, for a bright, hustling lad, could mean a quick release from a life of hard labor—if he understood the hopes of ordinary folks, if he could persuade and organize. It would help if he had a gift for "fair words and soft speech," the gift observed by Queen Elizabeth I in the lord of Blarney Castle.

It might take a bit of scrapping as well. The Irish were all but ignored at the New York City political club known as Tammany Hall—until 1817, when a band of 200 broke up a caucus of party leaders along with much of the furniture. Within a few decades, the Tammany tiger sported a shamrock. By the late 1860s Tammany was running a naturalization mill. Immigrants fresh off the boat were handed tickets reading, "Please naturalize the bearer," together with faked papers. And off to court they went for the ritual of instant citizenship.

But the political machines also aided struggling newcomers in a day when government offered no "safety net." Ward captains gave out food baskets, buckets of coal, jobs. Public works contractors hired quotas of approved laborers. The police and other public agencies became Irish strongholds.

As new immigrants arrived, the Irish cop, the Irish foreman, and the Irish pol became their guides to the inner workings of the city, to employment, to power. And as New York swelled into a multi-ethnic metropolis, a catchphrase made the rounds: that the city was "built by the Italians, run by the Irish, and owned by the Jews."

Meanwhile the boodle had piled up. Politics had enriched the bosses. The reformers hounded them, and often brought them to justice. But they were not the only scoundrels abroad and, measured against the corporate greed of the robber barons, maybe not the worst. Mr. Dooley put it all in perspective, warning a friend of his never to steal a doormat: "If ye do ye'll be invistigated, hanged, an' maybe ray-formed. Steal a bank, me boy, steal a bank." ◼

Above: An 1891 cartoon from *Judge* mocks the immigrant near-monopoly (mainly Irish) on the public payroll. Left: *Puck* in 1893 portrays New York in the grip of a shamrock-decked Tammany tiger.

Addams thought it possible "to devise some educational enterprise which should build a bridge between European and American experiences," and make both more meaningful. On that premise, she founded Hull-House in Chicago. Elsewhere, idealists and reformers emulated her work. Hull-House and other "settlements" served as employment agencies, social clubs, counseling services, educational institutions. Diverse cultural heritages were celebrated. Ethnic songs and dances, performed in costume, often made up the evening's entertainment. The still-popular *Settlement Cook Book*, containing ethnic recipes, was first published as a fund-raising effort for a Milwaukee settlement house.

By contrast, the charity's representative or the city's social worker was often a brisk stranger who "shows us how poor people should live without meat, without butter, without milk . . . why can't you yet learn us how to eat without eating?" If immigrants perceived such an individual as patronizing, they usually regarded Protestant church workers as thinly disguised missionaries. The latter met with little success among Italian or eastern European Catholics already struggling to preserve their religious practices in an Irish-dominated church, or among Jews trying to protect their ancient orthodoxy from the threats of a secular, materialistic culture.

Political machines frequently demonstrated more sensitivity to the needs of the immigrant poor. Tammany lawyers, noted the writer Alfred Kazin, "could always sprinkle a few tearful words of Yiddish solidarity during the campaign and so deliver the vote to the organization." The needy family might receive a Thanksgiving turkey from ward boss Big Tim Sullivan (unfortunately, "it was not *kosher*, and therefore forbidden to us"), or the rent or coal that saved it from disaster.

But the world of "outside" help remained remote to most immigrants. The resources of their own people provided more effective assistance. The community's own banker (offering unsecured loans), its doctor (making house calls for a dollar), and its other more affluent members, along with its religious leaders, padrones, saloonkeepers, and streetcorner scribes all helped the newcomers to adjust, and perhaps to forge an initial link to the world beyond the neighborhood.

Ethnic newspapers, by the hundred, were especially influential in that respect. The Ukrainian *Svoboda,* for instance, published articles entitled "Pictures of America" and "The Constitution of the United States of North America." The *Jewish Daily Forward* editorialized on tenement life ("Scandal is never far off where a boarder works his way in") but ranged far afield on the subject of life in America, especially in its "*Bintel Brief*—Bundle of Letters." A correspondent bemoaned his

There goes the neighborhood: Exotic Uncle Sams, drawn with poison pens, invite an endless stream of grotesques to America. As a latter-day Moses, the dark-browed, long-nosed Sam parts the waters of oppression, delivering the ungainly children of Israel. As a grim padrone, he welcomes ratty banditti, knives clenched pirate-fashion. In the smoke appears the assassinated President William McKinley, slain by an anarchist named Leon Czolgosz, the son of immigrants. Thus an unchecked tide of immigration roused fears that undesirables—"degenerate breeding stock"—would pollute the land.

Scientific studies purported to reinforce the stereotypes. Madison Grant, a leader of the scholarly bigots, saw New York becoming a "cloaca gentium—sewer of peoples." Researchers measured skulls and intelligence and discovered a "natural superiority" of northern Europeans over Alpine and Mediterranean peoples. In 1924 pseudoscience triumphed; a new law all but barred the door to immigrants from the soil that had nurtured Dante and Leonardo.

KERRY MILLS' TWO STEP MARCHES.
WHISTLING RUFUS
A CHARACTERISTIC MARCH
BY
KERRY MILLS
COMPOSER OF
"RASTUS ON PARADE."
"HAPPY DAYS IN DIXIE."
"AT A GEORGIA CAMPMEETING."
ETC. ETC.
F. A. Mills
MUSIC PUBLISHER
45 WEST 29TH STREET
NEW YORK CITY.
SONG 5.

son's passion for "this crazy game," baseball. Another wondered if it was "a sin" to use face powder. Editor Abraham Cahan approved of both baseball and powder—and with each cautious reply, helped, as other editors did, to illuminate the strange new culture.

Language remained an overwhelming barrier to the outside world. Sometimes it proved an internal one also, as for Italians who spoke different dialects, until a common, Americanized lingo emerged. All Italians would understand if the "storo" down the "stritto" needed to hire someone to do a "giobba." Croatians and Slovenians rode the "subvej," ate a "senvic" for lunch, and waited for the "bas" to pass out the "paycheki." Occasionally, an adult immigrant would tackle English at night school—but no student would be as enthusiastically misguided as Leo Rosten's fictional Hyman Kaplan, determined "by hook or cook" to master the new language. He admired American Presidents: Abram Lincohen, Judge Vashington, James Medicine. He learned that America was fringed by the "Atlantic and the Specific"; he even read Shakespeare's *"Julius Scissor."* His ambition had been to become "a physician and sergeant," but Kaplan spent his days as a "cotter in dress faktory."

Ambition, for many immigrants of all origins, yielded to the press of survival in the gray stone world. Their dreams, hoarded and then deferred, were finally willed to their American-born children. "As if it were an act of consecration," a father delivered his daughters to the public school—a place where perfect, unaccented English would be learned and ethnic heritages ignored. "In America, the children bring up the parents," went a ghetto proverb. But the proverb had an ironic underside, for the children sometimes refused to speak their parents' language at home, or discarded the Italian sandwich on the way to school, or demanded that their fathers shave off their long, white beards. Art did mirror life during countless performances of *The Jewish King Lear*, for the king had become a pious immigrant father and his daughters, Americanized tormentors.

The peddlers and shopgirls who wept for Lear also cried when they heard Yiddish songs like *"Ebiga Mama*—Eternal Mamma," or its Italian or Polish equivalent, and remembered their loved ones across the ocean. Now an ocean's worth of unfamiliar ways might separate them from children with whom they shared a few square feet of tenement. Nonetheless, the gap was usually bridged with hopes for the new generation. Somehow, somewhere, opportunity still glimmered for them. If the gold was not in the streets, it could still be, for the children, "in the dreams you will realize—in the golden dreams of the future."

Meet Whistling Rufus, whose "feet never missed a beat. . . . A great musician of high position." Or sing along with the jolly pick-and-shovel man. Entertainments based on folk traits or dialect made it big in days before ethnic self-awareness and good taste discovered mockery in much of the mimicry. Changing times brought new responses to folk experience. The world honored jazz as a unique art form, made in America, largely with black soul and black genius. And an Italian bricklayer in Pietro Di Donato's novel Christ in Concrete told his story in these words: "I have fought winds and cold. Hand to hand I have locked dumb stones in place and the great building rises. I have earned a bit of bread for me and mine."

Ethnic Theater

T
he lights dim, the curtain opens, and for a few hours Jewish immigrants of New York's Lower East Side live in a world of excitement and glamor. Enthralled by the lavish pageantry of *Der yidisher general*—*The Yiddish General*—they laugh, they weep, they cheer.

On any ethnic stage—in Yiddish or Slovak, Armenian or Latvian, Byelorussian or Ukrainian—the accents of the homeland were music after the

cated the alien, and—most important of all—gave pleasure.

An evening at the play was a festive one. Danes, who kept their homeland's tradition of comedy alive in America with amateur performances, often ended the show with a party.

Volunteer performers also supported the Finnish stage. Wherever Finns settled, they were soon giving plays to raise money for community projects. Some reached professional skill. A company from Fitchburg, Massachusetts, staged operas, including *Il Trovatore* and *Tosca*, in Finnish versions.

Believing that theater should instruct as well as entertain, Finnish-American playwrights stressed leftist ideology. Their audiences, however, like others across the ethnic spectrum, often preferred comedies or operettas as well as folk and historical plays.

Focusing on peasant life in the old country, folk dramas evoked nostalgia. Thus Swedes chuckled at Olle i Skratthult—Olle from Laughtersville —who specialized in country-bumpkin dialect roles.

Historical plays—with large casts, choruses, horses, and often a battle scene or two—created a living saga for the immigrant. The stories introduced his children to their ancestral heritage. Germans, for example, savored the exploits of Frederick the Great.

Greeks living near Hull-House in the Chicago slums took pride in presenting ancient classics. When they performed Sophocles' *Ajax*, said Jane Addams, they "felt that they were 'showing forth the glory of Greece' to 'ignorant Americans.'"

The Chinese enjoyed historical plays of epic proportions. A single performance might last five hours; a play in hundreds of acts might take several weeks to complete. In gorgeous robes and heavy makeup, male actors played all parts, the female roles in falsetto.

Visiting San Francisco in 1871, Auguste Bartholdi attended a Chinese theater; he disliked the music ("fantastic yapping and meowing") but greatly admired the colorful costumes. By 1880 the city had eight Chinese theaters.

When Old World companies came touring, famous artists appeared on the

strange sounds of the Americans. For the poor immigrant in the slum, ethnic theater helped to create an endurable world.

"I do not go to the theater to think, but to forget," confessed one; "the crowded tenement, the littered wash . . . ." On Thomashefsky's stage he could see "a beautiful room with expensive furniture" and pretend that the star "has invited me to his house"—luxury and escape, for only half a dollar.

Performed by immigrants for immigrants, theater met many needs. It expressed deep emotions, strengthened social bonds, kept traditions alive, edu-

Poster, New York, 1915

ethnic stage—Helena Modjeska in Chicago, Sarah Bernhardt in New Orleans. Impresarios with opera companies could count on a full house in Italian communities—and a temporary source of talent as well.

"Whenever we wanted singers for the chorus and hadn't time to train them, we used to go down to the wharf and get Eye-talian fishermen," reported a stagehand at an opulent opera house in San Francisco. "You'd find every one of 'em knowing their scores and singing *Ernani* and *Traviata.*"

Italian popular theater in America evolved from amateurs who met in clubs or cafes to sing. An immigrant named Eduardo Migliaccio, fired from a sweatshop, became the comedian Farfariello. He played the classic fruit vendor, the iceman, the garbageman, the ultimate greenhorn. His audience,

laughing at his gallant blunders, could relish their superiority: *They* had learned better! They were not greenhorns now!

Ethnic appeal was a standard of the vaudeville stage, whose motto was "cheap, wholesome entertainment for the masses." Ten cents bought as many as twelve hours of pleasure in 1898. Shows ran continuously, and always included acts that required little or no knowledge of English: jugglers, magicians, acrobats, and performing animals; the Strong Boy who played the violin with a bulldog suspended from his bow arm, or the artist who balanced parlor furniture on his nose.

In the vaudeville lineup, ethnic humor brought knowing guffaws. The typical routine featured a stereotype like the hard-drinking Irishman, who

satirized his own group. Vaudevillian Pat Rooney sang: "New York would be swimming in wine . . . If the White House and Capital were mine."

Flag-waving patriotism stirred the hearts of new Americans, and song-and-dance man George M. Cohan made a career with hit songs like "I'm a Yankee Doodle Dandy" and "You're a Grand Old Flag." Born in the States of Irish immigrant stock, he went on the stage before the age of ten.

Many famous entertainers got their start on the vaudeville circuit: Sophie Tucker, "The Last of the Red-Hot Mammas," born Sophie Abuza in Russia; escape artist Harry Houdini (Weiss) from Hungary; Al Jolson (Asa Yoelson) from Lithuania. Jack Benny and Eddie Cantor were born of Jewish immigrant parents, as was Fanny Brice.

When silent movies developed in

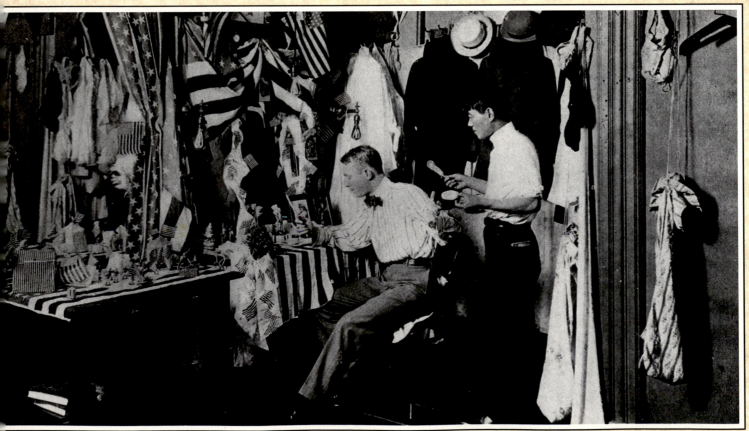

Entertainer George M. Cohan in a backstage dressing room (above); Fanny Brice in the Ziegfeld Follies, c. 1916 (right); Pat Rooney in costume for *Shamrocks,* 1924 (far right)

the early 1900s, more foreign-born stars emerged: Mary Pickford, Rudolph Valentino, Greta Garbo, Charlie Chaplin. A genius of slapstick, Chaplin gained enduring fame with his tragi-comic hero "the little fellow." In *The Immigrant* he turned the tribulations of many into art.

As films and radio replaced vaudeville, and as the children and grandchildren of "great wave" immigrants grew up as native-born Americans, ethnic theater began to fade.

Yet for many groups more recently arrived, their theater still holds a special importance. And in its heyday, from the late 1800s to the 1930s, ethnic theater brightened the lives of millions. It gave them a reason to laugh and a time to cry. It gave expression to their hopes, their fears, their pride, and their dreams.

in comedy roles—struggles in the gears of gigantic machinery, playing a hapless factory worker in his 1936 classic Modern Times.

Years of Hope and Struggle

I HAVE THE RIGHT!" The gritty cry was muted at first. Then it jangled to fullness in a babel of accents that rose from California canneries and Colorado coal mines, from Chicago stockyards and Massachusetts cotton mills, from looming tenements and cookie-cutter company towns. He had "the right," declared an Italian-born leader of thousands of immigrant mine workers, striking in 1897 against reduced wages and inhuman conditions in Pennsylvania's coalfields. "I am a Americano citizen," he told the local police chief. "I have my papers." His naturalization papers fluttered aloft with the flag; his enthusiastic supporters shouted "America!" Across the land, millions of other shirt-sleeved newcomers were also offering their new homeland a muscular embrace—and asking, in return, for its guarantees and assurances, for its promises.

"Who gave you the right?" The response came from hilltop mansions, from statehouses and law courts. Who had given her a permit to speak on the streets? A judge challenged Irish-born Mother Jones, arrested for rallying steelworkers in Homestead, Pennsylvania, in 1919. The 89-year-old labor leader had her answer ready: "Patrick Henry; Thomas Jefferson; John Adams!" In jail, on another occasion, she spoke of Washington, a "gentleman agitator" who had fought a powerful government; of Lincoln, agitating against powerful men, invested wealth, human slavery.

Adoptive Americans found their voice in varied settings. A little Jewish girl from Byelorussia, where "we had no flag to love," learns in a Boston school about the Revolution: "The people all desiring noble things, and striving for them together, defying their oppressors, giving their lives for each other—all this it was that made *my country*." In Pittsburgh, a new American from Wales warns: "Let the masters remember that the balance of power is in the hands of the sons of toil by the ballot box." In Braddock, Pennsylvania, a young Slovak steelworker discovers that his town is named for an English general who died nearby in 1755, defeated by the French after ignoring the advice of an aide from Virginia. The young aide, George Washington, "had been so obviously right" that the newcomer, caught up in the story, imagined himself "already half an American, and the Revolution inevitable."

Yet America seemed to have lost the revolutionary quality that shone, gem-bright, in the Founding Fathers' words. Ironically, its demise was signaled by unprecedented prosperity—a wealth based upon the dramatic rise of industry. "The old nations of the earth creep on at a snail's pace," wrote the Scottish-born steel magnate Andrew Carnegie in 1886. "The Republic thunders past with the speed of an express." It was racing along with new technology. America had few trains in 1830, no oil wells in 1850, few steel mills in 1870; but by the 1890s these industries had brought great-power status to America and mind-boggling fortunes to their owners. Now, to these men, came influence enough to defy the law. Cornelius Vanderbilt was typical, if unusually candid: "Law! What do I care about law? H'ain't I got the power?"

Many of these men—and their women—spent their new money on opulent display: on a $15,000 diamond collar for a dog; on a private carriage and a valet for a pet monkey; on cigarettes wrapped in $100 bills for a party. All of this stood in sharp contrast to the "rigid simplicity" of the old-money elite in preceding generations. For them, the ability "to limit display, to avoid pomp, was the mark of 'tone' and breeding." Nevertheless, the new style marked small cities as well as capitals of wealth like New York or San Francisco.

I n the metal-manufacturing center of Rome, New York, for instance, the change came rather late, when copper prices shot up at the beginning of World War I. Some of the new millionaires lived as before, in their family homes, but others built what one county judge indignantly described as "palaces, lady, palaces." Some continued to hunt and fish with old friends and neighbors, but others acquired a taste for the exclusivity of new country clubs, and took up golf.

In Rome, as across the nation, divisions of social class were growing starker. In the big mechanized workplace employer and employee no longer worked side by side. And if laissez-faire capitalism was bringing unheard-of wealth to some, it was testing the limits of deprivation among others at the bottom of the social scale. In Rome, prosperity depended on some 4,000 Italian immigrants—most of the city's labor force, on strike in 1919 for an eight-hour day, decent wages, and human respect. Nationwide, by 1910, more than half the unskilled workers in America's major industries were foreign-born.

The ratio was even higher in some cases. New England's textile mills were almost completely served by French-Canadians, Italians, Portuguese, Armenians, and other immigrants. Elsewhere, the mix was less eclectic. Confectioners often spoke Greek. The sturdy physique and high, grime-caked cheekbones of laborers in coal mines, steel mills, and stockyards usually bore the Slavic stamp. Foremen expected such a new immigrant to make "a better slave" than his predecessors.

Once-sleepy towns and mining camps proved as ill-equipped as great cities to cope with the new influx. At riverbank mill sites, ideal for commercial transportation, workers' shanties advanced precariously up steep hillsides, "a weary climb after the labor of the day." Or they

Belching smoke grays skies over the mills of U.S. Steel at Homestead, Pennsylvania, about 1905. This plant near Pittsburgh—Andrew Carnegie's from 1886 to 1901—boasted the most advanced technology of its day. Increased mechanization in the late 19th century lessened demand for skilled labor. Cuts in pay, and longer workdays, brought labor unrest. "I don't want the kids ever to work this way," one Scotch-Irish furnace boss said; "I'm goin' to educate them so they won't have to work twelve hours."

Managers sought eastern Europeans, considered more tractable, to replace feisty German and Irish workers. One mill specified "Syrians, Poles and Romanians preferred." By 1907 Slavs made up more than half the work force at Homestead, most of them in unskilled jobs. A bitter and bloody strike in 1892, quelled by militia, defeated unionism here, leaving an all-powerful mill that offered "wages and work under such conditions as it pleases."

hopscotched across crooked creeks that brought spring floods, the rotten-egg smell of sulphur, and often water so polluted that "no respectable microbe would live in it." When thrifty Slavs built their own abodes, the "hovels had roofs slanting in all directions, with eaves and without, sides of different lengths, and windows of various sizes appearing helter-skelter in the walls." On the other hand, in Braddock, "real-estate speculators put up the houses that became so characteristic of the steel towns, long, ugly rows like cell blocks, two rooms high and two deep, without water, gas or conveniences of any kind. . . ."

These were cities of smoke: iron mill smoke that settled "in black, slimy pools on the muddy streets. Smoke on the wharves, smoke on the dingy boats, on the yellow river. . . ." Smoke in summer: withering willow branches hung in doorways for an old-country festival. Smoke in winter: belching through western blizzards in miners' shacks, blackening somber family portraits and vivid insurance-company calendars,

clotting the wings of a mantelpiece angel. Smoke, and fire: licking at the night sky, high above purple arc lights, casting lurid shadows on the commotion below.

The noises of industry—staccato drilling, freight cars bumping, machines clattering—were ceaseless, almost natural, like the wind. The whistle or the siren dominated all other sounds. It announced death in the mine to shawled women who came running, each praying that her husband was not a victim. It brought the women to the mill on "Pay Friday," to escort their husbands' paychecks past the saloons and payday beggars. In predawn darkness it called the immigrant to work, and sent him home again in darkness 12 or 16 hours later—unless he was on the night shift that week, or on the 24-hour "long turn," the changeover shift in steel mills.

"At three o'clock in the morning of a long turn a man could die without knowing it," wrote a steelworker. "And go right on working till

Pay Friday at Homestead brings a long, patient queue of men and boys for biweekly wages. In 1907 most steel workers earned less than $2 a day— about 16½ cents an hour—for dangerous, back-breaking labor in searing, din-filled mills. Every two weeks came the "long turn," the deadly changeover from night to day shift when workers toiled 24 hours straight. Frugal Slavs paid little for housing, but did not stint on food. To round out income, families took single men as boarders in their homes. An eminently successful immigrant from Scotland, Carnegie had offered paternalistic benefits to his workers: cheap coal; low rents or loans to buy houses (like those opposite) near the Homestead plant; and, of course, a Carnegie Library. "We'd rather they hadn't cut our wages," some workers said of the last. "What use has a man who works twelve hours a day for a library, anyway?"

221

Women in babushkas and children in Sunday best crowd close to an open casket for a photograph, perhaps to send to relatives back in Slovakia. Flags wrapped in black frame the doorway of the deceased's home in Easton, Pennsylvania. On the way to the cemetery mourners will chant a dirge, "Už idem do hrobu—Now I am going to the grave." Uniform-clad members of the National Slovak Society, identified by their badges, attend their lost brother at the bdieť nad mŕtvym—the watching over the dead—and as pallbearers.

Such mutual benefit associations aided uprooted immigrants, helping to preserve old customs and to teach new. The Slovak Society, for instance, required members to become citizens. The lodges also offered real financial aid. Slavs, like the miner above, risked death and crippling at an alarming rate in coal mines and steel mills: 526 deaths in one year in the Pittsburgh area alone. Between 1890 and 1906 the National Slovak Society paid out 3.5 million dollars in death benefits.

the whistle blew." At three o'clock in the afternoon, noted a researcher in 1897, a child laborer could "no longer direct the tired fingers and aching arms with a degree of accuracy." The daily routine was as grueling for legions of immigrant children as for their parents. The coal mine was a school for the unschooled, whose graduates moved downward by stages. Twelve-year-olds tended ventilating doors; teenagers became coal haulers or mule keepers; at 18 or thereabouts they joined their fathers as helpers at the coal face.

The accident rate for children was triple that of their parents, which was appalling enough. In a factory job, a moment's distraction courted disaster. An Italian recalled the intricate drill of fastening tin tops onto containers: "Any false movement and the spinning tin would cut my index finger."

Employers bore little, if any, responsibility for accidents. Workmen's compensation laws did not become standard before World War I. In lawsuits, judges tended to favor employers: In a free society, they opined, an employee was at liberty to quit a dangerous job.

Some did. A few Slavs and Italians realized their dream of cultivating the land. Skilled Jews who escaped the sweatshop were more likely to become independent tradesmen or (Continued on page 232)

Molten steel explodes into sparks as workers pour it into molds at a Pittsburgh mill. Men in a Chicago meat-packing plant wield wooden poles, scalding hogs in a vat. In the late 1880s Polish workers predominated in the Chicago stockyards. Bohemians came in the 1890s, then Lithuanians, Russians, and Slovaks. "The foreman," an observer noted, "looks for round-toed shoes . . . [for men] fresh from the old country, not Americanized enough to wear factory-made footwear. When they are squeezed dry he can get other freshcomers."

Child Labor

Every day little children came . . . some with their hands off, some with the thumb missing . . . stooped little things, round-shouldered and skinny. Many . . . not over ten years of age"—so a labor activist described the children she found working in Pennsylvania's textile mills. Born in 1830 in Ireland, Mary Harris—better known as "Mother Jones"—had come to America as a child with her family. During most of her long life she served as an articulate defender of workers' causes.

In 1903, at age 73, she marched with a group of those mill children

Top: Injured mill boy, probably 12 years old, at Bessemer City, North Carolina, October 1912. Above: Spinning room of the Cornell Mill in Fall River, Massachusetts, January 11, 1912. Following pages: Breaker boys at lunchtime, South Pittston, Pennsylvania, January 1911.

all the way from Philadelphia to Theodore Roosevelt's home at Oyster Bay, New York. "I thought that President Roosevelt might see these mill children and compare them with his own little ones who were spending the summer on the seashore." Her little band did not see the President, but played their part in a campaign to end child labor in this country.

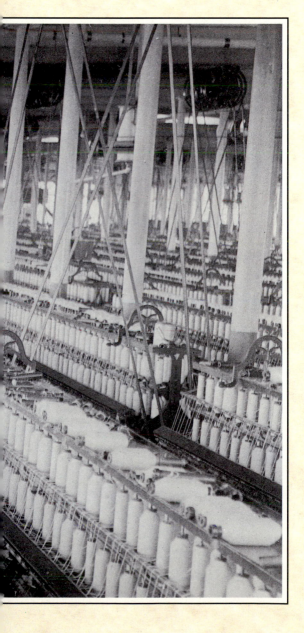

From 1870, when the census first recorded occupations of children age 10 to 15, until 1900, the number of children under 16 "gainfully employed" more than doubled—from about 750,000 to 1,750,000. Reform advocates put the number even higher, for children under 10 were not included.

Child labor was not strictly an immigrant question. Thousands of native-born children also worked in various industries. But unskilled immigrants often found themselves living from day to day. To survive, they depended on the meager wages their children added to the family income. In some cases parents lived off a child's labor. Jane Addams, the founder of Chicago's Hull-House settlement, encountered an Italian father grieving at the loss of his 12-year-old daughter—and the loss of her wages: "Now I shall have to go back to work again until the next one is able to take care of me."

The textile industry employed many children who worked long hours in din-and-dust-filled spinning rooms like that at Fall River, Massachusetts, photographed by the famed photojournalist Lewis Hine. Young boys, or "doffers," replaced full spools with empty ones. Girls tended the fast-spinning yarn. "The tangles were always worst when I was tiredest," explained one child on a night shift.

In the South, where the little boy at upper left injured his hand, perhaps a fourth of the mill workers were under the age of 16. Some, as young as six, earned only ten cents—the price of a two-pound loaf of bread—for a 12-hour day. Few immigrants settled in this region, and industry drew labor from impoverished native-born farm families.

But most of the child workers in the spinning room at Fall River were offspring of immigrants from Portugal, Greece, Italy, Russia, or Syria. They joined an early wave of English, Irish, and French-Canadian labor. By 1900, a full 90 percent of the cotton workers in Fall River were of foreign descent.

Work for children was not new to America. From colonial times the young had their duties in agriculture and apprenticeships. Labor was scarce, and the Protestant ethic deemed idleness "the mother and root of all . . . evil acts and other mischiefs." Early 19th-century New England factories often hired farmers' daughters. An 1828 Rhode Island newspaper advertised for a cotton mill: "Families wanted—. . . consisting of four or five children each, from nine to sixteen years of age." On the whole the system was paternalistic. "Operating machines was initially considered 'not half so hard' as many agricultural chores." And New England laws required some education for young workers.

But as the century wore on, long hours, low—even decreasing—wages, and a fast-growing factory system became dehumanizing for adult workers and a grave threat to the welfare of children, "blighting to body, mind, and spirit," in the words of one reformer.

During the laissez-faire era of the late 1880s, conservative businessmen seized upon a popular interpretation of Darwinian "survival of the fittest," as a social theory to justify unbridled competition. The hardships of rapid industrialization would winnow out the weak, they predicted, and develop an ever improving human race in better social conditions. Newly arrived immigrants were soon caught up in that expanding industrial system.

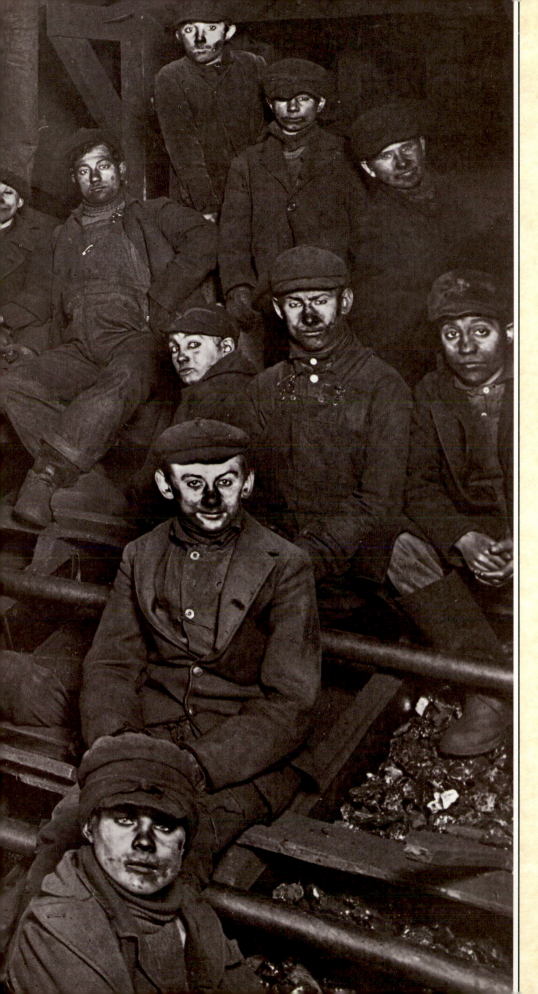

In his best-selling novels for the young, based on New York's destitute street urchins—bootblacks, newsboys, messengers, musicians—Horatio Alger became a prophet of optimism and the American Dream.

"I hope, my lad," said Ragged Dick's champion, Mr. Whitney, to Alger's bootblack hero, "you will prosper and rise in the world. You know in this free country poverty in early life is no bar to a man's advancement." Alger's plucky heroes bore adversity nobly, even with a certain humor. When asked by Whitney where he stayed, Ragged Dick replied, "The Box Hotel." "The Box Hotel?" "Yes, sir, I slept in a box on Spruce Street." "Suppose it had rained?" "Then I'd have wet my best clothes," answered Dick, who was not called ragged without reason.

There was little humor in real life for the 13-year-old boy who was docked two cents out of his 41-cent daily wage in 1906: He was ten minutes late. "Isn't that a bitter joke?" asked a letter reporting the incident to the editor of the *Jewish Daily Forward*.

Thousands of immigrant children worked in New York's garment sweatshops and so-called "home factories." Whole families—cigar-makers, garter makers, shirt makers, beaders of "cheap, dainty slippers for dainty ladies,"—crammed into tenement rooms and worked 16 or 18 hours a day for a pittance. *"Non dormire, Anetta! Solamente pochi altri. . . ."* were the words that reformer John Spargo heard at 11 o'clock at night in a slum dwelling. "Don't go to sleep, Anetta! Only a few more. . . ." An Italian mother was pleading with her four-year-old daughter to keep twisting wires—stems of artificial flowers for ladies' hats.

"A poor man stays a poor man, and the rest is nonsense." Thus one Slovak refuted Alger's myth of success. Another Slav would have added, "My people

229

do not live in America, they live underneath America." Rightly so in a broad sense, for Slavs like other immigrants often struggled at society's lowest levels. Literally true, as well, for many Poles worked deep in Pennsylvania's anthracite mines, along with Lithuanians and Hungarians. By 1900 eastern Europeans made up perhaps 40 percent of the laborers there, replacing Irish, Welsh, and Germans who came before.

Prosper they did, however, for they were hardworking and often frugal enough to save half their wages. For them "the valuable child was a working one." Their daughters worked in the mills. Their sons went to the coal breakers that some called the "nursery" because the workers were so young.

None of the boys with coal-dust-covered faces in Hine's 1911 photograph was older than 12, despite Pennsylvania's legal minimum work age of 14. For ten hours a day, six days a week, with only a short midday break, the boys sat hunched over the chutes in blinding dust, picking slate and rocks out of the rushing coal. "From the cramped position they have to assume," John Spargo wrote, "most become more or less deformed and bent-backed like old men."

Spargo tried the task for half an hour. "I could not do that work and live," he averred afterward, "but there were boys of ten and twelve doing it for fifty and sixty cents a day." Accidents were frequent: cuts, crushed fingers, even deaths. Parents lied to evade the minimum age law: "Wi'me pay so small, I was glad to give a quarter to have the papers [certificate of age] filled out so's he could bring in a trifle like the other boys," said one father of six.

Most of Horatio Alger's heroes on the way from rags to riches bore good "Anglo-Saxon" names like Frank Courtney or Tom Tracy. But even

Alger's relentless optimism faltered when he saw a terrified eight-year-old Italian boy die at the New York Newsboys Lodging House from beatings and starvation inflicted by his *padrone.* A padrone was a contract labor "boss" to whom, "for a few paltry ducats," some poor Italian peasant families sold their young sons. Many of these children died from abuse or malnutrition.

To expose such evils, Alger in 1871 wrote *Phil, the Fiddler,* a novel about street musicians Filippo and Giacomo who "were torn from their native hills [in Calabria] . . . doomed to walk the streets [of New York] from fourteen to sixteen hours in every twenty-four gathering money." Alger was instrumental in getting passage, in 1874 in New York, of the nation's first law for the prevention of cruelty to children.

The padrone system became significant in America as a result of an 1864 statute that attempted to fill labor shortages by encouraging immigration of workers under contract. In 1885 a law prohibited the much-abused practice. But among Greeks, Armenians, Syrians, as well as Italians, padrones continued to operate as middlemen for adult immigrants, and sometimes for children like little Johnnie. Hine found this nine-year-old shucking oysters in Louisiana under the stern gaze of his padrone. The labor contractor had brought the boy from Baltimore— quite possibly to earn as little as ten cents for a day that began at 6 a.m. and extended "till there ain't no more sun."

Reformers against the abuses in the seafood and canning industry mocked "tender laws" that protected oysters and shrimps, "dealing minutely with the crime of tearing them from their beds before they have attained a certain size," while no laws governed "ruthless employers who drag babies from their beds to labor in the shucking sheds."

As part of the Progressive Move-

ment that came in reaction to laissez-faire attitudes, agitation increased in the late 19th and early 20th century to end the worst abuses of child labor. Progressives believed that, through social and political action, the ills of society could be remedied. Jane Addams and other social activists had, in the 1880s, started the settlement-house movement to aid the urban poor. They took up the cause of child labor along with such publicists as Jacob Riis and Lewis Hine. In 1904 the newly founded National Child Labor Committee launched an inquiry and publicized the issue; it joined the fight for federal statutes to replace state laws that had proved ineffectual.

In a dramatic three-day speech in 1907, Indiana Senator Albert J. Beveridge led the battle in the U.S. Congress. "Does the Senate find that amusing . . . a girl going a mile or more across a windswept valley to begin work at half-past six at night and working until six in the morning for three cents an hour?" he asked. Beveridge then outlined the threats to health and the horrors of this "slow murder of these children." Despite his efforts, no law was passed until 1916. This statute, which utilized federal power to regulate interstate commerce, was declared unconstitutional by the Supreme Court in 1918. Attempts at other laws and a Constitutional amendment failed. Nevertheless, the use of child labor declined from the 1920s on, and in 1941 the Supreme Court reversed its earlier decisions on the child labor laws.

Today the question of the working child may seem a dead issue. But child labor exists today, particularly among migrant agricultural workers, many of whom are immigrants. Often these children lack education and health care, and they are caught in the cycle that early reformers denounced as "making human junk."

Nine-year-old Johnnie shucks oysters in Dunbar, Louisiana, March 2, 1911.

merchants. Representatives of other groups returned to the old country. But the newcomer who stayed at the mine or mill found that advancement eluded him not least because of the attitude of other workers.

Often the more successful, entrenched individual reflected immigration of an earlier era. As a "pusher" in a steel mill, he was noticeable because of a silver watch chain. One such Irish foreman warned a Slovak underling that "I don't like smart Hunkies"—slang for "Hungarians," and an all-purpose tag for Slavs as well. As a California construction boss, he refused to call an Italian anything but a "dago." As a Pennsylvania mine foreman, he might snub a dark-skinned southern Italian. Recalled one Sardinian: "As soon as they heard I was from the south I would not get the job."

Epithets were a minor irritant. The "Hunky" steelworker said that he had come "to find work and save money, not to make friends with the Irish." A greenhorn would compare himself at first not to the native but to "what he was in Lithuania" or in Italy—"always on the verge of starvation," as one immigrant remembered. "We were not poor in America; we just had a little less than the others."

Such attitudes provoked other workers, who claimed that greenhorns depressed wage scales by working for a pittance. As migratory "birds of passage," uncommitted to America, newcomers were compared to "Chinese coolies." They were thought to be dominated by sinister labor brokers. In reality, padrones did control half of New York City's Italian work force in 1900. Among Balkan and Lebanese immigrants, an all-powerful Greek from Sparta was known as the "Czar." Advertising himself as "The Reliable Labor Contractor," L. G. Skliris kept branch offices in seven cities across the continent. His headquarters were in Salt Lake City, which accounted for the heavy concentration of his countrymen in the mountain west.

Skliris enjoyed warm relationships with managers of mines and *sidheró dhramés* (rail lines), to whom he sent thousands of workers. Bosses made them sign a document in English, which none could read, authorizing payroll deductions in favor of Skliris. A sensible man would patronize coffeehouses owned by Skliris's agents—or else. Greeks at the Bingham copper mines in Utah rebuffed union organizers until the Western Federation of Labor offered to get Skliris out of their lives. Then, in 1912, "the Greeks joined [the union] in a body and jubilantly ran up and down the streets of Bingham shooting off guns."

Long before that, however, the new immigrants had gained a reputation for strikebreaking. Telegrams from Skliris to western coffeehouses, for instance, would send hundreds of unemployed Greeks to

Auto workers drop the engine into a Model T Ford in 1913 at Highland Park Michigan. Henry Ford's innovative assembly line—which moved the job to the man—speeded up production here and elsewhere. Cost savings helped the Model T, "a motorcar for the great multitude," revolutionize American life. Ford's generous wage of $5 for an eight-hour day—revolutionary in itself—attracted immigrant workers, particularly Hungarians and Finns. Though efficient, the assembly line, ever-larger factories, and monotonous work meant stress for workers. Decades later one steelworker described the anonymity of industrial toil: "you're not regarded. You're just a number out there. . . . They know you by your badge number."

strikebound mines and railheads. At harborside in New York, labor agents would intercept men just off the ship. A Pennsylvania miner recalled that when the Italians struck, "colored people, some Mexicans and many Spanish were shipped in . . . not knowing anything more than that they had a job."

Foreign laborers, wrote a French economist who visited America about 1900, "are incapable of organizing effectively. . . . They are a turbulent, violent, irrational population." If the newcomers were reluctant to organize and risk getting fired, irrationality was hardly to blame. As miner John Chessa recalled, those hired as strikebreakers were those "who did not know much about this country"—strangers to America and to its history of labor struggles. "America goes on over their heads," said a Ruthenian Greek-Catholic priest of his countrymen. "America does not begin till a man is a workingman, till he is earning two dollars a day. A laborer cannot afford to be an American."

Trade unions were the obvious route to better things. Union leaders, however, often saw the bewildered newcomers as the pawns of industrialists, and lobbied for immigration restriction. Most unions

accepted skilled workers only, thus barring the majority of newcomers. The cigar-chewing Samuel Gompers, himself an immigrant of Dutch Jewish stock, sought to enlist immigrants after 1881, when the organization that became the American Federation of Labor was founded. But the AFL was based on craft unions, and one Italian miner compared it to a private club for the "Anglo-Saxons."

Eventually, changes in the workplace itself mandated new union policies. Improved machinery was making skilled craftsmen obsolete. As skilled jobs disappeared and union membership declined, labor leaders turned to the newcomers to fill their ranks.

The task of organizing greenhorns grew easier with time. Birds of passage began to raise young broods; and the longer they remained, the keener their sense of their own worth. "While few . . . can talk English, they somehow learn mighty quick what the price of labor is and they demand and get it." Organizers learned too—to reach newcomers through their own leaders, and through union members like Paul Pulaski, who "speaks five different foreign languages . . . makes a good stagger at two more . . . and speaks good English too."

Once an ethnic group at a workplace decided to protest, it acted with fervor and unity. In the Pennsylvania coalfields in 1897, immigrant strikers went marching from town to town. They alarmed American workers, said a reporter, by "yelling and shouting like base ball rooters when the score is tied in the thirteenth inning with two out and Kelly at bat." The newcomers began to gripe about strikebreaking "foreign labor" or "Merica miners" who left the rough work to "Polanders."

Strikes led or sustained by immigrants began to make news—notably, the great Homestead steel strike of 1892. But there were also many small, unofficial actions. Italian railroad laborers, for example, answered a pay cut by cutting an inch off their shovels, "to shovel less dirt at the lower pay."

Diverse ethnic groups were able to discard old antagonisms and make common cause. The loyal followers of "Johnny D'Mitch"—John Mitchell, president of the United Mine Workers—were Poles, Lithuanians, Slovaks, Ruthenians, and others. They brought the coal mines to a standstill in 1902. President Theodore Roosevelt intervened; the miners got a 10 percent raise and a nine-hour day. Graveside eulogies for a striker might be heard in fifteen languages. Meetings of Chicago's Amalgamated Meat Cutters' Union were conducted in five. There, "common interests and brotherhood must include the Polack and the Sheeny," an Irish unionist had to admit.

"You ladies must remain steadfast!" urges labor leader Samuel Gompers at a 1909 meeting of striking New York shirtwaist makers. In protesting wages and work conditions, Jewish and Italian workers—mainly women— recited an old Jewish oath: Should one betray the cause, "may this hand wither from the arm I now raise."

The garment industry had long exploited many newly arrived immigrants in sweatshops. Women sew intently under the sharp eye of a contractor or "sweater" (opposite, top). Reporter Jacob Riis noted in the Jewish quarter of New York, "the whir of a thousand sewing-machines, worked at high pressure from earliest dawn till mind and muscle give out altogether." Bosses often required workers to buy their own sewing machines on time— for $50, roughly the equivalent of four weeks' pay. The boss charged, at a profit, for broken needles, spoiled fabric, even for chairs to sit on. The 1909 strike of 20,000 men and women united for the first time many garment workers. In 1911 the 146 deaths of the Triangle Shirtwaist Company fire in Manhattan stirred new passion in—and public support for— the industry's union movement.

If the union helped to blunt ethnic discord, it also forged links between the stranger and his new homeland. In a hall near Pittsburgh, men spoke "without stumbling over the words . . . about liberty and justice and freedom of speech." For a Lithuanian meatpacker in Upton Sinclair's muckraking novel *The Jungle,* the union made him "begin to pay attention to the country. It was the beginning of democracy with him. It was . . . a miniature republic; its affairs were every man's affairs, and every man had a real say about them."

As economic protest became a measure of Americanization, however, many union causes were denounced as foreign. Such was the movement for an eight-hour day—a coalfield ballad ran, "Eight hours we'd have for working, eight hours we'd have for play; Eight hours we'd have for sleeping in free Amerikay." This idea, said the *New York Times,* was "un-American." In 1886, in Chicago's Haymarket Square, a rally for the cause broke up when a bomb exploded among approaching policemen. Four labor radicals, convicted as conspirators and murderers, were hanged; three were German by birth, one of *Mayflower* stock.

Again the "foreign" Church of Rome stirred controversy when James Cardinal Gibbons, an Irish-American, denounced monopolies and "sanctimonious miserly" millionaires and defended unions. Moreover, in 1891 Pope Leo XIII issued an encyclical deploring "the hard-heartedness of employers and the greed of unchecked competition." (How far did papal infallibility extend, Gibbons was asked. "All I can say," he replied, "is that a few months ago in Rome His Holiness called me 'Jibbons.'")

Again, in 1901, America's unthinkable crime occurred: "Zolgotz, mean man/He shot MacKinley with his handkerchief in his hand/In Buffalo, in Buffalo. . . ." Actually, the President's assassin, who used the alias Fred Nobody, was American-born. But his Polish name and anarchist leanings reinforced a frightening stereotype of immigrants as agents of unrest. So did the flamboyance of the "Wobblies," the Industrial Workers of the World. Organized in 1905, the IWW called for "One Big Union" to include all workers, skilled or unskilled. The slogan attracted immigrants—especially the "snipes" and "jerries" on the railroads, "timber beasts" in the forests, "muckers" in the mines.

Among textile workers in the immigrant city of Lawrence, Massachusetts, the Wobblies scored their greatest victory, in 1912. With heavy sarcasm a judge blamed the strike on "gentlemen and ladies from abroad." In reality, the Wobblies' national leaders were mostly old-stock types with home-grown ideals of individualism, free speech, and frontier justice. They were men like "Big Bill" Haywood, a one-eyed

Backed up by signs in Yiddish and English that point out exploitation of labor, a speaker in New York's Madison Square exhorts boater-clad garment workers. Unionism grew in 19th-century America in the face of attitudes like that of the judge who sentenced one striker with the admonition, "You are on strike against God and Nature, whose firm law is that man shall earn his bread in the sweat of his brow." Critics accused President Theodore Roosevelt of meeting with "fomenters of anarchy" when he forced mine operators to negotiate with miners in the 1902 coal strike. "Green" immigrants soon learned loyalty to fellow workers in labor disputes. Unions became central to their Americanization, urging them to learn English. "The coal you dig isn't Slavish, or Polish or Irish coal," said John Mitchell, president of the United Mine Workers, "it's just coal."

ex-cowboy with "a face like a scarred battlefield." His acquaintance with violence dated from his childhood in a Utah mining camp. There was Father Thomas Hagerty, a black-bearded priest who told church officials that Marxism and Catholicism were compatible—and told railroad officials that "I have a brace of Colts and can hit a dime at twenty paces." There was the folk poet Joe Hill; born Joel Haaglund in Sweden, he declared himself a "citizen of the world."

Citizens of middle-of-the-road convictions had been jolted into paying attention to conditions in the workplace. President Theodore Roosevelt, alerted by what he read in *The Jungle,* urged passage of the new Pure Food and Drug Act. But all exposés paled in comparison to the Triangle Shirtwaist Company fire in 1911. Scraps of flaming fabric turned the top floors of a ten-story New York building into an inferno. Locked doors and a collapsing fire escape imprisoned many of the 146 victims—"bodies burned to bare bones. . . . skeletons bending over sewing machines." Others jumped to their deaths, hair aflame in the afternoon sky, bodies ripping through safety nets below. In the wake of the tragedy, protesters overflowed the streets. Marching beside young immigrant labor organizers like Rose Schneiderman and Pauline Newman were women of upright Yankee background—Frances Perkins,

"Abolition of the wage system" replaced, for the Industrial Workers of the World, the American Federation of Labor's goal of "A fair day's wage for a fair day's work." Lithuanian-born, an avowed anarchist, Alexander Berkman addresses a 1908 rally in New York's Union Square. Founded in 1905, the "Wobblies" called for one big industrial union, instead of trade unions that favored skilled and semiskilled workers. The Little Red Songbook (opposite, enlarged) contained rousing lyrics like "Ye sons of toil, awake to glory!"

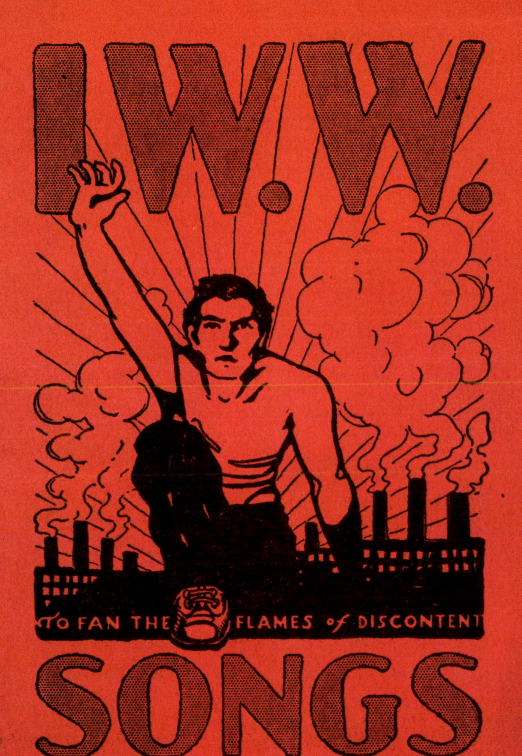

I.W.W.

TO FAN THE FLAMES of DISCONTENT

SONGS

10 CENTS

who would become the first female Cabinet member; Jeanette Rankin, the first Congresswoman. Church workers, civic leaders, philanthropists, socialites, and lawyers supported labor's "Great Revolt."

New safety regulations were instituted; the old sweatshop was on its way out. Rather than change working conditions, however, many industrialists sought to change—to "Americanize"—their immigrant employees. Henry Ford's auto company staged a pageant in which workers in old-country garb filed into a huge symbolic melting pot while others emerged wearing business suits and waving American flags.

Half a century earlier, nativists had sought to make citizenship more difficult to obtain; now their counterparts favored quick naturalization to neutralize the exotic masses. Many immigrants—especially Jews—responded eagerly. One of them, Moses Kirshblum from Poland,

understood hardly any English; when the judge asked if he was a bigamist he answered proudly, "yes." Then he identified the Fourth of July as "Labor Day." All his answers were wrong. Even so, the judge, deeply moved by the old man's pleading for citizenship, tearfully granted it. Many other immigrants, however, still felt a deep devotion to their native lands. As war clouds gathered over Europe, American nationalists became determined to sever those attachments.

In 1914, President Woodrow Wilson asserted neutrality so staunchly that movie audiences were urged not to cheer or hiss at newsreels. Nevertheless, Irish-Americans supported Germany out of hatred for England. Their oratory at social gatherings moved Mr. Dooley to say, "Be hivins, if Ireland cud be freed by a picnic, it'd not only be free today but an empire." Equally strong was German-America's pride in the *Kultur* of the fatherland. "Germany," remarked the *Houston Post* in 1915, "seems to have lost all of her foreign possessions with the exception of Milwaukee, St. Louis, and Cincinnati."

In 1917, the U.S. entered the war as an ally of Britain, Belgium, France, Russia, and Italy against Imperial Germany, Austria-Hungary, Turkey, and Bulgaria. Already Theodore Roosevelt had invented the term "hyphenated American"; he and Wilson had condemned Irish-American and German-American "hyphenism" as a sign of divided loyalty. Now zealots were demanding "100 percent Americanism."

Proudly bearing Old Glory—and supporting their striking fathers—children parade through the mining town of Calumet, Michigan, in the summer of 1913. Immigrants from 16 lands settled here, in the heart of Michigan's copper country, perhaps a third of them Finns. No longer "birds of passage," only here to hoard a nest egg, many had families and a stake in society. They struck in 1913, mostly against use of the new one-man air drill. Mine operators refused to negotiate, and violence increased. In December 1913, long into the strike, tragedy struck at a Christmas party of workers' children in the Italian Hall. A false cry of "Fire!" ended in a stampede in which 74 people died of suffocation, 62 of them children. The leftist, Finnish-language Lapatossu blamed the pro-management Citizens' Alliance. Mass funerals in four languages drew wide attention. Disheartened, workers eventually gave up the strike.

As radicalism increased, industry set up programs like English-language classes for their workers. Teachers (below) line up by their blackboards along with rows of workers at one factory. Henry Ford made classes compulsory: "Our one great aim is to impress these men that they are, or should be, Americans, and that former racial, national, and linguistic differences are to be forgotten." At right, a teacher acts out a sentence. A manual for Italians asserts that knowledge of English will bring prosperity. The shabby immigrant arrives toting one small satchel. English-speaking, and now smartly dressed, he returns to Italy requiring a porter to carry his trunk, umbrella, and hatbox.

ENGLISH FOR COMING AMERICANS

Series A --- Fourth Lesson

PREPARING BREAKFAST

gets	The wife gets the kettle.
takes off	She takes off the lid.
is	The kettle is empty.
puts on	She puts on the lid.
fills	The wife fills the kettle with water
is placed	The kettle is placed on the fire.
burns	The fire burns brightly.
gets	The water gets hot in the kettle.
boils	The water boils.
is taken	The kettle is taken off the stove.
pours	The wife pours boiling water on the coffee.
puts	She puts the coffee pot on the stove.
pours	She pours boiling water into a saucepan.
cooks	She cooks the eggs in the pan.
are	The eggs are done.
takes	She takes the eggs out of the pan.
are placed	The eggs are placed on the table.
pours out	The wife pours out the coffee.

Published by ASSOCIATION PRESS, 124 East 28th Street, New York
Copyright, 1909, by the International Committee of Young Men's Christian Associations

The popular clamor for "Americanization" rose to the level of frenzy.

Suspicion fell on Americans as well as aliens. Socialist leader Eugene Debs, a critic of the war, went to jail for his views; a Texas judge declared that Robert La Follette and five other Senators should be shot for theirs. But the worst indignities befell the Germans. In many schools the teaching of German was dropped, and German books were burned in Oklahoma. Anything "German" was renamed. Manhattan's German Hospital became Lenox Hill Hospital. Walking a dachshund was a risky venture. Wild accusations—that German-Americans were putting ground glass in Red Cross bandages, for example—sometimes inspired violence. At least one lynching occurred, in Collinsville, Illinois. The victim, a German immigrant, had hoped for citizenship.

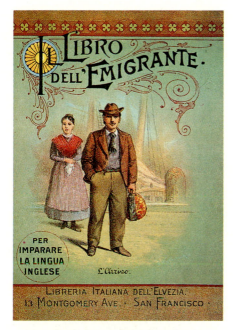

Wartime xenophobia dealt a blow to German-America from which it would not recover. Slavic groups, meanwhile, gained new status for their support of the Allies against their old overlords. Moreover, peace fulfilled old dreams for many with the appearance of new states: Poland, Czechoslovakia, Finland, Estonia, Latvia, Lithuania, the Kingdom of Serbs, Croats, and Slovenes (now Yugoslavia). Still, ethnic groups nitpicked the terms of the peace treaty until Wilson charged that "Hyphens are the knives that are being stuck into this document." Immigrants lobbied on behalf of their native lands, and dismayed Americans saw this as a failure of Americanization. And as peace brought fresh waves of immigrants, despite a new literacy test, demands for stiff new restrictions gained fervor.

The war and its aftermath marked a turning point in America's attitude toward immigration. Wilson the idealist had led the nation into the conflict to make the world "safe for democracy." The battlefield with its "monstrous killing matches" caused more than 320,000 American casualties—and a sense that the world's ills had become the nation's burden. Gone was the innocent optimism of small-town front porches and ice cream parlors. Evil, it seemed, came from foreign lands—and from foreigners in America. As attention shifted from the "mechanized production of death" in Europe to the production of goods at home, labor unrest erupted anew. Businessmen blamed the strikes on "long-haired Slavs and unwashed East Side Jews." Unions called for "an American standard of living." Employers countered with the open shop—"the American plan."

Wartime rhetoric had flavored the idiom of protest. A complaining copper miner was "an emissary of the Kaiser." Mother Jones denounced bosses as Kaisers with "hearts of steel and tears of steel."

THAT LIBERTY SHALL NOT
PERISH FROM THE EARTH
BUY LIBERTY BONDS
FOURTH   LIBERTY   LOAN

Beheaded, the Statue of Liberty rises before New York City engulfed in flames. German planes attack both in a 1918 poster urging citizens to buy government bonds during World War I.

Chinese-Americans portray Uncle Sam, Miss Liberty, and China at a 1917 bond rally in New York. Immigrant Americans played their part for their adopted country. Poles at a special rally in New York declared that "in proportion to population . . . the military . . . had in it more Poles than Germans, French or other nationality." Stylish women of New York sign up East Side citizens for the draft. As for anyone "heartily . . . loyal to this republic," asserted Theodore Roosevelt in 1915, "no matter where he was born, he is just as good an American as anyone else." Despite their loyalty, German-Americans faced wartime prejudice, burning of German books, even lynchings. And sauerkraut became, briefly, "liberty cabbage."

Mounted police attacking strikers were "Cossacks." Conditions in Pennsylvania's coal towns were summed up as "despotic tyranny reminiscent of Czar-ridden Siberia at its worst."

All these terms of insult made way for the damning "Bolshevist," a new catchall word for radicals. In 1917, Americans had welcomed the downfall of tsardom, but they soon learned to detest its Soviet successors. What if the revolutionary ideas of Communism crossed the Atlantic?

Within and without the labor movement, immigrants seemed the likeliest Bolshevists. A clergyman suggested deporting them "in ships of stone with sails of lead, with the wrath of God for a breeze and with hell for their first port." The Red Scare had broken out in 1919 when bombs were sent to prominent businessmen and government officials. In Washington, D. C., one blew up the front of Attorney General Mitchell Palmer's house—and the bomb-thrower along with it. When the assassin turned out to have been an Italian-born anarchist from Philadelphia, the worst fears of immigrant radicalism seemed confirmed. Nonconformists of any stripe were branded as "Bolshevists" in a nation one visiting Englishman described as "hag-ridden. . . . by a thousand phantoms of destruction." Palmer and an ambitious young assistant, J. Edgar Hoover, set out to deal with the "Reds." Rights were devalued, as the *Washington Post* explained: "There is no time to waste on hairsplitting over infringement of liberty. . . ."

In late 1919, 249 deportees from Ellis Island sailed, Russia bound, on a creaky Army transport nicknamed the "Soviet Ark." Flying squads without warrants invaded homes, union halls, clubs, bowling alleys. In Boston, 400 prisoners were marched off in chains. In Newark, a man was arrested because he "looked like a radical." In all, the Palmer raids netted several thousand aliens, of whom fewer than a third were deported. Many proved to be perfectly inoffensive innocents.

Palmer's own excesses discredited him, and the Red Scare subsided abruptly in 1920. Yet an obscure trial in the next year became a famous one because it suggested that an alien of unpopular opinions could not expect impartial justice. Two avowed anarchists, Nicola Sacco and Bartolomeo Vanzetti, were convicted of murdering a paymaster and his guard during the robbery of a Massachusetts shoe company. The guilt of either remains debatable. But their Italian origins and political views clearly weighed against them. Judge Webster Thayer made plain what Vanzetti called "despisement against us." As defense counsel fought to save them, they became world-famous. Thousands of citizens and many distinguished foreigners—George Bernard Shaw and Albert Einstein

O, LADY! LADY!

Crowding the decks of the Cunard liner Mauretania, *5,000 soldiers—native and foreign-born—await landing at New York in December 1918. Tooting sirens, megaphones, and wireless signals welcomed the men home. To the idea of a parade on Fifth Avenue, an officer of the 167th Aero Squadron replied, "I don't know how we'll march; we are better mechanics than soldiers." Miss Liberty greets her doughboys in a cartoon of the day. "Take a good look at me, Old Girl," they joked on their way home to the heartland. "If you ever see me again, you'll have to do an about-face!"*

among them—were protesting when they were finally executed in 1927, still defending their ideals.

Most immigrants had no greater fondness for radical ideology than did, say, Calvin Coolidge. Yet indiscriminate bigotry assailed American minorities in these years. Henry Ford's newspaper, the *Dearborn Independent,* vilified Jews. Oregon outlawed parochial schools (until the Supreme Court erased the statute). In big cities, whites rioted against blacks, the nation's "home-grown aliens." In smaller cities and rural areas, a reorganized Ku Klux Klan resorted to terror. To its "native born, white, gentile" members, the black was "a servant of humanity," the Jew an "un-American parasite," the Catholic "a curse to humanity and the freedom of conscience." The Klansman seemed, like Joe Hill's legendary diehard Scissor Bill, "down on everybody, the Hottentots, the bushmen and the man in the moon." And citizens who scorned the Klan could be just as contemptuous of the immigrant.

Crude bigotry had a sophisticated counterpart in eugenics. This school of thought purported to prove that race—defined as ethnic background—gave different peoples inherited traits that no environment could overcome. Thus, said men like Madison Grant, the inferior folk of the new immigration would pollute the superior Nordic stock at the pinnacle of civilization. Grant, chairman of the New York Zoological Society, was one of the patrician intellectuals who gave prestige to the Immigration Restriction League. Men of this sort had influence in Congress.

In 1911, Senator William Dillingham's commission on immigration had released a 42-volume report laced with condemnation of the new immigrants. It proposed that immigration be restricted according to nationality. By mid-1920, with 50,000 newcomers a month pouring in, Congress favored the idea. Dillingham drafted an emergency measure: Each European nation might annually provide the equivalent of 3 percent of its natives living in the U.S. in 1910.

Over Wilson's veto, the bill was passed in 1921. It was extended a year later. In 1924, the Johnson-Reed Act stiffened the law. Permanent quotas would be allotted on the basis of the ethnic backgrounds of the nation's white population. It would prevent "beer, bolshevism, unassimilating settlements," remarked an approving Congressman, and would uphold constitutional government.

The annual total would be about 154,000. Great Britain had a quota of 65,721, Germany 25,957, Italy 5,802. Africans were excluded. So were most Orientals. For the Europeans of the new immigration, however, the law meant the most drastic change. Henceforth, the Statue of

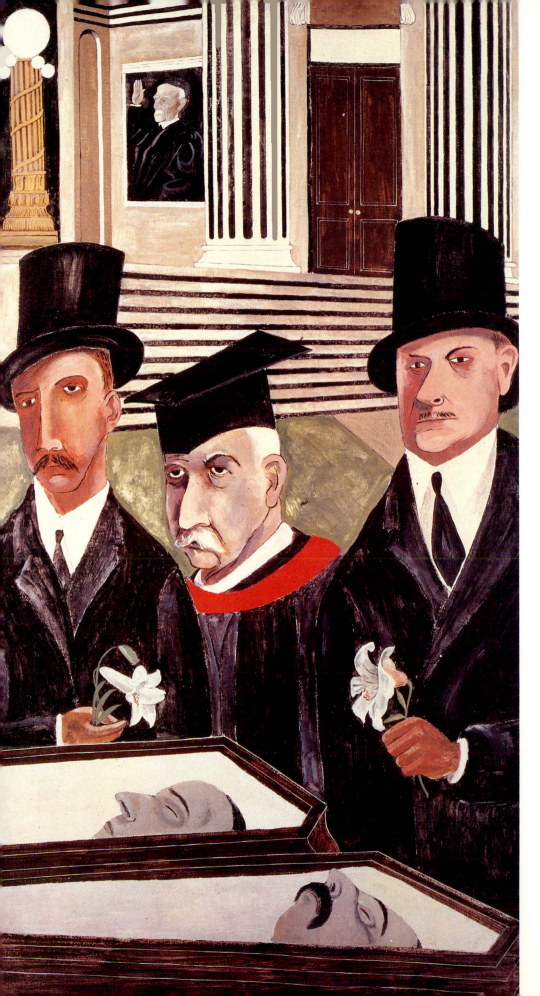

Glowering triumvirate holds lilies over the coffins of Nicola Sacco and Bartolomeo Vanzetti: immigrants from Italy, avowed anarchists, convicted murderers, and—in the eyes of many—martyrs to bigotry. The committee of three, men of New England's intellectual elite, concluded that the two had received a fair trial before their execution in 1927. A niche in the background of Ben Shahn's painting frames Judge Webster Thayer, who presided. At the time he called the accused "anarchist bastards." He told the jury that although Vanzetti "may not actually have committed the crime," he was "morally culpable . . . the enemy of our existing institutions." Their guilt remains a matter of debate; historians agree that the trial in 1921 was unfair. It came soon after the post-war Red Scare, in part a reaction to the success of the Bolsheviks in the Russian Revolution.

In a 1919 drawing, a stereotypical agitator confronts American Liberty. U.S. Attorney General A. Mitchell Palmer likened the "blaze of revolution" to "a prairie fire . . . sweeping over every institution of law and order . . . eating its way into the homes of the American workman . . . burning up the foundations of Society." A rash of deportations of radical immigrants followed.

The Klan attacked immigrants—especially Jews, Catholics, and radicals—as well as blacks, asserting white Protestant supremacy.

Liberty would fix a cold guardian gaze upon her harbor. Shut out, the war-scarred "huddled masses" of fallen empires would become captives of imitation emperors—*der Führer, il Duce, Vozhd*—who would render old definitions of cruelty obsolete.

Immigration from New World nations was unrestricted. (The Philippines, controlled by the U.S. since the Spanish-American War, also escaped quotas until 1934, and supplied labor for Hawaii.) At least half a million incoming Mexicans were counted at the southern border during the 1920s. In the same decade, nearly a million blacks moved north. They took the unskilled jobs vacated by upwardly mobile Europeans, as those newcomers had once replaced the old immigrants.

In the Great Depression, old Americans and new, men and women, were thrown out of work in hundreds of thousands. Half a million people returned to Mexico; almost as many Europeans left America as arrived. In 1930, American consuls had begun requiring prospective immigrants to show substantial means of support.

In the presidential campaign of 1932, Herbert Hoover declared that political persecution abroad had "largely ceased. There is no longer a necessity for the United States to provide an asylum. . . ." Adolf Hitler came to power in Germany the following year. As his assault on the Jews grew increasingly vicious, thousands sought a place of safety, and the United States—like most countries—did not want them.

Denied entry at liberty's door, "undesirable aliens" board a Coast Guard cutter for deportation from New York in 1938. Growing out of unionism, theories of racial superiority, and Red Scare politics, an America-for-Americans movement curtailed immigration into the U.S. In 1917 the Congress required a literacy test for newcomers. A 1924 law— favorable to folk of northern and western Europe—established a temporary quota system based on estimates of the foreign-born in the U.S. in 1890. A Swedish immigrant arrives in New York complete with number on his collar and suitcase in hand, on the cover of a program for a 1923 ballet-revue called "Within the Quota." This jazz musical, by Cole Porter and Gerald Murphy, satirized the new law and elements of American life an immigrant would encounter. In 1929, the national origins of the white population in the U.S. in 1920 became the basis for quotas. "It will preserve the blood of the United States in its present proportions," claimed a restrictionist Congressman.

American law made no provision for refugees. Albert Einstein, Thomas Mann, Enrico Fermi, Paul Tillich, and hundreds of other men and women, Jews and Christians, hardly less distinguished—they were among some 250,000 potential victims who reached America between 1933 and 1945. Many of them, as academics, were exempt from quotas. Trapped in Europe, others shared the doom of six million Jews. (Estimated deaths for the Allies of World War II, military and civilian, have been reckoned as high as fifty million.)

At the end of the war, the magnitude of human suffering brought new legislation. First, war brides, fiancées, and foreign-born children of servicemen were freed from quotas. The Displaced Persons Acts of 1948 and 1950 admitted 405,000 Europeans (out of five million uprooted by the war). In 1953, Congress voted to admit another 205,000, some from behind the Iron Curtain. These laws would smooth the way for Hungarian and Cuban anti-Communists a few years later.

In more profound ways, the war affected American attitudes toward immigration. The Holocaust proved the depths to which ethnic hatred could be carried. Thoughtful citizens were disquieted when they remembered the wartime internment of Japanese-Americans. Old biases lingered, but calls for immigration reform were mounting. In 1952, President Harry Truman said the quota system rested on the idea "that Americans with English or Irish names were better people and better citizens than Americans with Italian or Greek or Polish names."

Over Truman's veto, Senator Patrick McCarran's bill became law in that same year. The McCarran-Walter Act preserved the quota system, but shifted justification for it from ethnic terms to political ones. Relaxing quotas, argued the bill's supporters, would flood America with Communist subversives. Cold War alliances, however, resulted in new if tiny quotas for Asian nations, with 100 per year the usual total. Moreover, for the first time, an immigration law gave preference to applicants of "exceptional" skill or ability.

Many such individuals had arrived as wartime refugees, helping to dissolve the old myths about the inferiority of immigrants. Time, moreover, had blurred such ideas. Between 1925 and 1948, fewer than three million quota immigrants arrived. As in the early 1800s, when few newcomers entered, old-country languages and customs waned and disappeared, and stereotypes faded with them. Still, Americanization remained a personal matter, incomplete for most immigrants and some of their children. "We live between memory and reality," a Norwegian clergyman could say. Echoed a Bulgarian writer: "I shall always be the adopted child, not the real son." But with equal conviction a writer

Warm smile and American flags welcome a Jewish family to America about 1940. Tags identify them for a Jewish social service group. Thus a few fortunate families escaped persecution and war in the tragic Europe of the 1930s and '40s. But in general the immigration laws and quota system had no provision for refugees. In 1938 President Franklin D. Roosevelt extended temporary visas for 15,000 refugees already in the U.S. But the mood of the country—still in the Depression—remained isolationist, and unions feared immigration would add to unemployment. Attempts failed in 1939 to admit 20,000 German children —mostly Jewish. "We used to be more sensitive to human need," said Eleanor Roosevelt when the Child Refugee Bill came to naught. Though directed by FDR to give refugees "the most humane and favorable treatment possible under the law," consular officials, asserts a historian, "threw one legalistic roadblock after another into the path of rescue."

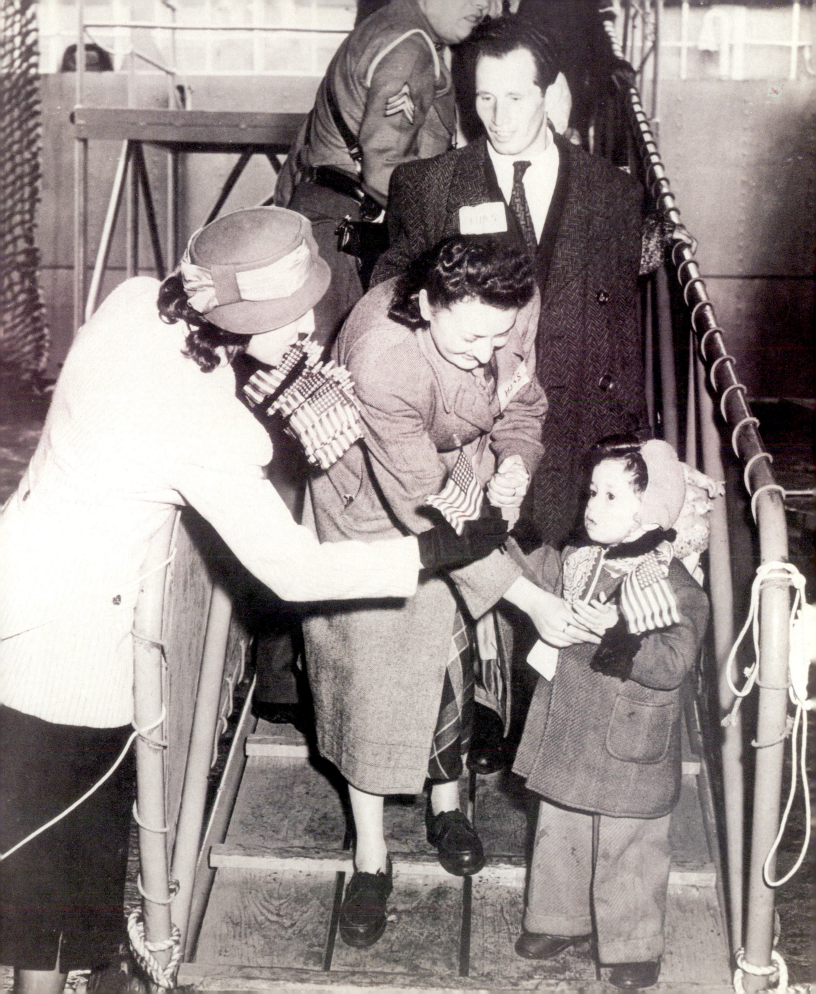

Internment

With the bomber raid on Pearl Harbor on December 7, 1941, anger against the Japanese swept the West Coast. Panic and fury generated by Japan's early victories in the Pacific inspired wild rumors of spying and sabotage by Japanese-Americans. Such newspaper headlines as "Caps on Japanese Tomato Plants Point to Air Base" reflect the hysteria of the times.

Accusations of radio signals to Japanese warships proved groundless; no Japanese-American was ever brought to court for aiding the enemy's war effort. Yet to some, like California's Attorney General Earl Warren (later Chief Justice of the United States), even this innocence was suspect. "It is a studied effort not to have any [sabotage] until the zero hour arrives," he told state law-enforcement officers on February 2, 1942.

In the weeks after the attack, the FBI rounded up those it considered "dangerous" among the Issei—immigrant Japanese, by law ineligible for citizenship. Homes were searched on the slightest pretext; the military imposed an 8 p.m.-to-6 a.m. curfew on all ethnic Japanese. On February 19, President Roosevelt as Commander in Chief issued Executive Order 9066, permitting the military to designate areas "from which any or all persons may be excluded."

Enemy aliens from Germany or Italy, and citizens of such background, were hardly affected—a total of 254 individuals were barred from specific areas, and about 2,000 interned—but the War Department uprooted nearly 120,000 Japanese-Americans on the

West Coast, banishing them from their homes and imprisoning them behind barbed wire in ten desolate "sand and cactus" camps in the interior. Nearly 63 percent were Nisei—born in America and therefore U.S. citizens. In Hawaii, ironically, where 157,000 ethnic Japanese were a third of the population, the military never ordered evacuation—and Japanese-Americans proved completely loyal.

On the mainland, exclusion orders "To All Persons of Japanese Ancestry" let the evacuees take with them only the clothes, bedding, and personal effects they could carry by hand. Many had only a few days' notice to wind up their affairs, harvest crops, and store or sell their belongings.

In addition to losses estimated at hundreds of millions in 1942 dollars, the Japanese suffered humiliation at forced sales. Buyers came in droves to get property at a fraction of its value—25 cents for a table, $25 for a truck; $50 for a grand piano, $500 for a house—"knowing we had no recourse but to accept," said Yasuko Ito of San Francisco. Mike Umeda worked his farm until he

had to leave; strangers harvested his crops and he, like many others, received nothing for his labor.

The Army moved evacuees to assembly centers such as the Portland fairgrounds, where some 2,000 people were packed into one building.

In permanent camps run by the civilian War Relocation Authority, guarded by armed soldiers, residents lived in tarpaper barracks: one 20-by-25-foot room for each family. Life was highly regimented—"rushing to the wash basin . . . rushing to the mess hall. . . ." Razors, scissors, and radios were forbidden. To many the greatest hardship was lack of privacy.

Within months schools were provided for the younger students. One teenager never forgot an essay assignment: "Write why you are proud to be an American." Hundreds of older Nisei resumed their college education on campuses in the Midwest and the East. Others were granted leave for farm work or jobs in inland cities.

Early in 1943 the War Department decided to form an all-Nisei unit, the 442nd Regimental Combat Team, of volunteers from the camps and Hawaii. In heavy fighting in Europe the "go for broke" Nisei fought with bravery and distinction, suffering many casualties.

For example, five sons in the Masaoka family earned more than 30 medals. Four survived; but their mother was not allowed to leave camp to receive the posthumous award for Pvt. Ben Frank Masaoka, killed in the fight to rescue a "Lost Battalion" of Texans, who had been surrounded by German forces in the French Vosges Mountains in October 1944.

Few Americans questioned the constitutionality of detaining citizens without specific charges. The first legal

Opposite: A soldier posts exclusion and evacuation orders at Bainbridge Island, Washington, March 23, 1942
Below: A child waits to be taken to an assembly center, April 11, 1942

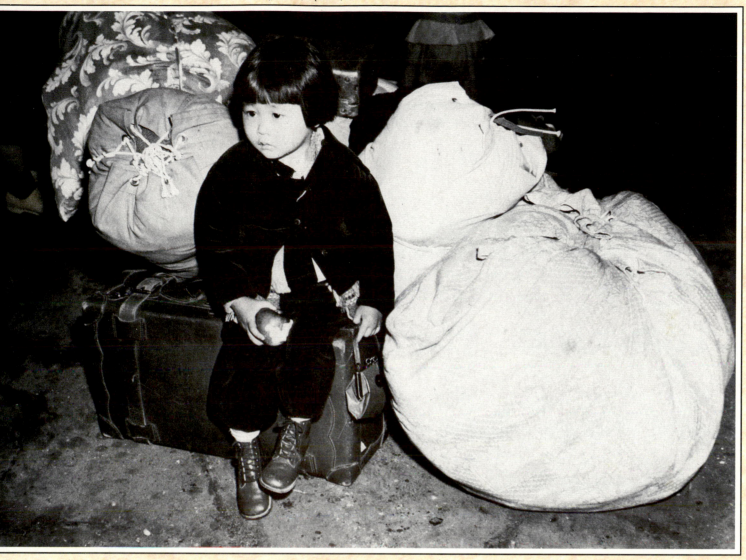

challenge came with the case of *Hirabayashi* v. *U.S.* in the spring of 1943. Gordon K. Hirabayashi, a Nisei college student convicted of breaking the curfew and failing to register for evacuation, contended that the orders violated his rights as a citizen. The Supreme Court, ruling only on the curfew, held unanimously that national security could warrant depriving an ethnic group of its civil rights. Chief Justice Harlan F. Stone expressed the Court's opinion that "one national extraction may menace that [public] safety more than others."

On December 18, 1944, the Court decided the *Korematsu* case, on the question of the government's power to order the evacuation of civilians. Split six to three, it upheld the government, citing "the gravest imminent danger to the public safety" in 1942. In a dissenting opinion, Justice Frank Murphy called this "the legalization of racism."

Ruling on the *Endo* case that same day, all nine Justices ordered the release of Mitsuye Endo from camp, decreeing that war or no war, the government has no power to confine a citizen of undisputed loyalty, charged with no offense.

At the very same time the Army revoked its exclusion orders, allowing the release of all trustworthy Nisei. But not until 1976 did a President, Gerald R. Ford, issue a formal apology.

Even later, in 1983, a federal commission recommended reparations of $20,000 to each surviving evacuee. Endorsing the plan, the American Civil Liberties Union described that wartime episode as "the greatest deprivation of civil liberties by government in this country since slavery."

from Byelorussia could call her girlhood home "a toy of memory."

Whatever their degree of assimilation, however warm or chilly their welcome, newcomers received one of the nation's most cherished gifts: options. Not that these were always given freely. Some surnames and not others identified distinguished law firms. For many years, talented Jews struggled against rigid quotas that limited their numbers at prestigious universities. But the barriers fell. As a young boy, Stanislaus Kowaleski struggled against a foreclosed future in the Pennsylvania mine where he worked on a 12-hour shift. In the evening darkness, he threw stones at tin cans; his accuracy attracted attention; in the 1920 World Series, Stan Coveleski pitched three winning games for Cleveland. English-born novelist Wilfrid Sheed spoke for hundreds who found baseball "a social passport"—"The Statue of Liberty, bat in hand, said, 'Try this, kid.'"

The Statue doled out balls, books, footlights, microscopes, patents, gavels, even Saturday-night specials (the option of lawlessness outlived the frontier). Perhaps most important of all, she handed out ballots—even to women as of 1920. When Fiorello La Guardia became New York's mayor in 1934, it was the first time the city elected a man who was neither Irish nor old-stock Protestant. When Prague-born Tony Cermak ran for mayor of Chicago in 1931, an opponent taunted him: "Tony, Tony, where's your pushcart at?" Cermak's reply won victory cheers from his multi-ethnic supporters. "It's true," he said, "I didn't come over with the *Mayflower*, but I came over as soon as I could." When Al Smith (part-Italian, part-German, part-Irish, part-English) ran for President as a Democrat in 1928, however, his Catholic faith worked against him.

In 1960, voters did elect a Catholic President. And it was appropriate that John F. Kennedy, proud of his own ethnic background, was the first postwar President to present Congress with legislative proposals to replace the old quota system. Under the existing law, as he had pointed out earlier, the "huddled masses" were welcomed only "as long as they come from northern Europe, are not too tired or too poor or slightly ill, never stole a loaf of bread, never joined any questionable organization, and can document their activities for the past two years."

Two years after Kennedy's assassination, his goal became reality. Congress overhauled the McCarran-Walter Act and discarded quotas framed by national origins. Henceforth, the Western Hemisphere might provide as many as 120,000 immigrants annually and the Eastern Hemisphere 170,000. No Old World nation might send more than 20,000 a year. Outside these limits, however, and not charged

"What Happened To The One We Used To Have?"

U.S. IMMIGRATION POLICY

"Those who can contribute most to this country—to its growth, to its strength, to its spirit—will be the first that are admitted," declared President Lyndon B. Johnson, signing the 1965 Immigration Act on Liberty Island. By abolishing the national-origins quota system, the law removed the last cultural and racial barriers to immigration. A 1946 cartoon, above, spoofs a snooty Liberty who rejects displaced persons and refugees. The 1965 Act set an annual ceiling with a maximum of 20,000 from any Old World nation.

against them, were parents, spouses, and unmarried children of American citizens. Preference under the limits shifted to other relatives of citizens as defined by the law, and a lesser priority went to bearers of exceptional skills.

On October 3, 1965, when President Lyndon Johnson signed the bill into law at the base of the Statue of Liberty, he cautioned that it would bring no major changes to America. Still, he continued, it was one of his administration's most important acts.

"For it does repair a very deep and painful flaw in the fabric of American justice. . . . [It] will really make us truer to ourselves both as a country and as a people. . . . The days of unlimited immigration are past. But those who do come will come because of what they are, and not because of the land from which they sprung."

The Enduring Dream

New groups of immigrants, new patterns of residence for the native-born mark the U.S. today. A mural on Mexican themes covers a wall of Willowbrook Junior High School in Los Angeles County, where more than two million Hispanics make their home.

he contest has epic proportions and outsize odds. On one side of a river, a Mexican peasant awaits the cloak of dusk to steal across the border. On the other, night scopes and helicopters are readied to foil his kind. On one side of a guarded gate in Hong Kong, an endless line of men and women awaits the opening of the consulate. On the other, an American official prepares to inform the hopeful that more than 30,000 already stand ahead of them on the U.S. waiting list. On one side of the earth, a leaky little boat lies hidden among rice stems in a paddy that has been a combat zone. On the other, a placid farmscape rolls to the horizon. In between: waters that swallow the boat, pirates who murder the passengers.

The story can begin in any place, at any moment. It has a million variations. A single strand links them all: the ferocious attachment to a dream, often improbable, of a better life. The results make for lively conversation among employees of the United States Immigration and Naturalization Service. They discuss counterfeiters who fake the *tarjeta verde*, the coveted "green card" of the legal resident alien. They mention the illegal alien from Mexico who was apprehended and deported six times—the same day. And the one who was deported 37 times before he established a successful business in Los Angeles and was allowed to stay. They also know the wreckage of thwarted dreams, the black bodies washed ashore on Florida's white sands.

One thing that makes the contest—against terrors and dangers, laws and borders, hunger and exhaustion—uniquely American is the fact that the underdog wins sometimes. And whether he does or not, regardless of his origins, he can be cheered. When Florida spectators applauded the Swedish tennis star Bjorn Borg as enthusiastically as the American Jimmy Connors, a retired-player-turned-commentator could say, "I've played in a lot of countries, and this is the only country where the crowd roots for the other guy."

It can happen elsewhere—but the United States is preeminently a nation of "other guys." They were, and are, venturesome men and women who distinguished themselves from their compatriots by leaving the fold of the familiar. An Englishman arriving in Virginia's wilderness almost four centuries ago had something in common with today's newcomer from India, growing raspberries and blueberries on a farm in Washington State. Both had the imagination and courage to will a place they had never seen into reality. Their independence of spirit, multiplied by millions, has both shaped the national character and given American immigration its dramatic quality. "The decision to settle

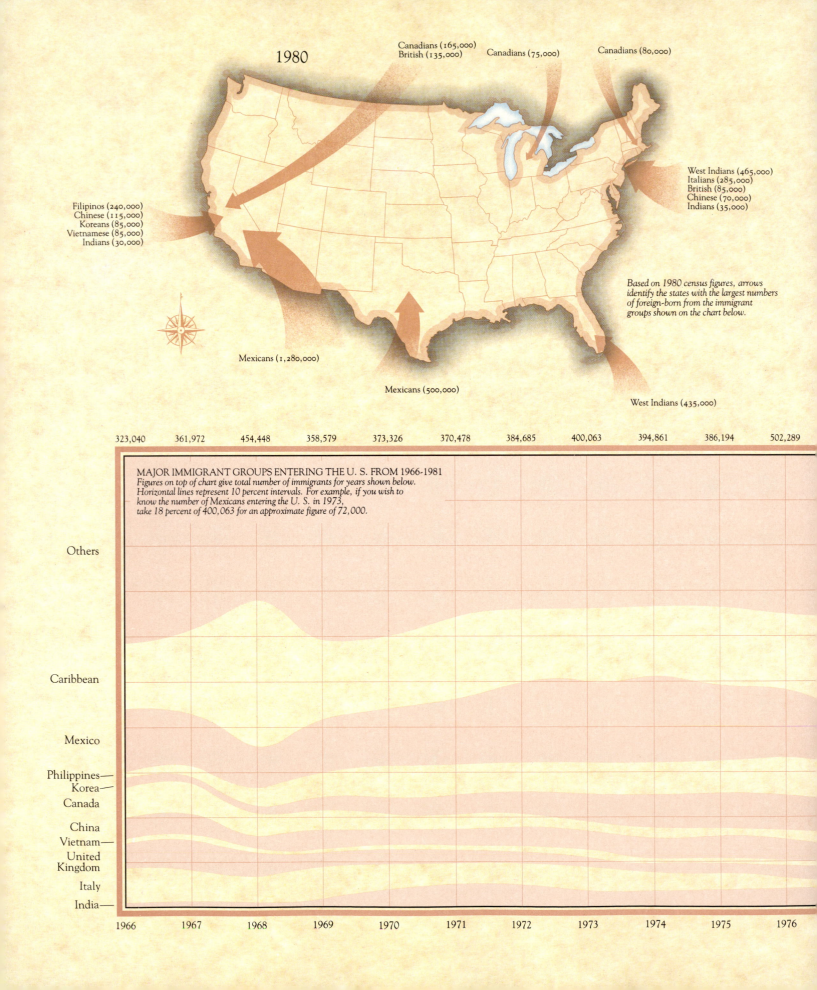

1980

Canadians (165,000)
British (135,000)

Canadians (75,000)

Canadians (80,000)

West Indians (465,000)
Italians (285,000)
British (85,000)
Chinese (70,000)
Indians (35,000)

Filipinos (240,000)
Chinese (115,000)
Koreans (85,000)
Vietnamese (85,000)
Indians (30,000)

Based on 1980 census figures, arrows
identify the states with the largest numbers
of foreign-born from the immigrant
groups shown on the chart below.

Mexicans (1,280,000)

Mexicans (500,000)

West Indians (435,000)

| 323,040 | 361,972 | 454,448 | 358,579 | 373,326 | 370,478 | 384,685 | 400,063 | 394,861 | 386,194 | 502,289 |

MAJOR IMMIGRANT GROUPS ENTERING THE U. S. FROM 1966-1981
Figures on top of chart give total number of immigrants for years shown below.
Horizontal lines represent 10 percent intervals. For example, if you wish to
know the number of Mexicans entering the U. S. in 1973,
take 18 percent of 400,063 for an approximate figure of 72,000.

Others

Caribbean

Mexico

Philippines
Korea
Canada

China
Vietnam
United
Kingdom
Italy
India

| 1966 | 1967 | 1968 | 1969 | 1970 | 1971 | 1972 | 1973 | 1974 | 1975 | 1976 |

Many-channeled Stream

The year 1965 brought major changes in immigration policy. The old quota system came to an end. The new legislation set up new "preference categories." These favored family ties and the skills an individual immigrant might offer in a high-technology economy. Although the new policy incurred criticism for promoting a "brain drain" of talent from other societies, it offered opportunity to some who lacked it in their own countries.

As the chart indicates, of earlier major lands of origin, only Mexico, Britain, Canada, and Italy remain among the top ten. And they show only as narrow ribbons except for Mexico—which now contributes more immigrants than any other single country. The wide band that delineates Caribbean immigration includes a score of small island nations. About 35 percent of all immigrants now come from the lands grouped as "other."

From 1931 through 1960, more than half of all arrivals came from Europe. In 1980, 44 percent came from Asia and 29 percent from Latin America; Europeans made up less than 14 percent. In 1910, fifty states and empires figured on the world scene; in 1980, immigrants came from 194 nations. Now the stream of immigration has split into many strands. These include more than fifty African nations, with 2 persons each from Djibouti and Gabon in 1980, 6 from Chad, 7 from Rwanda, 2,833 from Egypt. Tiny island nations in the Pacific also contribute a share.

In the 1980 census, the largest numbers of foreign-born from the ten major groups show up on the coasts, as the map suggests. West Indians, mainly Cubans, concentrate in Florida. The wide arrow indicates Mexicans in California, a third of its foreign-born residents. A fourth of all the foreign-born —and a third of all Asian-born—appear in California. Some 14 percent of the population of Hawaii, a state since 1959, are foreign-born; a meager 4 percent in Alaska, admitted to the Union in the same year.

With the 1965 law, Western Hemisphere nations were no longer exempted from numerical ceilings. This change has certainly affected the controversial issue of illegal immigration. Some "illegals" are students or visitors from far-off lands who have overstayed their visas, but about half are Mexicans who have entered without formalities. Daily tens of thousands of Mexicans legally commute to work in the U.S. But the scale of the illegal problem is massive and of long standing. More than a million Mexicans without papers were rounded up in Operation Wetback in the summer of 1954. No one has accurate current figures. Sober estimates of all illegal residents range from three to six million, with perhaps half a million entering each year.

The problem of refugees has also increased in scale. The 1965 law's preference category for refugees soon became inadequate in the wake of the Vietnam War, with turmoil elsewhere in Southeast Asia, Latin America, Afghanistan, and Iran. Special provisions had to be made. In 1978 Vietnamese immigration reached a peak of nearly 90,000, some of these the desperate "boat people." In 1980 legal refugees pushed the total of those granted admission above 808,000. (INS includes refugees in its total for the year they become legal residents—which is not necessarily the year of arrival.) Actual entries in 1980 were the highest since 1924. The numbers of these refugees and the disparities of cultural background—as in the case of Hmong tribesmen from Laos—lead thoughtful citizens to wonder if "the cultural fabric will stretch as it has before, or finally be torn."

The plight of refugees raises poignant questions. "Even though America's upraised torch of liberty is the noblest part of its role in the world," as one writer has observed, "the U.S. cannot provide a new home for all the oppressed. To whom, then, should it offer shelter?"

462,315   601,442   460,348   530,639   596,600

1977   1978   1979   1980   1981

in America must come from a man's own power of will and deed," declared the 19th-century German immigrant John Roebling, a famous bridge-builder. "Otherwise he is not suited for America."

In this sense, as the historian Marcus Lee Hansen pointed out, the immigrants were Americans before they arrived. And in another sense, they have always been the truest Americans, for their nationality was theirs by choice and not by birthright. Such was the decision of the first citizens, those rebellious subjects of King George III. The King's ministers recognized that newcomers in America might increase the threat to the old order—and in 1773 tried to make naturalization more difficult. Among the grievances charged to the King in the Declaration of Independence is this: "He has endeavoured to prevent the population of these States; for that Purpose obstructing the Laws of Naturalization of Foreigners; refusing to pass others to encourage their migration hither, and raising the conditions of new Appropriations of Lands."

Perhaps these words measure the passions of their time and not a commitment to unrestricted immigration. The chilly waters that grew "black with unexpected tea" had also lapped Plymouth Rock when the Pilgrims came ashore with visions of a God-given preserve in the New World. A few years later, the Puritan newcomers required strangers to obtain permission before settling in their model community, a "city that is set on an hill." "No Trespassing" was the Bay Colony's message to other sects, including that "cursed set of hereticks lately risen up in the world," the Quakers. Those upstarts, on the other hand, welcomed all comers when they established Pennsylvania in 1681. Immigration policy as controversy easily became a homegrown tradition.

Nevertheless, the framework of nationhood was erected in a mood of confidence, and the "Welcome" sign was hung out. The Constitution gave Congress the power to establish "an uniform Rule of Naturalization." When the authors of that document were debating it, phrase by phrase, some argued that only the native-born should serve in Congress. George Mason was unwilling to bar the foreign-born from the Senate because many "had acquired great merit during the Revolution." Benjamin Franklin agreed with him. But no one expected that a grasp of American affairs comes easily. A shoemaker would need seven years to learn his craft, said Gouverneur Morris: "fourteen at least are necessary to learn to be an American legislator. . . ." The compromise: seven years of citizenship for a Representative, nine for a Senator. And, with no debate at all, the one great distinction: A President of the United States must be native-born.

"Men love power," said Alexander Hamilton (born in the West Indies). "Give all power to the many, they will oppress the few. Give all power to the few, they will oppress the many." The Constitution—adopted by the votes of a majority—included provisions to defend the states against the Union, small states against large. The Bill of Rights—added at the insistence of a minority—enshrined "otherness." The customs and creeds of the majority had the inherent strength of a mainstream current. Any unpopular minority might need protection. After all, the rebellious colonists had themselves been a minority within the British realm. Or, occasionally, they had been a minority within a minority. Paul Revere's father had changed the family name from Rivoire, because, according to tradition, he thought "the bumpkins should pronounce it easier." As President Franklin Delano (originally De la Noye) Roosevelt reminded the Daughters of the American Revolution, "Remember, remember always that all of us, and you and I especially, are descended from immigrants and revolutionists."

Even so, many have argued that the lessons illuminated by memory no longer serve a changed reality. Others have tried to look forward as well as backward—to test the limits of their own imaginations as well

FOTOS DE
NINOS Y GRUPOS
EN 1 MINUTO

Prevalence of Spanish attests the growing numbers and power of Mexican-Americans in Los Angeles. At a fast-photo studio, doting parents wait to have their children's pictures taken. Family-oriented Hispanics have a birthrate more than twice that of "Anglo" women— a trend that would help make them the majority in the city by A.D. 2000. For many, bilingual signs (opposite, upper) don't go far enough. They want their children educated in both English and Spanish to bring them the best of both cultures. A newsstand displays two of the Spanish dailies published locally.

as the continuing relevance of America's first principles. "Self-evident" truths are not universally evident, and may have a broad or narrow meaning: ". . . that all men are created equal. . . ." The imaginations of the new republic did not assign equal status to women, or blacks, or Native Americans.

Article I of the Bill of Rights begins: "Congress shall make no law respecting an establishment of religion, or prohibiting the free exercise thereof. . . ." The Founding Fathers could imagine the silence of the Quaker meeting as well as the stately prose of the Anglican service, the rabbi's fringed prayer shawl as well as the minister's gown. The vestments of the Catholic priest might suggest a tradition of tolerance in Maryland—or a hostile power in Quebec. But what would the Founders have thought of some of America's religious figures today? Could they accept a Buddhist monk who wears saffron robes or a Rastafarian who wears dreadlocks, the crimson-garbed followers of a Bhagwan in Oregon who boasts of 90 Rolls-Royces, the Reverend Sun Myung Moon or a 13-year-old Perfect Master? If they approved of formalized prayer in a public school, what would they say to a devout Muslim student, required by his faith to prostrate himself toward Mecca in prayer?

In the 1850s, even as ardent a supporter of immigration as the philosopher Ralph Waldo Emerson rejoiced that most newcomers were "the fair-haired, the blue-eyed." He had trouble imagining an America peopled by "the Europe of Europe," the swarthy "new" immigrants who came later. Could they, or the Chinese, become equal in citizenship? What would Emerson make of the Hmong tribal folk from the hills of Laos and Vietnam, who traditionally defined the world as the distance a man could walk from his own village? There have always been failures and triumphs of imagination; and so it is today.

In general, the Republic's founding principles have proven far more elastic than rigid on the subject of immigration. Of course, national self-interest has supported the historical welcome given to most newcomers. The taming of a vast wilderness and its peopling, the building of industry—all have been made possible by immigrant muscle and intellect. But even the America of today is, despite its restrictive laws, remarkably receptive to strangers. Canada and Australia, considering the size of their populations, take in a larger percentage of aliens; the United States receives a much larger number. Which should be called more generous is debatable.

Australia, for instance, a spacious and democratic land, has traditionally needed settlers. Until recently its 20th-century immigration policies have been highly selective. Its goal of a "White Australia" was aided, as of 1901, by a "dictation test" for unwelcome new arrivals. Though these were usually Asians, the test was given in a European language of an official's choosing. In 1973, Australia formally disavowed its preference for Europeans. Its ethnic character, overwhelmingly British, has not yet changed dramatically. But in 1974 roughly one in nine of its immigrants came from Asia; ten years later, one in three.

Crowded, prosperous lands in western Europe have favored different policies. There thousands of "guest workers"—from southern and eastern Europe, Africa, Asia—answer a pressing demand for labor. Their presence is seen as a temporary expedient and they can remain for years as sojourners on the fringes of society. France encourages its North African "guests" to return home eventually; Switzerland requires alien workers to go home at least once a year. Wariness or dislike of foreigners is hardly peculiar to the industrialized world or to our times.

America, however, has welcomed a wide array of outsiders—and made their peaceful coexistence a national goal. An incredible task: One study discussed 106 ethnic groups (and 173 distinct American Indian groups) as of the 1970s. By any historical comparison—and the

Fiesta of Cinco de Mayo: Diminutive folk dancers in colorful costumes entertain visitors to Olvera Street in Los Angeles at the Fifth of May celebrations. The festivities commemorate a victory in 1862 over French troops on Mexican soil. Merchants sponsor performances and craft shows that not only draw customers to shops and restaurants but also fortify the sense of community among Mexican-Americans. Dressed up for the occasion, a youngster begins to learn the history of his people. "It is important to imbue our children with a pride in their heritage. Our strength as a people comes from a knowledge of our past," declares Adán Medrano, a spokesman for the Hispanic

Telecommunications Network. A puppet show teaches its young audience about the Day of the Dead, November 2—All Souls' Day in other traditions. In Mexico, families observe this as a religious holiday marked by scoffing at death as well as by honoring and praying for one's ancestors. Hispanics have no desire to lose their ethnic identity. "Retaining our language and culture does not conflict with our being good Americans," says Medrano.

Roman Empire may be the only example available—it would seem a reckless, outlandish proposition merely to test such an explosive mix.

Yet America's peculiar genius consists in making the outlandish commonplace. This is the definition of the phrase "Only in America." Unlikely juxtapositions hardly raise an eyebrow. Near the Capitol in Washington, descendants of Virginia's First Families wheel their polo ponies. In the adjacent playing field, West Indians in immaculate white spend the afternoon at cricket. Next to them are softball players whose native language is Spanish (which holds true for dozens of major-league baseball players). A large contingent of Vietnamese picnickers divides its attention among the games. The scene is as American as apple pie (from Elizabethan England), as natural as hot dogs (from Germany) on the Fourth of July, as plausible as the black customers buying kosher burritos from a Korean in a Los Angeles cafe. Only in America.

America is the land of incongruities, of adrenalin-pumping change, of reversals, of the second or third or tenth chance. A poor boy born in a log cabin grows up to lose a Senate race and win the Presidency and become world-famous as the Great Emancipator. A poor man wins a fortune and loses it and makes another. In a California court, an ex-convict presides as a respected judge. The dream—of a fresh start, of yet another try—is the same the world over. Yet nowhere is the

Protecting herself from dust and contamination by pesticides, a union field hand harvests lettuce in California's Salinas Valley. To the south in the Imperial Valley, watermelons go one by one into a truck. Until Cesar Chavez succeeded in organizing the farm workers in the 1960s, migrants, nearly all of them Mexican-Americans, earned wages far below the minimum standard. Many employers found—and still find—even cheaper labor by exploiting illegal aliens (called wetbacks because originally many waded across the Rio Grande) who would not dare to seek official help.

juxtaposition of reality and possibility more poignant than along the 1,950-mile border that separates the United States from Mexico. There the prosperity of the First World confronts the aspirations of the Third World. In some respects, Mexico's difficulties, like those of developing countries elsewhere, parallel those that created "America fever" in 19th-century Europe. The population soars; tiny plots of farmland no longer support families; scores of little villages are depopulated. In his dirt-poor mountainside *aldea,* said one 55-year-old former inhabitant, the only men left "are those that are older than me." But the overcrowded cities offer little hope to most, as 40 percent of Mexico's work force is underemployed or without a job.

Enterprising people cross the Rio Grande or the deserts to the west. Such workers can earn five or ten times as much in *El Norte* as in Mexico—if they can find work in Mexico. Among those who choose to leave their homeland each year are almost 65,000 legal immigrants, giving Mexico a greater share of America's total influx than any other country. In addition, about 100,000 Mexicans legally cross the border to work every day. Others, technically illegal, are tolerated by the authorities because they go home every night. A few cross the Rio Grande pickaback on the shoulders of the "Old Capitalist," a man well known to the Border Patrol at El Paso. He never leaves the water to step onto U.S. soil—and perhaps now and then he brings someone who means to stay. Estimating the number of illegal arrivals is difficult; it is said that 250,000 cross each year and stay for some time. The border is a torn net; but as one Mexican citizen explained, even if an electrified fence stretched from the Gulf of Mexico to the Pacific, people are so desperate in Mexico that they would manage to cross it anyway. They already find their way through reeking sewers. They may be guided across the desert by the stars, or by smugglers to whom they pay hundreds of dollars. They hide behind false panels in a van. At most, one in five is apprehended at the border. One Border Patrol agent compared his job to trying to bail the ocean with a bucket—and throwing each pailful back into the surf.

The issues surrounding "imported labor," legal or otherwise, are almost as old as the American republic—older, considering the slave trade. Whether or not such labor depresses wage scales, whether it means unemployment for the native-born—the questions have been answered differently at different times. Today the situation in the Southwest poses new questions, because Hispanic culture has marked the region since Santa Fe was founded in 1610 by colonists from Mexico. It remained Mexican until Texas won independence in 1836 and

Red gateway leads to a bit of Chinese-Americana, a mall in Los Angeles. For Chinese newcomers life in the U.S. often begins in the nation's Chinatowns, from which the America-born tend to move away. The immigration law of 1965 allowed thousands of Chinese from Hong Kong, Taiwan, and Indochina to join family members already in the U.S. Later Congress admitted people directly from the People's Republic of China. A travel advertisement in Chinatown's mall reflects a degree of affluence. In general, educated professionals have prospered; bias has slowed the progress of others.

Holding joss sticks and bell, a Vietnamese Buddhist high priest blesses a dragon boat

before a race on a lake in Los Angeles' Echo Park. Thousands of East Asians gather here in summer for the annual Lotus Festival.

the United States wrested away other great expanses in 1848. Today, Mexican-Americans are one-fourth of New Mexico's population, one-sixth of Texas', one-eighth of Arizona's and California's.

Across the Southwest there are flourishing Spanish-language newspapers, magazines, radio and TV stations. Their audiences are a boon to advertisers: Beer is *cerveza*, and "*es para usted*" equals "this one's for you." In San Antonio, the *norteño* music on the radio reveals cultural melding of a different sort. The lyrics are in Spanish, but the steady beat of accordion and guitar create a sort of Mexican country-western with a twang.

The border is a paradox: It separates, it joins, and as a cultural dividing line it all but disappears. The journalist and historian Carey McWilliams called the borderlands "a binational, bicultural, bilingual regional complex or entity. . . . Nothing quite like this zone of interlocking economic, social and cultural interests can be found along any other border of comparable length in the world."

"*Una nación indivisible*" pledge the schoolchildren in Brownsville, Texas, right on the border. But their classroom can symbolize a deeply divisive issue—bilingual education. For years, Mexican-American activists cited the language of instruction as one factor in their children's high dropout rate. (The rate for Spanish-speaking students is almost three times that of English-speakers.) In 1968, Congress concurred: The Bilingual Education Act provided money for new programs designed to let Hispanic-American children with limited proficiency in English use Spanish as necessary to proceed with their schoolwork.

Today the languages of these programs, about a hundred in all, range from Cantonese to Lithuanian, Armenian to Estonian; roughly half are Native American languages such as Tewa, Navajo, Blackfoot, and Inupiaq. But the programs for Spanish-speaking pupils draw the most attention because they affect about a million children. (The Hispanic population of about 15 million is the nation's second largest minority, after 26.5 million blacks.) Mexican-Americans, like other concerned groups, argue the educational merits. The symbolic aspect provokes more wide-ranging contention. To some Hispanic activists, bilingual education symbolizes pride in a traditional culture of the Southwest. But many other Americans would agree with the comment that "It sounds like a threat not to assimilate"—and they point to French-speaking Quebec for comparison.

"My nationality," wrote the Polish-born novelist Joseph Conrad, "is the language I write in." For Conrad, who became a naturalized

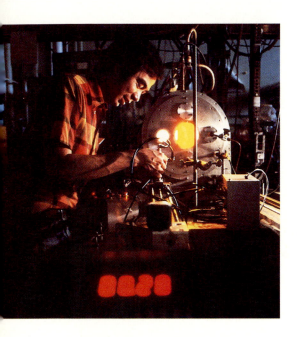

"*Most Asian youngsters have a great respect for learning. Their families place such a premium on education that they motivate their children to work very hard,*" says Jo-Ellen Tannenbaum (opposite, upper), who specializes in teaching English to immigrant elementary pupils in Takoma Park, Maryland. Experiments in chemistry challenge a class at New York City's highly selective Bronx High School of Science (opposite, lower), where Asian-Americans make up 20 percent of the student body. Philip Leung (above) from Hong Kong adjusts his apparatus for plasma physics research at the University of California, Los Angeles. He has earned his Ph.D. in physics, and has become a U.S. citizen.

British subject, that language was English. For many Americans over the years, language has been a powerful symbol of national unity, while different immigrant groups have had varied experiences with English. Those speaking a closely related tongue would have an advantage. Those boasting many highly educated individuals have, not surprisingly, tended to learn it quickly. Many of today's Asian immigrants are in the latter position—not least because of familiarity with English as an international language of science.

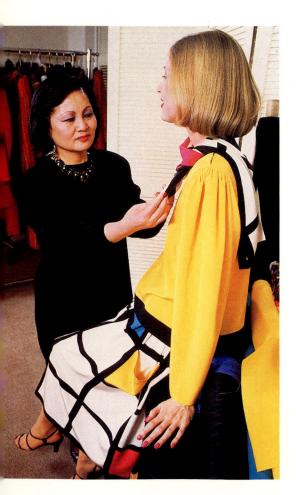

Moreover, those newcomers who expected to return to their homelands seldom bothered with trying to master the quirks of American custom, including language. Those who fled persecution and expected to stay have usually adapted more quickly and more completely. A family from Vietnam, reunited in Washington, D. C., offers a stunning example. They arrived in 1980, penniless, exhausted, heartbroken, and bewildered by the English language. Five years later, the four oldest of twelve children had earned engineering degrees and were holding jobs with large companies; three more were in college studying engineering (on full scholarships) and another was majoring in computer science; a ninth, studying and working, was planning to go into business for himself; the three youngest were in public schools.

As one survivor of Kampuchea's death camps explained, "I have to be an American now." Since 1980, the law has followed the United Nations' definition of a refugee: "any person unable or unwilling" to return to his or her homeland "because of persecution or a well-founded fear of persecution on account of race, religion, nationality, membership in a particular social group, or political opinion." The Refugee Act also established an annual limit of 50,000 admissions, but gave the President power to admit more when he thought it "justified by grave humanitarian concerns or in the national interest."

In the past, refugees from Communist countries could reasonably expect to find a haven. Under the new law everyone living in a dictatorship became a candidate. Thousands of Salvadorans, escaping carnage in their homeland, have claimed a "well-founded fear of persecution." Guatemalans have sought safety here. Haitians fleeing the hemisphere's poorest nation—and one frequently described as highly oppressive—have often applied for refugee status as well. Many have been refused. An Afghan may be accepted, an Ethiopian denied.

Whatever the preferences of the law or the decisions of officials, one immigrant describes Americans as "one vast rescue committee for the rest of the world." The ideal of "asylum" expounded by the

Founding Fathers finds expression in the efforts of relief organizations, civic groups, religious bodies, and countless private citizens. In 1975 the State of Iowa began a resettlement program that one spokesman compares to an adoption service for refugee adults, and Idaho quickly followed suit. At the opposite extreme of legality, churches across the country follow medieval precedent in offering sanctuary—sheltering illegal aliens from Central America. Some of the movement's leaders compare their campaign to the civil-rights agitation of the 1960s and the Underground Railroad of the 1850s.

There is, of course, another side to the story, as there always has been. Vietnamese refugees encountered a nasty antagonism along parts of the Gulf coast when their industrious work—and their ignorance of local ways—angered American fishermen and shrimpers. Before tensions eased, the signs had begun to appear: No Vietnamese Wanted.

They recall other signs: No Colored. . . . No Irish Wanted . . . No Jews Need Apply. Though most immigrants now come not from Europe but from Latin America or Asia, Americans' attitudes have changed little. The open hand and the clenched fist are equally characteristic.

To make a success of their supermarket in Falls Church, Virginia, Hoc Tran and his wife, Kim Dung, refugees from Vietnam, work every day of the year. A former diplomat with a master's degree in political science, Hoc has the hard-driving determination typical of many who fled. Often individuals hold two jobs, pooling family savings to start a business. For the talented and ambitious, like Korean-born designer Soo Yung Lee (opposite), America remains the land of opportunity.

In many ways, the motives for immigration have also changed but little. For most newcomers, the goal is still economic; for many others, it is political or religious freedom. "In Poland, we had surrealism for every day," explains a filmmaker in New York. In the opinion of a Salvadoran, "People aren't leaving with dreams of money, they're leaving the country because they're fearing for their lives."

For the "boat people" from Southeast Asia or Haiti, or the "feet people" from Mexico and Central America, the passage is often as harrowing as it ever was in the coffin ships of the Irish famine. Possibly half of the Vietnamese did not survive the sea voyage to neighboring lands. One who did recalled that starvation and thirst claimed so many that "there was no need for enemies"—but the boats encountered murderous pirates. Others encounter the old-style human parasites in newfangled guises. These are the *coyotes* and *polleros*—professional smugglers of people—who sometimes rob and rape and then abandon their hapless customers; the officials along the way who extort exorbitant *mordidas*, or bribes; the airline ticket agent in San Diego who double-charged one frightened illegal alien.

And the Man at the Gate is still there, riding a helicopter or a horse or a Coast Guard cutter. On the Mexican border, he ferrets out the ineligible with starlight-powered goggles as fearsome as the eyelid-flipping buttonhooks of Ellis Island. Off the Florida coast his radar scans the horizon for a leaky little sailing vessel. Its occupants may have prayed to Simbi—Haitian counterpart of St. Raphael—for a safe voyage; and at sight of the cutter on the horizon they might call upon a *lwa*, a powerful spirit, to bring fog and mist to hide them.

"We thought by coming here / We would be in paradise . . . ," goes a Haitian song of America. "It's only and simply / A daily battle for survival." As cane-cutters in Florida or melon-pickers in Maryland,

For Tet, the Vietnamese lunar New Year, a girl in Biloxi, Mississippi, appears in her holiday best. Drawn by the warm climate and jobs in the seafood processing plants, several thousand Vietnamese have made a home for themselves along the Gulf coast from Florida to Texas. Many of them, fishermen by trade, scraped together their savings to buy or build boats to bring in their own catches of shrimp. A bumper sticker reflects the hard feelings that developed as refugees competed with locals in the heavily fished waters. Newcomers' ignorance of fishing rules and customs made the problem worse, but tensions diminished as refugee agencies and officials worked to clear up misunderstandings. In some places along the coast, local fishermen have left shrimping to the Vietnamese, who over time have earned respect for their diligence and honesty.

Desperate Haitians reach Florida shores after risking a 600-mile voyage, only to be caught

Haitian and other migrant workers often labor under conditions close to peonage. Hispanic or Asian, job-hungry newcomers meet exploitation in the garment industry—a California investigation, in its first six months, found "violations of the labor laws and the rights of workers in 96 percent of the shops." Still, immigrants expect to work long, hard hours. A university graduate from the Soviet Union, with a white-collar job, was amazed that his office "empties at five o'clock"—American colleagues were going home, spurning generous overtime pay.

Despite their usually poor wages, the newcomers scrimp and save for their families back home. As Leonel Castillo, a former director of INS, has explained, a poor Mexican family will send its brightest, strongest, most promising child to the United States: "He doesn't speak a word of English . . . but he's gonna save that family. A lot rides on that kid who's a busboy in some hotel." El Salvador has its "Washington houses," homes built with money sent from the District of Columbia. In America—in a Koreatown, a Little Havana, a Little Odessa—the newcomers save for their own dreams also: for a washing machine or a college education, a new business or an old car, the car that takes a breadwinner to a better job or a teenager on that first thrilling drive. Says Castillo: "Every new group comes in believing more firmly in the American Dream than the one that came a few years before. Every new group is scared of being in the welfare line or the unemployment office. They go to night school, they learn about America. We'd be lost without them."

Their successes, large and small, help to perpetuate the ideal of a fluid, mobile, bountiful society. Of course, the United States is not the only land of possibility. In a strictly material sense, industrialization elsewhere, along with the export of U.S. goods and culture, has "Americanized" much of the world, even Communist states. Young Muscovites long for black-market Levi's; Cubans read American magazines and tune in Bob Dylan or major-league baseball games. About a third of Central America's TV programs come from the U.S.A.

All this has helped to ease many immigrants' transition into American life. To Soviet newcomers, America might seem "another planet." Nevertheless, as one systems analyst explained, the Russians had copied their computer software from the States, so he already knew the necessary languages. American-owned companies in developing nations have let thousands of women master less-skilled jobs. The Korean immigrant who has spent years sewing pajamas in a factory in Seoul understands her work on her first job in Los Angeles.

Immigration—its numbers and sources—has probably not changed more than the world itself has. The jumbo jet that whisks the Korean from Seoul to California in hours has shrunk the world; so have

Art enhances a sign in Miami, where some 40,000 Creole-speaking Haitians live. Over the last 20 years about half a million Haitians have come to the U.S.—many of them paying smugglers exorbitant fees to board overcrowded, decrepit boats. The flood of illegal immigration reached a peak in 1980; it declined after Haiti agreed to let the U.S. Coast Guard intercept Haitian vessels. Some of these refugees still manage to slip through—providing cheap labor, working for almost anything on jobs Americans won't do.

the satellite-linked phone systems that allow the traveler to call home with news of a safe arrival. But in a shrinking world, political dissidents from any number of countries may live in fear of government agents who have also crossed the ocean. Some things know no borders: The threat of nuclear annihilation equalizes humanity in a single nightmare vision. As the pace of technical change accelerates, all of the planet's residents become immigrants of time, whirled ever faster into the unknown land of the future.

As the world grows smaller, its nations grow more interconnected. America's policies have a more pronounced effect on other lands. Its special laws permit temporary residence for unskilled hands in agriculture—guest workers of a sort. Immigration laws, however, state a preference for the highly skilled and well educated, and this may be to America's advantage. It may help the foreign professional leave a place like the Philippines; there, one immigrant physician remarked, "the people are so poor that they can't support all these professionals." Nonetheless, it contributes to a "brain drain" of talent and skills from other countries.

Once America's manufacturers could choose between native-born or immigrant workers; today they can also decide to take their jobs abroad, to places where wages are low and unions weak. But if job prospects narrow at home, resentment may focus on the aliens in the country, especially the illegals, as strangers and scapegoats.

While the Third World population doubles every thirty years, and the work force far outruns the available jobs, America remains for many the ideal—in distant continents, the standard of the good life; in nearby lands, the accessible refuge. Some experts believe that immigration policy cannot be successful without adjustments of foreign policy, and argue that America must offer massive aid for economic development in other countries. Some insist that American diplomacy must do its utmost to make life more tolerable in lands ruled by oppression.

"The best thing that I love this country for," says an illegal refugee, "is that you have the right to speak out against injustice, and I love that; and I ask myself why we cannot have a country like that. I want to take this back to my country."

A plurality of questions, a multitude of conflicting answers: Debate comes naturally to America, especially on a subject as important as immigration. The historian Oscar Handlin wrote: "Once I thought to write a history of the immigrants in America. Then I discovered that the immigrants *were* American history." If history repeats itself—as it has in the experience of the immigrants and the attitudes of the

native-born—it also inspires new assessments. And Americans have discovered a new value in ethnicity itself—a strong pulse, a life force. The old concept of the melting pot has lost its standing as an ideal.

An immigrant once defined the symbolism of the cauldron with ironic wit: "This is my pot—now you do the melting." The appearance of "unmeltable ethnics" in the late 1960s followed the rise of black awareness and pride in the early 1960s. Today, ethnicity can mean many different things: the focus of a life, or merely the sweet memory of a half-forgotten lullaby that a grandmother sang.

Thus it no longer seems necessary—or even possible—to single out "immigrant contributions" like so many staples or spices in a recipe. All of America's "contributors" have been immigrants or their descendants since Siberian hunters wandered into the Western Hemisphere. Some have been famous, many forgotten. But historian Philip Taylor found the deepest fascination in sketches and photographs of immigrants whose names went unrecorded: "Now and again from the faceless crowd, there emerge . . . features more striking, more noble even, than

At a high school soccer match in Miami, Florida, a predominantly Cuban team scores a goal. Some 810,000 refugees have reached the U.S. since Fidel Castro came to power in 1959. The majority settled in Miami, where nearly 20,000 Cuban-owned businesses—banks, stores, restaurants, Spanish-language television and radio stations and daily newspapers— have created a Little Havana. Those who came in the initial exodus included many college-educated professionals who spoke English and adjusted quickly to life in the U.S., but people from all walks of life have fled Castro's revolution. At first the Cubans considered themselves temporary exiles, and they expected to return to their homeland after the overthrow of the Communist regime. Only in the 1970s did large numbers of Cubans decide to make this country their home and begin applying for citizenship.

those of the generals and the prelates, the politicians and the magnates, of whom most history is told."

Patriots of such undaunted character sustained the Revolution. They gave substance and life to the idea of human equality. And the success of that unlikely contest—a coalition of rebels against the greatest empire of its time—suggested that anyone could become not only American, but equally American.

Becoming American has never been instantaneous or easy. It has always been characterized by imperfection, ragged edges, asymmetry, tension, imbalance. It has also bespoken a national willingness to make and admit mistakes, change course or start afresh. Some have argued with passion that open immigration was a mistake. And the Founders might have agreed, had they been able to see into the future.

On the other hand, they might simply have smiled and repeated the words that drew 13 British colonies together into something unique: *E Pluribus Unum*—Out of Many, One—a whole unimaginably greater than its parts.

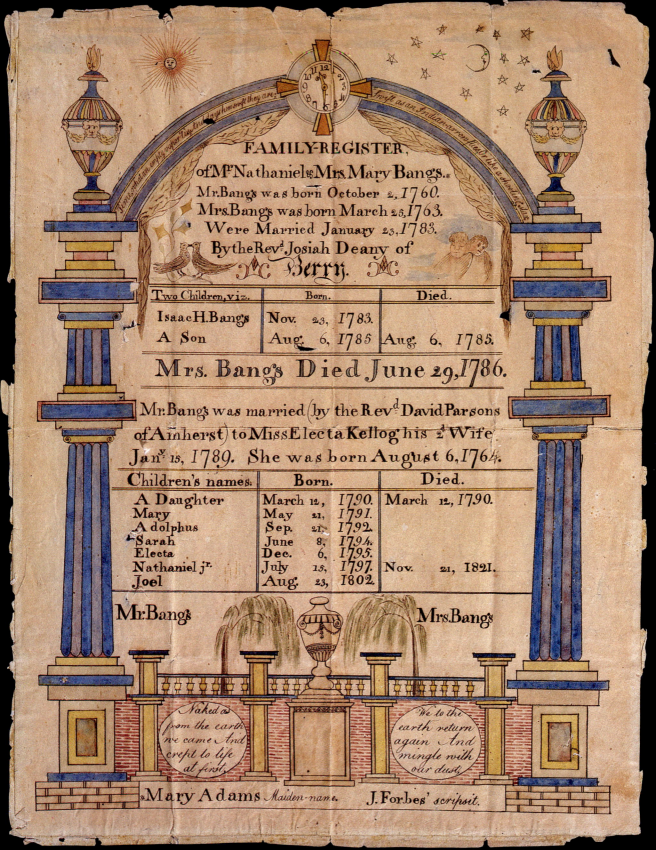

FAMILY-REGISTER,

of Mr Nathaniel & Mrs Mary Bangs.*

Mr. Bangs was born October 2, 1760.

Mrs. Bangs was born March 26, 1763.

Were Married January 23, 1783.

By the Revd Josiah Deany of

Berry.

Two Children, viz.	Born.	Died.
Isaac H. Bangs	Nov. 23, 1783.	
A Son	Aug. 6, 1785	Aug. 6, 1785.

Mrs. Bangs Died June 29, 1786.

Mr. Bangs was married (by the Revd David Parsons

of Amherst) to Miss Electa Kellog his 2d Wife

Jany 15, 1789. She was born August 6, 1764.

Children's names.	Born.		Died.
A Daughter	March 12,	1790.	March 12, 1790.
Mary	May 21,	1791.	
Adolphus	Sep. 21,	1792.	
Sarah	June 8,	1794.	
Electa	Dec. 6,	1795.	
Nathaniel jr.	July 15,	1797.	Nov. 21, 1821.
Joel	Aug. 23,	1802.	

Mr. Bangs   Mrs. Bangs

Naked as from the earth we came And crept to life at first.

We to the earth return again And mingle with our dust.

* Mary Adams *Maiden-name.*   J. Forbes' *scripsit.*

Afterword: Tracing the Family

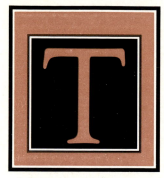

National Archives files contain this meticulously embellished "Family-Register," submitted to the government by Revolutionary War veteran Nathaniel Bangs with his pension application.

hree stories above the Declaration of Independence and the Constitution, in Room 400 of the National Archives in Washington, 57 people sit before large machines, cranking rolls of microfilm and peering at little bits of history that pour across the screens. A woman finds her grandfather's name written in the elegant hand of a Philadelphia census taker in 1900. Two members of the youngest generation crawl about their mother's legs as she scrolls the passenger list of a ship that carried immigrants to Ellis Island.

At a desk near the door, an Archives worker welcomes a newcomer to his first day as an ancestor hunter. She glances at his notebook and says, "You'll need quite a few 1860s." She begins patiently explaining the mysteries of the microfilmed 1860 census records and sends him off to one of the 93 machines. He has just joined the 40 million Americans who are doing their own genealogical research.

The National Archives, which calls itself the nation's memory, is a treasury of American genealogy. The records, brimming with names, form a collage of America's immigration history. Brighton, New York, 1900: Here is Catherine Daly, of Irish stock. When the census taker counted her, she was working as a "kitchen girl"; she was 19 years old; she could read and write. All of this is one line on a census page. Nicolas P. Sinnis, an 11-year-old Greek schoolboy, left Europe on the S.S. *St. Louis* on March 9, 1907, and arrived in New York on March 17. With $15 in his pocket, he headed for Springfield, Ohio, to join his father. Nicolas stood 4 feet 10 inches tall, was in good health, and had black hair and gray eyes. All of this is on one page of a passenger list.

The Archives also reveal the anonymous struggles of some Americans. Slave ship manifests, bearing no names, yield little information for black genealogists. But files of the Freedmen's Bureau, established to help ex-slaves after the Civil War, mark an end to anonymity. The Bureau's marriage register, for instance, helps in the search for black ancestors. A typical record: 34-year-old Richard Downing and 23-year-old Melinda Holmes, both former slaves in Vicksburg, Mississippi, were married on August 4, 1864. Americans of Indian descent find sparse genealogical records. Not until 1885 did the Bureau of Indian Affairs order its agents to send in annual census lists. These censuses continued until 1940, but often left out whole tribes.

Few of the 40 million Americans seeking their roots begin at the National Archives. The best sources for family history are the memories of older relatives, local offices of vital records, and public libraries. (For some ideas on how you can search for your past, see the next two pages.)

GENEALOGICAL RESEARCH starts at home. Ask your elders about their childhood; you may get the names of relatives you never knew. Births, marriages, and deaths may have been recorded in a mislaid family Bible. An old desk may yield a 19th-century deed, a military discharge, a packet of letters. Soon your search becomes a marathon through time: The going gets harder the farther you go. You'll need what genealogists call a pedigree chart. An example of a standard type appears below.

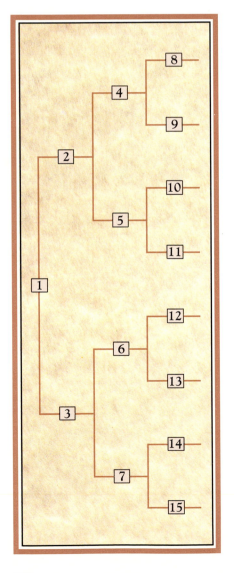

Each relative gets a code number, beginning with *1* for you, as the person compiling the genealogy. Your father's number is *2*, your mother's *3*, and so on through the generations, with males assigned even numbers and females odd numbers. (So 6 and 7 are your grandparents on your mother's side.) Make individual records on each family member and on each family group. The code numbers will help you sort out your findings.

Your records can fill rapidly with names and vital statistics. And family trees sprout more and more branches as you cultivate your past. If, for example, you continue your chart to your great-great-grandparents' generation, you will go well back into the 19th century and you will be seeking information on 30 relatives—assuming that none of them married cousins—and on *their* relatives.

The four keys to your family's past are *names*, *dates*, *places*, and *relationships*. Record every date of birth, death, marriage, and divorce. Track down real estate transactions and records of military service—solid information to augment what you get from sometimes hazy memories.

Don't forget old photographs, especially the backs, where you might find the name of a studio still in business or a cryptic *Aunt Dorothy, Atlantic City, 1932*. That will tell you Aunt Dorothy was alive in 1932, and the reference to Atlantic City may jog somebody's memory. Local historical societies may help you identify clues in a picture.

You may have to send for copies of lost birth, marriage, and death certificates. In most states, county offices keep such records. Your search may also take you to local courthouses for such documents as wills, deeds, mort-gages, and records of divorces, adoptions, the appointment of guardians, and legal changes of name. These are invaluable for the years before certificates became standard.

Public libraries often have genealogical sections. You can look up names and addresses in old telephone books or city directories. An obituary in an old newspaper may list survivors and pallbearers. Names from cemetery records and gravestones may also produce clues for solving your mystery story.

The National Archives cannot help you unless you have some information on which to build. To tap the Archives' census, military, immigration, and land records, you will need more than a name. If you, for example, believe an ancestor homesteaded or otherwise acquired land from the federal government, you should know the approximate date of the transaction, the state in which it took place, and whether it was before or after 1908.

If your ancestors lived in the United States between 1790 and 1910, you may find their names on one of the decennial national censuses. (The 1910 is the latest available, because none is opened for research until 72 years after the census was taken.) Names can be hard to find, and misspellings are frequent. " 'Bobbie' in one census," an exasperated searcher says, "was 'Barbara' in the next. She was five years old in one census and listed as *eight* years old ten years later. And this in handwriting almost impossible to read!"

Records of naturalization are scattered in many institutions nationwide. Even if you know where and when an ancestor became a citizen, you may face a long search.

But if your ancestors came on a ship that docked at an East Coast or Gulf port, you may find their names—quite likely misspelled—on a ship passenger list at the Archives.

The Archives' military records begin with the Revolution and continue through the Spanish-American War. To see military records since then, you should follow rules set forth in *Getting Started: Beginning Your Genealogical Research in the National Archives,* available free from the National Archives and Record Administration (800 Pennsylvania Ave. N.W. Washington, D. C. 20408). The pamphlet guides you through the genealogical records, lists locations of Archives branches outside of Washington, and suggests federal publications for novice genealogists.

Other aids: *Guide to Genealogical Research in the National Archives* (available from Archives at the address above); *How to Trace Your Family Tree,* by the American Genealogical Research Institute Staff. Also: Gilbert H. Doane and James B. Bell, *Searching for Your Ancestors;* Charles L. Blockson, *Black Genealogy;* Val D. Greenwood, *The Researcher's Guide to American Genealogy;* Bill R. Linder, *How to Trace Your Family History;* Dan Rottenberg, *Finding Our Fathers: A Guidebook to Jewish Genealogy.*

You might also want to consult the *Harvard Encyclopedia of American Ethnic Groups,* edited by Stephan Thernstrom.

The National Genealogical Society (4527 17th St. North, Arlington, Va. 22207) offers tips and a free bibliography.

The Library of Congress (Washington, D. C. 20540) has some international material and a major collection of U.S. local history and genealogy. This includes many rare books, long out of print. The staff will respond to queries about specific areas or families that might be represented in their holdings. For example: "Do you have a history of Tipton County, Indiana?" "Is there a book on a family named Jordan?"

If you want the help of a professional genealogist, the National Archives suggests that you write the Board for Certification of Genealogists, P.O. Box 19165, Washington, D. C. 20036. You may especially want to use a professional for searching overseas. If you do go to an ancestral land, you will most likely need help deciphering foreign handwriting and understanding local record-keeping.

Knowing an ancestor's religious faith may lead you to appropriate records. Several Christian denominations have centralized their historic records. You can find out about these repositories from local church sources.

For information about American Jewish congregations, inquire at American Jewish Archives, 3101 Clifton Ave., Cincinnati, Ohio 45220, or American Jewish Historical Society, 2 Thornton Rd., Waltham, Mass. 02154; Yivo Institute for Jewish Research, 1048 Fifth Ave., New York, N.Y. 10028; Leo Baeck Institute, 129 East 73rd St., New York, N.Y. 10021. Victims and survivors of the Holocaust can be sought through Yad Vashem, P.O. Box 3477, Jerusalem, Israel; and International Tracing Service, 3548 Arolsen, Federal Republic of Germany.

Mormons, who believe that family life endures forever, have a profound religious interest in genealogy and will help non-Mormons search. The Church of Jesus Christ of Latter-day Saints maintains the largest genealogical library in the world. Deep within a mountain near Salt Lake City is a vault containing 1,450,000 rolls of microfilm. Mormon records contain more than 1.5 *billion* names. Included are church and synagogue records from many foreign countries and documents from about a thousand county courthouses. Write to the Genealogical Library of the Church at 50 East North Temple St., Salt Lake City, Utah 84150.

Genealogical Helper (Everton Publishers, Inc., P.O. Box 368, Logan, Utah 84321) advertises genealogical searches and alerts readers to people looking for members of the same family. The Daughters of the American Revolution Library (1776 D Street N.W., Washington, D. C. 20006-5392) has on microfilm many family genealogies, federal censuses from 1850 to 1900, and miscellany including copies of all DAR membership applications.

Check for your ancestors' membership in patriotic societies, professional groups, or ethnic organizations. And always be ready for surprises. A woman in a small New England town found that middle names on some birth certificates did not jibe with middle names on family baptismal records. She got the answer from an old town clerk: A mischievous midwife sometimes slipped the name of her grandchild into the registry when she reported births. "It was sort of her trademark," the clerk said.

We, the People

"T he bosom of America is open to receive not only the opulent and respectable stranger," declares a statement attributed to George Washington, "but the oppressed and persecuted of all nations and religions."

A haven since its very beginnings, America would in the century and a half after the Founding Fathers absorb an astonishing number of people within its expanding borders. Large, sparsely populated lands lay open elsewhere in those years—in Canada and Australia, Argentina and Brazil. But it was the United States that took in by far the greatest number of newcomers.

In Europe, political turmoil and socio-economic upheavals marked nations entering the industrial age. A basic cause of change was the unprecedented population explosion that stemmed from better health conditions. Aliens continue to enter the U.S. today—many for similar reasons.

The graph below tracks immigration in five-year intervals between 1820 and 1980. Its totals cannot be exact, because of variations in record-keeping. Still, official sources show that by 1981 a total of 50 million had come into the area now encompassed by the U.S.

How many stayed? In technical terms, what is the net total of immigration? No one is sure. The net total may well be the most significant figure of all; from it have come new citizens. But if the figures for those entering the U.S.

are imperfect, the figures for those leaving are worse—for early decades, almost nonexistent. Experts estimate that only one migrant left for every eight who entered during the 19th century. Between 1908 and 1924, a period that does offer some documentation, 3,574,974 people are known to have left—roughly, a third of the number that entered. By the 1880s, cheap steamship fares had made it possible for workers to think of America as a place of short-term employment.

Poles and Italians, in particular, were apt to come as temporary visitors, to earn enough money in America to establish themselves comfortably in the homeland. In the years 1899 to 1924, nearly four million Italians entered the U.S.—but more than two million departed. Some individuals

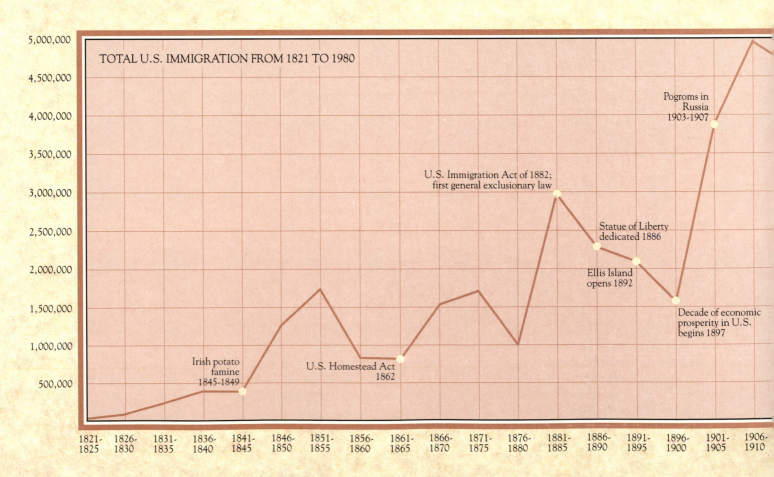

TOTAL U.S. IMMIGRATION FROM 1821 TO 1980

Irish potato famine 1845-1849

U.S. Homestead Act 1862

U.S. Immigration Act of 1882; first general exclusionary law

Statue of Liberty dedicated 1886

Ellis Island opens 1892

Pogroms in Russia 1903-1907

Decade of economic prosperity in U.S. begins 1897

1821-1825 · 1826-1830 · 1831-1835 · 1836-1840 · 1841-1845 · 1846-1850 · 1851-1855 · 1856-1860 · 1861-1865 · 1866-1870 · 1871-1875 · 1876-1880 · 1881-1885 · 1886-1890 · 1891-1895 · 1896-1900 · 1901-1905 · 1906-1910

undoubtedly traveled back and forth more than once. Moreover, Canadians and Mexicans had always moved freely across the borders.

Thus the sharp peaks and deep troughs on the graph indicate abrupt changes in gross immigration only. One-year intervals would give a more ragged profile—the all-time high of 1,285,349 in the fiscal year 1907 contributes to the spike for 1905-1909. In two other years of this period the tally topped 1,000,000. (That five-year peak of nearly 5,000,000, if it recorded net immigration, would shrink to about 3,300,000.)

Of events noted on the graph, two—the dedication of the Statue and the opening of Ellis Island—mark a time frame. Others affected immigration to some degree. Sharp dips indicate the falling numbers associated with the world wars, the Great Depression, and the quota laws of the 1920s. (In two brief intervals, 1918-19 and 1932-36, more people left the U.S. than entered it.) The rise in recorded immigration since 1965 is also apparent. It has helped to bring the ratio of the foreign-born in the current population to about 6 percent.

"Providence has been pleased to give this one connected country to one united people," proclaimed the *Federalist Papers* in 1787, "a people descended from the same ancestors, speaking the same language, professing the same religion, attached to the same principles of government, very similar in their manners and customs." In succeeding years this society based on similarities would become a heterogenous mixture, and yet it would retain its underlying bond of principles, goals, ideas of freedom.

Sometimes the native-born child of immigrants would ignore the parents' heritage. Then sons and daughters of the next generation in America would grow up eager to hear stories of the old country, to revive a holiday custom, to trace their ancestry or revisit a place of origin. "What the son wishes to forget, the grandson wishes to remember," notes one historian. Thus the cultural strands of individual and family are woven into a single fabric that forms the living richness of the nation.

The United States has accepted millions of people over the years, those who sought a better life, and those who fled oppression or natural disaster or pernicious combinations of both. At times fear has emerged among the citizens: that these immigrants may overwhelm the civilization they find, take jobs from those already here, diminish the wealth of the land, destroy the ideals on which the nation is founded.

Yet consistently the newcomers have accepted the discipline of citizenship. And, in one writer's summary, "the immigrant's grit and courage, and even his anxieties, impart productive energy" to America. Artists, inventors, unskilled workers, musicians, scholars, and artisans—all have made their contribution.

"A willingness of the heart"—in this phrase the perceptive novelist Scott Fitzgerald defined America. Perhaps the willingness is that of those already here to give newcomers a place, to accept their ideas and cultural contributions. Perhaps it is the willingness, too, of those courageous ones who came to stay—who struggled to succeed, to enrich and, finally, to belong to their adopted land.

World War I begins
August 1914

U.S. Immigration Act of 1921;
national-origin quotas begin

Great Depression
1929-1941

U.S. Immigration Act of 1965;
national-origin quotas end

World War I ends
November 1918

World War II ends
August 1945

| 1911- | 1916- | 1921- | 1926- | 1931- | 1936- | 1941- | 1946- | 1951- | 1956- | 1961- | 1966- | 1971- | 1976- |
| 1915 | 1920 | 1925 | 1930 | 1935 | 1940 | 1945 | 1950 | 1955 | 1960 | 1965 | 1970 | 1975 | 1980 |

Author's Note

Leslie Allen, a native of the District of Columbia, acquired unusual sensitivity to aspects of the immigrant experience by growing up abroad in a Foreign Service family. She spent a year of her childhood in Paris, and lived for nine years in South America. She attended the Chinese University of Hong Kong for a year, and traveled in Southeast Asia, before graduating from Bryn Mawr with honors in English in 1975. She worked as a free-lance writer before joining the staff of the National Geographic Society in 1978. As a member of the Special Publications Division, she visited Tierra del Fuego for *Secret Corners of the World*. She has described modern techniques of maritime preservation in *Preserving America's Past*, and traditional ways of the Chesapeake Bay watermen in *America's Hidden Corners*. For a chapter in *Exploring America's Scenic Highways*, she returned to New England—a region significant in her own family background. She now lives in Washington, D. C.

Illustrations Credits

Note: The following abbreviations are used in this list:
(t) Top, (b) Bottom, (l) Left, (r) Right
BA—The Bettmann Archive, Inc.
Brown—Brown Brothers
Culver—Culver Pictures, Inc.
LC—Library of Congress
MCNY—Museum of the City of New York
NA—National Archives
NGA—National Geographic Archives
NGP—National Geographic Photographer
NYHS—New-York Historical Society
NYPL—New York Public Library
SHSW—State Historical Society of Wisconsin
SI—Smithsonian Institution

Endpapers—Temple-Balch Center for Migration Research, Philadelphia

CHAPTER I
2, 3 Peter B. Kaplan. 5 Keystone/Mast Collection, University of California. 6, 7, 8 Peter B. Kaplan. 12, 13 International Ladies Garment Workers Union. 14 Peter B. Kaplan. 16 Library Company of Philadelphia. 17(t) LC. (b) Musée National de Blérancourt; Photo Agraci, Paris. 18, 19 Musée Bartholdi, Colmar; Comet's. (r) Union League Club, New York. 20, 21 Musée Bartholdi, Colmar. 22 Bibliothèque du Conservatoire National des Arts et Métiers, Paris; Comet's. 23 NYHS. 24 NYPL. 26(t) LC. (b) National Park Service, Statue of Liberty National Monument. 27 Musée Carnavalet, Paris; Giraudon/Art Resource. 28 Graduate School of Journalism, Columbia University; Victor R. Boswell, Jr., NGP. 29(t) NYHS. (b) Courtesy Joseph P. Pulitzer, Jr., St. Louis. 30 BA/BBC Hulton. 31 Peter Turnley/RAPHO. 33 BA. 34, 35 Collection of Andrew J. Spano. 36, 37 LC. 38 SHSW. 39(l) Museum of Modern Art/Film Stills Archive. (r) BA. 40, 41 Peter B. Kaplan.

CHAPTER II
42 NYHS. 46 Granger Collection. 47(t) BA. (b) BA/BBC Hulton. 48, 49 Bildarchiv Preussischer Kulturbesitz, Berlin. 50 Minnesota Historical Society. 51 NYHS. 52(b) Verlag Moos & Partner. 54 Statens Museum for Kunst, Copenhagen. 56, 57 From *Auswanderer*, by Hermann von Freeden and George Smolka, Leipzig. 58 Royal Danish Embassy, Washington, D. C. 59 Collection of E. Morgan Williams. 60, 61 Culver.

CHAPTER III
62 Birmingham Museum and Art Gallery, England. 64(t) Rhine Navigation Museum, 'Our Way To The Sea,' Basel. (b) Collection of Albert Hümmerich, Berlin. 66, 67 Museum für Hamburgische Geschichte. 69(t) Verlag Moos & Partner. (b) Peabody Museum of Salem. 70, 71 Chicago Historical Society. 71(t) BA. (b) From *Nach America!* by Friedrich Gerstäcker, Leipzig,

1855. 72, 73 Museum für Hamburgische Geschichte. 74 Fr. Dominik Lutz, Staffelstein, Upper Franconia. 75 Staatsarchiv, Hamburg. 76 NYPL. 77 LC. 78, 79 Metropolitan Museum of Art, New York. 80 Balch Institute for Ethnic Research. 81 Granger Collection. 82 Encyclopaedia Britannica, Inc. 83 BA. 84, 85 Collection of Business Americana, SI.

CHAPTER IV
86 LC. 90 SHSW. 91 Kansas State Historical Society. 92 Collection of Business Americana, SI. 93 Beinecke Rare Book and Manuscript Library, Yale University. 94, 95 SHSW. 96, 97 Collection of Business Americana, SI. 98, 99 Collection of James M. Bjerk. (b), 100, 101 Nebraska State Historical Society. 102, 103 Bishop Hill State Historic Site, Illinois. 104(t) Kansas State Historical Society. (b) NYPL. 105 BA. 106, 107 Kansas State Historical Society. 108 SHSW. 110 From The *People of Georgia*, by Mills Lane © 1975, The Beehive Press. 111, 112 Keystone/Mast Collection, University of California. 113 NYHS. 114 through 117 SHSW. 118 NYHS. 119(t) Sixty-Ninth Regiment Armory, New York. (b) LC. 120, 121 Cincinnati Historical Society. 123(t) Royal Danish Embassy, Washington, D. C. (b) Watertown Historical Society, Wisconsin. 124, 125 Milwaukee County Historical Society. 126 SHSW. 127 Margaret Woodbury Strong Museum, Rochester. 128, 129 Caroline B. Krane Collection, Western Michigan University.

CHAPTER V
130 MCNY. 132, 133 LC. 134 University of Washington Libraries. 135 Burlington Northern. 136, 137 University of Washington Libraries. 138, 139 NYHS. 140 National Maritime Museum, San Francisco. 141(t) Collection of Thomas W. Chinn. (b) California Historical Society, San Francisco. 142 Granger Collection. 144 Chinese Culture Center of San Francisco. 145 Bancroft Library, University of California. 146 Keystone/Mast Collection, University of California. 147 California Historical Society, San Francisco.

CHAPTER VI
148 Scala/Art Resource. 152, 153 LC. 156(t) Culver. (b) NGA. 158, 159 Brown. 160 NYPL. 162 through 165 NGA. 166 Keystone/Mast Collection, University of California. 167 Brown. 168(t) NGA. (b) Brown. 169 United Methodist Church. 170(t) Culver. (b) Brown. 171 BA. 172, 173 Brown. 174 NGA. 175 Brown. 177 Keystone/Mast Collection, University of California. 178 Dan Cornish. 180 through 183 Peter B. Kaplan.

CHAPTER VII
184 Granger Collection. 186 Culver. 187 BA. 189 Keystone/Mast Collection, University of California. 190, 191 NGA. 193(t) LC. (b) BA.

194 NYPL. 195 MCNY. 196, 197 NYPL. 198, 199 NYPL. (b) Chicago Historical Society. 201 MCNY. 202, 203 LC. 204 BA. 205(t) Collection of Business Americana, SI. (b) NYPL. 207 LC. 208 Collection of Business Americana, SI. 209 Balch Institute for Ethnic Research. 210, 211 YIVO Institute for Jewish Research. (r) American Jewish Historical Society. 212 MCNY. 213(l) Culver. (r) MCNY. 214 Museum of Modern Art/Film Stills Archive.

CHAPTER VIII
216 Collection of Lee Baxandall. 219 through 221 Keystone/Mast Collection, University of California. 222, 223 Culver. (r) NYPL. 224 LC. 225 NYPL. 226(t) LC. 226, 227 NA. 228 through 230, NYPL. 233 Henry Ford Museum, Greenfield Village. 234 Brown. 237 NGA. 238 LC. 239 Collection of Mary Ann Harrell. 240 Tamiment Collection, New York University. 241 Michigan Department of State Archives. 242 NGA. 243 American Museum in Britain, Bath. 244 NA. 245(t) Encyclopaedia Britannica, Inc. (b) NA. 246 MCNY. 247 Peabody Museum of Salem. 248 Culver. 249 Whitney Gallery of Art, New York. 250, 251 From The *People of Georgia*, by Mills Lane © 1975, The Beehive Press. 252 Dance Museum, Stockholm. 253 Reuters/Bettmann Newsphotos. 255 National Committee of Jewish Women. 256 *Seattle Post-Intelligencer*. 257 NA. 258 From *The Herblock Book*, 1952, Beacon Press. 259 UPI/Bettmann Newsphotos.

CHAPTER IX
260 Danny Lehman. 265 Courtesy of USAF. 266 through 269 Jodi Cobb, NGP. 270 William A. Allard. 271 Craig Aurness. 273 through 276 Jodi Cobb, NGP. 277(t) Linda Bartlett. (b) Scott Thode, *U. S. News & World Report*. 278 Scott Thode, *U. S. News & World Report*. 279 Timothy A. Murphy, *U. S. News & World Report*. 280, 281 Steve Wall. 282, 283 Nathan Benn. 284 J. P. Laffont/SYGMA. 286, 287 Nathan Benn. 288, 289 Chick Harrity, *U. S. News & World Report*. 290; NA; Sisse Brimberg. 296, 297 Peter B. Kaplan.

STATEMENT OF ACKNOWLEDGMENT

The National Geographic Society gratefully acknowledges the invaluable assistance which its staff members have received during the preparation of this book from many individuals and institutions. Among them: embassies, officials, and repositories of art in numerous nations; departments and agencies of the United States Government; state and local departments and officials; historical and ethnic societies throughout the country; universities and other institutions of learning; religious bodies; persons in private life, native- and foreign-born.

Index

Library of Congress CIP Data

Allen, Leslie.
    Liberty : the statue and the American dream.
    Includes index.
    1. United States—Emigration and immigration—History. 2. Statue of Liberty (New York, N.Y.)—History. I. Title.
JV6450.A565 1985   325.73   85-17304
ISBN 0-87044-583-9 (regular edition)
ISBN 0-87044-584-7 (deluxe edition)
ISBN 0-87044-622-3 (library edition)
ISBN 0-87044-623-1 (limited collector's edition)

Composition for *Liberty: The Statue and the American Dream* by National Geographic's Photographic Services, Carl M. Shrader, Director, Lawrence F. Ludwig, Assistant Director. Printed in Saratoga Springs, N.Y., by QuadGraphics Inc., Pewaukee, Wis. Bound by Holladay-Tyler Printing Corp., Rockville, Md. Film preparation by Catharine Cooke Studio, Inc., New York, N.Y. Color separations by the Lanman Progressive Company, Washington, D. C.; Lincoln Graphics, Inc., Cherry Hill, N.J.; and NEC, Inc., Nashville, Tenn.

OFFICIAL CENTENNIAL SOUVENIR: The Statue of Liberty-Ellis Island Foundation, Inc., offers a souvenir envelope bearing the Auguste Bartholdi commemorative postage stamp with first-day-of-issue cancellation. An enclosed card carries the Centennial seal, embossed in foil containing copper derived from the statue's restoration. To order, send $10.50 to Statue of Liberty Cover, Philatelic Sales Division, Washington, D. C. 20265-9978.